Fifty Shades
and Popular Culture

Fifty Shades
and Popular Culture

Yuya Kiuchi

McFarland & Company, Inc., Publishers
Jefferson, North Carolina

ISBN (print) 978-1-4766-6317-3
ISBN (ebook) 978-1-4766-2839-4

LIBRARY OF CONGRESS CATALOGUING DATA ARE AVAILABLE

BRITISH LIBRARY CATALOGUING DATA ARE AVAILABLE

Front cover image of blue smoke © 2017 ILLUSIANA/iStock

Printed in the United States of America

McFarland & Company, Inc., Publishers
Box 611, Jefferson, North Carolina 28640
www.mcfarlandpub.com

Acknowledgments

First and foremost, I would like to thank Dr. Amy Bonomi. When I first met Amy in August 2013, she had just joined the Department of Human Development and Family Studies at Michigan State University as the new department chair. By then, she was already a superstar researcher on the novel version of *Fifty Shades of Grey*. As we discussed our research topics, she noticed the similarities that existed between her own research and my interests in popular culture. Later, she kindly invited me to join her study team to investigate young women's perception about the *Fifty Shades* film. It was later published in the *Journal of Women's Health*. Although this book and the *JWH* article are two separate projects with different disciplinary approaches, methods, premises, and objectives, Amy's input and insights have been intellectually stimulating. In addition, I would like to thank the other members of the research team at Michigan State University with whom I had the pleasure to work as we prepared our manuscripts for *The Journal of Women's Health*. Thank you, Emily, Christin, and Samantha.

This book is different from my previous works in that it aims to represent the field of popular culture studies as widely as possible. My previous books have been much narrower in methodological focus. As I mention in the introduction, I do not pretend that this volume is comprehensive. But as I reflected on various approaches in the field, I hoped that it will be useful for others who are interested in popular culture studies.

In order to make such a project possible, I relied on what I had learned from many scholars in the field. Some of the methods were familiar to me, but not all. In the process, I gained even more of the valuable lessons taught to me by my professors and mentors, including Drs. Carlo Rotella, Rachel Rubin, Ann Larabee, and Gary Hoppenstand. A special nod should be given to the late Prof. Kumi Inoue, who provided my initial introduction to popular culture back in the late 1990s when I was a freshman student at Sophia University, Tokyo, Japan. May you rest in peace.

Last, but not least, I would like to thank my friends and family. Ms. Ava Kiblawi, whom I met through my wife, read a part of Chapter Eight and offered advice. My mother, Noriko Kiuchi, continues to support my academic and professional endeavors, over 6,500 miles away from home. To my late father, Tsuneo Kiuchi, I owe much of my work ethic. My in-laws, Rich and Dee Kramer, encourage my publication projects by having my books represented in their personal library. As always, I cannot thank my wife, Nichole Kramer-Kiuchi, enough. She read the entire manuscript closely, and gave me valuable feedback. I would also like to thank her for agreeing to go watch *Fifty Shades of Grey* with me on the opening night at our local movie theater in Holland, Michigan, just so I did not have to be the only guy who would have been alone. She is always understanding, even when I feel overwhelmed with work. Thank you, Nicki.

Table of Contents

Introduction

On one level, this is a book about the *Fifty Shades* trilogy and its film. It will explore the genre, adaptation, music, business schemes, merchandizing, and other facets of this hugely successful popular cultural icon, originally written by E. L. James in the early 2010s. But on another level, it is a book about the ecology surrounding the trilogy. Many fans loved the series. Many others loved to hate it. The reception depended on the social sentiments about romance (a trifling genre for housewives), pornography (a moral evil that needs to be controlled), scapegoating *Fifty Shades* for various crimes, and many others. Regardless of one's perceptions and opinions about the books and film adaptations, there is no denying that James's work attracted the attention of millions of readers around the world. In this book, I will dissect *Fifty Shades* from eleven different perspectives, each of which comprises a chapter.

Although the focus of this book is on *Fifty Shades*, it is, more generally, an introductory study in popular culture. I do not claim that this book is comprehensive in reflecting all the theories and approaches available in the discipline, however, it is designed, instead, to show some of the ways in which scholars in the field can dissect a popular cultural text and explore its meaning and significance.

In particular, this book falls into the category of what I term the era of customized information. On the one hand, it is convenient when a shopping website suggests more than one item for sale. Entertainment websites—from YouTube to Netflix—are often effective in recommending a host of videos that might interest the viewer. But it can also mean that one is less likely to face perspectives that challenge our preconceived ideas. News websites, for example, share stories and viewpoints with which the average viewer agrees, leading us to erroneously believe that everyone shares the same thoughts and beliefs. We are surprised when we realize there are others who have completely opposing views. They are shocked about our existence, as well. Rather than dismissing the others and their beliefs, it is vital that we recognize how a text or an event can be read in multiple ways.

Fifty Shades *and Its Popularity*

Originally written as a *Twilight* fan fiction by a British writer, E. L. James, in 2011, *Fifty Shades of Grey* became an international best seller. Along with its two sequels, *Fifty Shades Darker* and *Fifty Shades Freed*, published in 2012, the trilogy has entered the lexicon of pop culture. Categorized as an erotic romance novel, the books trace the relationship between a college student (later a college graduate), Anastasia Steel, and a young billionaire named Christian Grey. Christian is obsessed with bondage, discipline, sadism, and masochism (hereafter referred to as BDSM), subjects with which Anastasia is conflicted. Various scholars, critics, and fans have described the characters' relationship as romantic and/or abusive; such perceptions will be discussed later in this book. Sexually explicit depictions of the relationship resulted in James removing her earlier versions of the novel from the fan website.

The trilogy's success is clear from its publication records. Anecdotally, one would remember feeling as though *everyone* was talking about *Fifty Shades* after the books came out. Despite the description of the novels as "mommy porn," the Associated Press reported that James's work appealed to a wide-ranging audience. The readers include "young and old, doctors and churchgoers, gay and straight" ("'Fifty Shades of Grey' Draws," para. 1). The article also explains that there were "men who have devoured oh-so-naughty 'Fifty Shades of Grey'" (para. 1). One such reader, David Shobin, a sixty-six-year-old man from Smithtown, New York, commented, "At my age, my arthritis flared up just reading about Ana's sexual gymnastics." He continued to admit that the story had a "definite infectiousness" ("'Fifty Shades of Grey' Draws," para. 11). The book has even been sought out by detainees at Camp Seven, the most secure part of the Guantanamo Bay detention camp. The camp's inmates, including those responsible for the September 11 attacks, read the entire trilogy in English. James's books stand alongside *The Odyssey, The Hunger Games*, the *Star Trek* novels, and others at the on-site lending library (Hicks; "Fifty Shades a Must Read"). Indeed, the book reaches beyond the predictable demographics.

The fervor around the 2015 Valentine's Day season with the release of the film was also evident. Because so many people bought all three books, second-hand stores are now inundated with used copies. In March 2016, a charity shop in England released a picture of a "fort" made entirely out of *Fifty Shades* paperbacks. Piled on top of another, thousands of copies of James's work now need a new home ("Charity Shop"). Writing for the *Guardian*, Alison Flood explains that *Fifty Shades of Grey* has sold over 100 million copies internationally and has been translated into more than fifty languages. In the U.S., 45 million copies have been sold. The U.K. and its commonwealth have reported the sales of 27 million copies. International sales were aided by translation into Thai, Hebrew, Icelandic, Latvian, and other languages (Flood). In the U.K., the first volume became the fastest selling paperback book in history (Bentley). Supported by this popularity, in 2015, *Fifty Shades of Grey* appeared as a film adaptation. The film made almost $250 million during the first week, internationally. Although it saw a sharp decline in box office during the following week, within the first month after the launch, the film had grossed over $500 million (Child). There are only two other films directed by a female director—namely *Kung Fu Panda 2* and *Mamma Mia!*—to attain this level of box-office success (Mendelson).

The success and popularity of *Fifty Shades* is an avenue to understanding how we consume popular culture. For example, the simple fact that it was acceptable to read an erotic novel in public reflects shifting social norms. Reading *Playboy* is still not acceptable on a public transit system in the U.S., but many of us have read or have seen others read *Fifty Shades* on a bus or a plane. It also raised other questions. Will it be acceptable to watch it on your laptop while travelling on a plane? Is it okay to admit to your children you enjoy reading what is considered an erotic novel? Many young people have voiced ambivalent feelings when they learned that one or both of their parents read and liked *Fifty Shades*. There is a cultural parallel between the *Fifty Shades* phenomenon and what happened with *Deep Throat* (1972). As I have noted elsewhere, *Deep Throat* marked the first time in American history that people openly admitted going to see a pornographic film without having to worry about being stigmatized (Bartkowiak and Kiuchi). Many readers in the early 2010s similarly admitted enjoying a novel that included thirteen explicit sex scenes, some involving BDSM. Many readers admitted they liked the book.

But it is not just the popularity of the book that calls for an in-depth look at this publishing phenomenon. As a literary work, it enables us to conduct a genre study. From the genre perspective, the books are just the combination of the romance and vampire fiction. This is partially due to the fact that the trilogy began as a fan fiction. The film version of *Fifty Shades* also enables popular culture scholars to examine the role of music or of Hollywood as a business industry. It is also an effective means to understand how various biases and prejudices of class, race, and gender play out in popular culture. Did the trilogy's being labeled as "mommy porn" lead some reviewers to negatively evaluate James's work? Would the story be as attractive if Christian Grey were poor? What if he were not white? How would that affect the ways in which the audience perceives the storyline?

Fans and members of the media have also reacted to the film in ways that deserve scholarly exploration. Merchandizing efforts resulted in a surge in the sale of sex toys, a new product lineup at fashion accessory stores targeting teenage girls, and a series of spinoff novels. It has also demonstrated how certain countries embraced or censored the film. A high school teacher from a mid-sized city in Michigan expressed that teachers sometimes "cringe" at what their students are reading, including *Fifty Shades*. Her student commented that they would not be interested in reading a book unless there is something inappropriate in it (9). Although the book itself is a work of fiction, what fans, media, and Dakota Johnson (the actress who played Anastasia) have voiced reflects how contemporary society views women's agency.

Why Study Popular Culture?

Before further discussing how to dissect *Fifty Shades*, it is important to understand why we must be concerned about popular culture. For many scholars and students of popular culture studies, the significance is clear. The passion one can feel among the attendees at the annual national conference at the PCA/ACA (Popular Culture Association/American Culture Association) is just one example of how engaged these scholars are. But how do we explain the importance of the discipline for someone who is unfamiliar with the field? Fortunately, intellectual giants of the discipline, from Ray Browne to Gary Hoppenstand, have answered the question. Michel de Certeau discussed the importance of studying texts to understand the world we live in. He wrote, "The text is society itself" (167). The text does not live independently of its social context. He also continued to argue that text should not be studied alone. When a text is examined, its reader's reaction also needs to be explored (xii).

Jack Nachbar and Kevin Lause investigated the nature of prejudices and negative definitions about popular culture. Out of four misconceptions they address and investigate, the second tenet is that "popular culture is trivial." They prove otherwise. Popular culture is not trivial because it carries "the underlying cultural mindset which those [popular cultural] artifacts and events both reflect and mold." In addition, popular culture surrounds the mass and "forms the great majority of [their] cultural experiences" (32–33). Just as elite culture contained the mindset of the elite class and surrounded them, popular culture possessed the values of the popular mass.

Popular culture is not only relevant to zeitgeist; it also reflects it. Nachbar and Lause explain that "it tells us what we are now, what we have been in the past and where the two overlap to define what we may always be." They argue that popular culture topics we examine (e.g., football, MTV, television programs, fast food, etc.) are chosen because they provide "means of unlocking their meaning in the culture" and advance the knowledge of what the spirit of the era is (5). Browne similarly claims that "popular culture is the way in which and by which most people in any society live" (6). Study of popular culture, therefore, does not strive to understand the culture itself, nor does it treat it as an end. Instead, it examines popular culture to comprehend the society it reflects.

Furthermore, not only is popular culture relevant and reflective of zeitgeist, but also formative and manipulative. Popular culture works as "hidden persuaders" because it conveys the values embedded therein. Nachbar and Lause's analysis that the increasing violence in movies not only reflects an increasingly violent society, but also leads society to be more accepting of violence is one of such examples (7). Of course, we must not carelessly assume that *Fifty Shades*—or any other popular culture example, for that matter—make its audience violent or kind, stupid or smart, selfish or caring. Popular culture is just a part of a larger social system which reflects who we are and which reinforces who we have been. It also shows us what we want to be and what we become.

Chapter Outlines

Chapter One is a recognition of the value of fans. It starts by revisiting the origin of the trilogy. It is no secret that *Fifty Shades of Grey* started as fan fiction, entitled *Master of the Universe*, written under the pen name of Snowqueen Icedragon. The book, sold originally as an on-demand e-book, was a huge success. As the author of the fan fiction,

E. L. James (another pen name; her real name is Erica Mitchell) asked herself so-called "what-if" questions about the two main characters of *Twilight*, Bella and Edward. Basically, she wondered what would happen if Bella and Edward were mortal, and Edward was a billionaire. This venture proved to be a huge international success. The story's popularity was due to the ready accessibility of digital technology. Although fan fiction long predated the Internet, the e-society enabled James's work to spread rapidly and widely, reaching an unprecedented level. The increasing popularity of e-books late in the first decade of the 2000s enabled many fans to discreetly purchase and read *Fifty Shades*, even in public places. But the visibility of James's fan fiction also led to cultural, and even legal, criticism. Not only were critics claiming that James's writing was of poor quality, questions about copyrights and ownership inevitably were raised. In short, *did* James infringe upon Stephenie Meyer's work? Did she "steal" her intellectual property? If she did, then does that mean fans' creativity is disregarded when they write fan fiction? Can fans exercise their own creativity through this outlet? So far, there is no agreement on fan works and their legal implications. But if society recognizes the value of fan works, it can also recognize fans as more than just a passive audience. This would be a more appropriate perspective in the age of what Don Tapscott calls "prosumption."

Chapter Two attempts to look at the trilogy by exploring what genre it might fit. Although the book itself says "erotic romance" on its back cover, the book has been called pornographic, and even pornography. Some have called it simply a romance novel, or erotica. Based on scholarships on romance novels, represented by Pamela Regis, Janice Radway, and many others, the *Fifty Shades* storyline actually follows the conventions of a romance novel very closely. However, it is also true that there is a group of people who claim that the trilogy is nothing but pornography. A problem with such a claim, though, is that despite the large number of attempts to define the genre, there is no consensus as to what constitutes pornography. Explicit depictions of sex, a lack of story, and some other factors tend to characterize the pornography genre. But the line between pornography and erotica is unclear. Because the history of attempting to define pornography is filled with examples of censorship and control, the debate about the book as pornography also shows social inclination to control, or ban, what some deem inappropriate. The label of pornography is conveniently used to justify such a claim.

Chapter Three examines what made *Fifty Shades* unique and what other aspects of the trilogy are unprecedented. There is a tendency to believe that we are witnessing a significant moment in history. From the popularization of social media to the election of the first African American president, and to a list of international threats and opportunities, we hear similar arguments made repeatedly—we are at a special moment in history, and nothing like this—whatever "this" might be—has ever happened before. Many of these claims, however, turn out to be inaccurate. In the last fifty to sixty years of popular culture history, there have been many examples of novels and movies that were as edgy or controversial as *Fifty Shades of Grey*. The 1986 *9½ Weeks* involved an affair that revolved around sex games. *Secretary* (2002) portrayed a BDSM relationship. As far as *Fifty Shades'* content is concerned, the story is not unique. What makes the trilogy notable—but still not very unique—is its high visibility. Of course, fans talked about it both online and off. They shared books at work. There were online book clubs. International book tours by E. L. James were organized. What is particularly interesting is how the books' many dissenters also talked about it. Reaction by youths who discovered that their older family members were reading the book appeared in many places online. Their sense of panic was widely shared and retweeted. Furthermore, the advancement and popularization of e-readers helped boost the visibility of the book. Not only did it allow what was a small on-demand e-publication to gain momentum and be noticed by Vintage, or the publisher of the book, it also kept enhancing its popularity after its mass market publication. Therefore, what made *Fifty Shades* different from similar works was its high visibility enhanced by fan and non-fan reactions and its popularity on e-reading devices that enabled readers to enjoy the book privately.

Chapter Four focuses on resistance to the work. Although the trilogy and the film were a major success internationally, they also witnessed a great amount of rejection and criticism. It was expected that parents with adolescent and younger children voiced their concerns about the visibility of *Fifty Shades*. But resistance was also from faith-based groups claiming that it was against God's will. Some argued that *Fifty Shades* was pornographic, a reason in itself for resistance. Others understood it was erotica or a romance novel, but nonetheless inappropriate because only their spouse should drive their sexual arousal. Similarly, some libraries banned the trilogy, claiming that it was pornography and that they did not collect pornographic materials. Such a decision led to debates on censorship and the First Amendment. The *Fifty Shades* resistance and censorship controversy shows America's general ambivalence about sex and sexuality. The U.S. appears to be a society open to exploring sexuality. Young people's attitude towards sex—from internationally known spring breaks among college students to hook-up cultures—supports this view. But Americans also tend to be conservative in their views on sexuality, especially compared to their European counterparts. Michel Foucault's idea of sexual repression continues to be true in many parts of American society. Furthermore, some very religious people turned out to be avid fans of James's work. Although this appears counterintuitive, it shows how they managed to balance organized and traditional authority and their individual choice. The *Fifty Shades* controversy allows us to discuss the meaning of sex and sexuality in contemporary society.

Chapter Five looks at the trilogy in relation to BDSM. Although there is no scholarly consensus as to how popular BDSM is, it is expected to be more popular and mainstream than its frequent characterization as dark, subcultural, and deviant. In reality, BDSM seems to—at least in part—drive the curiosity of many (Busby 346). Therefore, it is not surprising that E. L. James's story, which prominently features BDSM, attracted so many fans. But actual BDSM practitioners and experts argue that James failed to portray BDSM correctly. In reality, BDSM is based on safety and consent. As for Christian and Anastasia, a close read of the story reveals that their relationship lacked these two main basic foundations. Furthermore, arguing that Anastasia voluntarily agreed to be in a relationship with Christian that lacked safety and that she allowed him to be violent toward her reflects the continuing trend that "no" means "no," although sometimes "no" may mean "maybe" or even "yes." Overly emphasizing Anastasia's free will and agency as she faces pain and life uncertainties ignores her—and victims of other similar situations—vulnerability and need for help. In addition, even though BDSM sex is based on a pretend-play of power hierarchy, *Fifty Shades*' depiction of the power relations between its two main characters go far beyond the confines of their bedroom or the Red Room of Pain and is based on stereotypical views on male and female sexualities. Christian is portrayed as all-knowing and all-capable. He knows what Anastasia wants, even if she says otherwise. According to James, he can allegedly make her happy with a few touches on her back or with a glider ride. On the other hand, Anastasia is confined to the submissive role both inside and outside the Red Room of Pain. These misrepresentations of BDSM by James alone is not a significant issue for a fiction novel. But what could be problematic is how readers and critics might approach the novel and discuss it. They might consciously or subconsciously read the story while reaffirming the so-called rape fantasy. They might discuss the responsibility of Anastasia and not hold Christian—a wealthy white male—accountable.

Chapter Six is about scapegoating and moral panic. After the publication of the trilogy and the release of the film, various news media outlets reported sex-related incidents allegedly inspired by *Fifty Shades*. In some cases, perpetrators forced BDSM-like sex on their victims. In other instances, couples were caught having sex in public, and teenagers were caught with *Fifty Shades* games at school. Regardless of the specific situations, critics were quick to blame the book as the cause of the problem. However, any kind of sexual abuse or sexual behaviors characterized as inspired by *Fifty Shades* predates the trilogy. James did not invent rape, sexual violence, public indecency, and the idea of teenagers experimenting with sex games. Popular culture simply reflects who we are and what our society is like. Numerous overlaps also exist between the ways in which *Fifty Shades* was scapegoated for these social concerns and the ways in which other popular culture examples in history were blamed as the cause of widely spread social concerns. Usually, scapegoating does not last long, and is highly exaggerated. The concerns may be justified, even though the blame is misplaced. It is understandable that avid churchgoers disapprove of their neighbors reading a novel with so much premarital sex. It is also understandable that caring parents would wonder how the novel might influence their children's views on sex. But blaming *Fifty Shades* for both criminal and non-criminal cases show that it is just another example of moral panic, one that masks a problem that is far larger than a popular culture text. The problem is systemic. But moral panic and scapegoating makes the problem someone else's fault—e.g., filmmakers—and enable others to be innocent victims even though they themselves have the responsibility to address and work on the social problem.

Chapter Seven examines fan fiction, book club experiences, and parodies relating to this publishing phenomenon. Popular culture is not just produced by some and consumed by others. But the blurring line between the producers and the consumers—as attested by the concept of prosumers—does not sufficiently describe the current status of popular culture. The reality is far more complex. As we know well, *Fifty Shades of Grey* started as a *Twilight* fan fiction. But once the trilogy was out, they became the cultural object about which fans began to write fan fiction. Just as was the case with *Twilight*, in some instances, fans asked "what-if" questions to write their version of the story. In other instances, they tried to fill a gap in the story on which James did not elaborate. When fans wrote versions of *Fifty Shades* from Christian's perspective, they were released before E. L. James published the novel known as *Grey*. Many fans reacted to *Grey* with a sense of doubt and distrust. Many expressed that they preferred Christian's accounts of *Fifty Shades of Grey* written by fan fiction writers, especially because they were available first and James's version was secondary. Some readers interacted with the fictional world by participating in a book club. Guiding question lists and reports on book club meetings in which *Fifty Shades of Grey* was discussed provided a forum in which to discuss sex in a way that few outside of the book club community imagined to happen. Our prejudice about sex as a taboo topic—especially for women—shows through strongly in the ways people talked about these book club meetings. The *Fifty Shades* ecology went further than books. Online memes and other popular culture references show how the movie was perceived by the public in general.

Chapter Eight focuses on the music in the film. Both critics and fans had mixed reactions to the soundtrack. Some believed that it was one of the best soundtracks in recent film history, while others strongly disagreed. The dissenters generally disliked the inclusion of two older songs—The Rolling Stones' "Beast of Burden" (1978) and Frank Sinatra's "Witchcraft" (1957)—and two remixes of Beyoncé's songs. Despite its shortcomings, the soundtrack CD is filled with contemporary songs by Sia, Ellie Goulding, Vaults, and The Weeknd, to name a few. For some artists, even including Beyoncé, the film was an opportunity to advance their brand. For others, the film enabled them to be a part of the mainstream music scene. The songs compiled in the soundtrack tend to underscore the romance between Christian and Anastasia while downplaying the negative side of their relationship. For Danny Elfman, the prolific composer who has scored numerous Tim Burton films as well as the theme song to the long-running cartoon *The Simpsons*, *Fifty Shades* represented a new genre. His score reflects the tension between the two main characters in the film. It also mirrors the relationship that fails to develop smoothly. In general, reviewers agree that the soundtrack—which characterizes Christian and Anastasia's relationship as romantic—outperformed the novel and the film. Because music is an integral driver of a film's story, it is understandable that many viewers perceived the film as a romantic story.

Chapter Nine looks at *Fifty Shades*-based merchandizing. Of course, the book itself is an advanced version of *Master of the Universe*, which was a spinoff of *Twilight*. Therefore, the trilogy is not, in the purest sense, "original." But *Fifty Shades* also generated numerous spinoff products. Its movie and CDs are best known. In addition, E. L. James has lists of *Fifty Shades* wine as well as two brands of wine—one red and one white—that are sold as the novel's official wine. Unofficial products, from apparel to jewelry and sex toys, reveal how fans created their own versions of the novels. Many of these products are barely connected to the story. For example, it is just the word "grey" that E. L. James's trilogy and Fifty Shades of Earl Grey tea have in common. Nonetheless, both fans and non-fans have bought such products. These consumerist behaviors suggest that fans are not passive. Many entrepreneurs make their own *Fifty Shades* products as a way of becoming a tangible part of the franchise. It is a form of active participation in a community, and cannot—and should not—be underestimated as meaningless or mindless.

Chapter Ten is also about commercialism. Unlike the previous chapter that looked at the productization of the *Fifty Shades* brand, this chapter looks at Christian Grey as a brand and brands that appeared in the film. This chapter is about commerce. It is almost rare for a movie or a TV show today not to feature brands. Product placement is an expected practice. In the *Fifty Shades* movie, Apple, Audi, Omega, and many other popular aspirational brands appear. These not only helped the moviemakers depict Christian as a wealthy man with exclusive tastes, but also benefited from significant media exposure. Audi, for example, was proud to announce that the movie's high-class image helped the German car brand underscore its cultural values. Even though product placement of this kind seems to benefit multiple parties involved, it is also important to note that the image of wealth could distort the reality. In other words, would Anastasia and many *Fifty Shades* fans be attracted to Christian if he drove a 1995 Honda Civic? Would the fans find Anastasia and Christian's relationship romantic if they spent nights at a Holiday Inn? The allure of certain brands, therefore, can easily affect the way we look at a relationship and romanticize a story that otherwise would not be as appealing.

Chapter Eleven particularly examines how Japanese readers and audiences reacted to E. L. James's work. Japan's movie industry, in general, has been prosperous in recent years. The proportion of profit made by foreign films to overall industry profit has shrunk in the last decade. *Fifty Shades of Grey*, however, was widely discussed well before its release. due partly to the popularity of the original trilogy. Many Japanese fans agreed with non–Japanese counterparts that the story was rather shallow, that Dakota Johnson's acting was better than Jamie Dornan's, and that the movie's soundtrack outperformed the movie itself. But there are also a few themes unique to Japanese audiences. The first concerns the poor quality of censorship efforts. In order to make the film accessible to a wider audience, a list of changes was ordered to be made prior to distribution. Blurred images, pixilation, and black bars were employed to the point that they interfered with the integrity of the film. At times, more than half the screen was covered by what many fans called a "black hole." The second issue concerns Japan's attitudes toward sex, specifically relating to women's desires. On the one hand, Japanese fans expressed their interest in a man like Christian: rich, strong, and enigmatic. On the other hand, such a view points out the fact that Japanese moviegoers rarely discuss relationship violence in a non-spousal context.

Popular Culture Matters

Fifty Shades of Grey is not one of the more prestigious literary works of the early twenty-first century. Nor is its reputation likely to improve in the future. Still, it has its own role in the literary world. As Dira Sudis notes: "Even the most cringe-worthy stories might have a deeper connection for some readers (Crouch para. 22). Sudis continues:

> Somewhere out there is a person who genuinely actually needs to read that badly punctuated story about two Transformers getting it on…. Maybe because their gender identity or sexual orientation or abuse history or some other thing going on in their life makes them feel uncomfortable thinking about sex involving squishy vulnerable human bodies, and robots having sex helps them to express, or understand, something about their own identity or desire that they can't get at any other way [para. 23].

The Associated Press quoted Dr. Mehmet Oz, who argued that the trilogy enabled people to have "an honest conversation about what sex should be like, what makes it feel better, what are the timing issues, how do we make it an important issue in our life rather than an afterthought?" ("'Fifty Shades of Grey' Draws," para. 24).

Laura Berman also argued that *Fifty Shades* could have a positive impact on a relationship. Arguing that the trilogy "has something for everyone" (para. 5), the books "show that monogamy can be naughty" (para. 6), and that they "get couples talking" (para. 7), Berman believes that "women are reconnecting with their mates and turning up the heat in the bedroom." She continues, stating that the trilogy is "acting as foreplay, and, in some cases, as training manuals for some couples who are actually acting out some of the hot scenes in the book in the safety of their own bedrooms—and marriage" (para. 1). Deborah Whitehead also claims that even religious people, who were assumed to have resisted *Fifty Shades*, actually read the novels. According to Whitehead, there are

> internal disagreements as well as ongoing negotiations of the respective weights of institutional and traditional authority, scripture, and individual experience in arriving at decisions about what aspect of the vast smorgasbord of popular culture to consume. So, ... it is not so much that one book is being replaced with another, but that both books, the Bible and *Fifty Shades*, are being read *together* [emphasis in original; 927].

The above statements show that *Fifty Shades* mattered to many, partly because popular culture both reflects and reinforces social norms. As Ryan Goodman stated about same-sex relationships, people with sexual preferences and tastes that are considered marginal "are ultimately encouraged to discipline themselves" (643). Such disciplining partly comes from what we experience in our daily lives (Moon 184). Of course, a significant part of such experience comes from our exposure to popular culture that reflects "institutionally anchored, hierarchical forms of power and the power that works through discourse to limit what kinds of personhood are thinkable and what seems unimaginable and inhuman" (Moon 197). Those aforementioned couples and individuals who felt comfortable trying new sexual ideas and who were able to feel safe when discussing sex (thanks to James's work) are testaments of how popular culture reflects an existing system of control while providing opportunities at the same time to reverse the hierarchy.

Many of the previous high-profile romantic stories have been far less controversial than *Fifty Shades*. Its high media exposure—due to the advancement in communication and media technologies—explain, in part, the intensity of the controversy. But depictions of BDSM and other marginalized sexual orientations and preferences undoubtedly fueled the controversy. What James's work attained was to provide an alternative to a "commonsense theory" about sexuality based on "assumptions about the purposes of sexual behavior" (DeLamater 266). To be labeled as "marginal" or "deviant" is consequential. How others perceive you is assumed to reflect "a piece of information on [your] character, preferences, or other intrinsic property," at least according to the signaling theory advanced by Eric Posner (Engart 336). Because popular culture, with its wide reach, can make its audience feel what they frequently see is socially normative, and what they rarely see is not, texts like *Fifty Shades* give voice to those whose preferences have been quieted.

This point must be read carefully because popular culture does not establish norms. It simply reflects what society has established as a norm and underlines it through its reach and power. To borrow Raimo Tuomela's words, this is "collective acceptance." Members of society establish an idea of what is normal sexuality. Then the idea is seemingly supported by much of popular culture, even though such popular culture texts are created because the very idea was already in place. Nonetheless, society as a whole acts upon what it learned as a norm (124). As DeLamater argues, "Norms are the principal mode of control" (267). In addition, norms, just like laws, serve "as foundations of social order, helping to ensure that people will act in ways considered pro-social by their society" (Etzioni 159).

It is not just the academics and theorists who were made aware of the matter of normalization and control with the release of *Fifty Shades*. Writing for the *Christian Science Monitor*, Gloria Goodale argued that the important issue with sexuality is "not the debate over conservative or liberal views on human sexuality ... but rather a deeper awareness of who is controlling what we think" (para. 6). The fact that women discussing BDSM captured so much attention as seen with *Fifty Shades* also suggests whose voice continues to dominate in our society, namely men's. As has long been the case with romance novels and, more recently, with social media websites like Pinterest, the audience of which is predominantly female, male-dominated society tends to have "a more general cultural snobbery towards 'women's texts'" that they are less worthy (Hunter 969). Mark Ritson's commentary about the film and its product placement, for example, reflects such a hint of aloofness.

This aloofness can explain not only the lack of recognition paid to what the female popular culture audience appreciates, but also the failure of *Fifty Shades* to serve as an agent for social change. As discussed later in this book, *Fifty Shades* could highlight more effectively how certain sexual tastes are marginalized, how signs of wealth tend to mask—and even glorify—what might otherwise be considered risky, or how systems of male control continue to be pervasive, both inside and outside of the bedroom. The idea that women's literature is trivial leaves little room for serious discussions on sexuality, control, or equality.

Alex Dymock posits that BDSM had been a topic of discussion in women's magazines well before *Fifty Shades* (888). More importantly, a close examination of merchandizing and productization efforts of *Fifty Shades* by various companies does not address concerns of many women. Dymock argues:

> The question of women's sexual desires has been appropriated and answered for through the mechanisms of capitalism and consumerism, establishing a link between the governance of femininity and private affirmation of sexual limits.

What woman wants, according to the *Fifty Shades* phenomenon, is to uncover and disclose new limits of sexuality and femininity in an infinite process that, rather than liberating the self from the apparatus of social power, instead imposes new limits that must be transgressed [892].

Indeed, James's work leads Anastasia to "conform to [Christian's] desire" (Fahs 282).

The trilogy surely enabled many people to feel more adventurous with their sexuality and comfortable when discussing sex. The sheer number of media appearances of Dakota Johnson and Jamie Dornan from morning TV shows like NBC's *Today* to late-night comedy programs like Jimmy Fallon's *The Tonight Show* enabled discussions on sex, BDSM, and a text that some claimed to be pornographic to be a part of mainstream. After all, even First Lady Michelle Obama observed, "You can't live in this society without hearing about *Fifty Shades of Grey*" (McDevitt para. 2). Examining a popular culture text reveals who we are. It also reveals our values in an honest way. Although it is easy to dismiss popular culture as trifling, it is a powerful witness of social reality.

CHAPTER ONE

From *Twilight* to *Master of the Universe* to *Fifty Shades*
Fan Fiction, Ownership and Agency

For many unsuspecting fans, *Fifty Shades of Grey* and *Twilight* may appear to be two completely different stories. On the one hand, *Fifty Shades* is about a sexually inexperienced female college student who meets a young billionaire. The student, Anastasia Steele, and the young billionaire, Christian Grey, engage in BDSM, the depictions of which have earned the *Fifty Shades* trilogy an erotic romance novel category, or, more commonly, the derisive label "mommy porn." On the other hand, *Twilight* is about a female high school female student who falls in love with a vampire. The storyline lacks explicit sexual depictions. If Christian and Anastasia keep pushing the boundaries through their sexual explorations, Edward and Bella are in a relationship of abstinence. These two worlds do not seem to cross paths.

Of course, both the *Fifty Shades* and *Twilight* brands were immense hits, both as books and films. *Fifty Shades of Grey*, published in 2011 and its two sequels published in 2012, have jointly sold over 100 million copies by early 2014 (Bosman "For 'Fifty Shades,'" para. 1). In a similar way, the *Twilight* series, whose first novel was published in 2005, has sold over 100 million copies in thirty-seven languages. Thirty-five million copies have been sold in the U.S., and sixty-five million copies elsewhere. Its four books were the best-selling novels in 2008 according to the *USA Today* (Cochrane para. 2; Deahl para. 3). Its five films took in over $1.3 billion gross sales at the box office in North America alone ("Twilight"). Stephenie Meyer's four-book series and E. L. James's three-book series are, therefore, irrefutable commercial successes.

What really connects the two highly successful works is the fact that *Fifty Shades* started as *Twilight* fan fiction. Pugh explains that fan fiction is "based on a situation and characters originally created by someone else." He continues, stating that readers

> had a canon of stories invented by others, but [they] wanted more, sometimes because the existing stories did not satisfy [them] in some way, sometimes because there are simply never enough stories and [they] did not want them to come to an end. So [they] invented the ones [they] wanted" [9].

Erica Mitchell, better known by her pen name E. L. James, the British-born author of the *Fifty Shades* trilogy and a fan of *Twilight*, wrote her works based on the world, or the canon, created by Stephenie Meyer. James was not the only one to do so. As of early 2011, the year James wrote her first book, there were over 175,000 fan-fiction stories based on *Twilight* on FanFiction.net, one of the largest such archives (Leavenworth 69). This was only second to about 500,000 fan fiction stories based on *Harry Potter* (Leavenworth 79).

Recognizing *Fifty Shades'* origin as fan fiction and examining it as it relates to *Twilight* helps reveal several issues, such as copyrights and creativity, definition of quality, and agency that are pertinent to the world in which digital technology has made it much easier for fan fiction to be recognized outside of the traditional small circles of fans. This is not to say that all fan fiction writers wish to have recognition of general society as E. L. James attained in the early 2010s. But it is to say that such an opportunity is there, and more importantly, it has become easier for major publishing houses—such as Vintage, the publisher of James's work—to find similar venues.

Fans and Fan Fiction

Not all fans are created equal. Furthermore, not all kinds of fans are treated equally. For example, in the U.S., along with other Western societies, sports fandom "is widely normalized," while "fandom centered around fictional narratives … are still often considered the domain of socially hopeless geeks" (Tosenberger 6). This is because "sport embodies many elements of dominant value systems, including masculinity, meritocracy and patriotism" (Schimmel, Harrington, and Bielby 590). However, fandom for fictional narratives is considered to be for men who fail to live up to the hegemonic masculinity, or for young women (Tosenberger 6). Or, according to Schimmel, Harrington, and Bielby, they are imagined to be "out-of-touch loners, losers or lunatics" (582). This unfair treatment about fandom can be seen in popular TV shows including *The Big Bang Theory*, in which following college sports is characterized as cool and debating on comic books is seen as nerdy and geeky, and, therefore, uncool. TBS's *King of the Nerds*, during its three-season lifespan, emphasized the contestants' quirks in a way that was far different from how sports fans are celebrated for their knowledge about team and player statistics and history.

Since fan fiction, as its name suggests, deals with fictional narratives, this type of literature had long been seen as a part of the "uncool." Cavicchi even comments that many considered such fan behaviors as "abnormal" (52). Due partially to the view that fandom is uncool and less worthy of study, the "novelty of modern fan communities is often overestimated in research that sometimes seems to assume that fandom began with *Star Trek*" (Reagin and Rubenstein para. 5.3). In reality, the history of fandom dates back much further than the mid-1960s. Cavicchi traces it back to the seventeenth century, while identifying the end of the nineteenth century to be the beginning of the use of the word, "fan" (which is short for fanatic). He also argues that by the early twentieth century, the concept of fans has become a part of the mainstream American consciousness (54–55).

With the modern origin of fans dating back to the turn of the twentieth century, these individuals started producing fan fiction soon after, sometime around the 1920s and '30s (Thomas 1; Coppa 42–43). Of course, this is not to disregard the existence of fan fiction in the nineteenth century and before. Derecho discusses that a form of fan fiction existed in the fifteenth century (66). Published in 1740, Samuel Richardson's *Pamela, or the Virtue Rewarded*, saw many parodies that can be considered fan fiction by today's standards ("*Pamela* the Novel," para. 10). Furthermore, Pugh hints that when small children use their imagination and creativity to imagine the "what if?" world for their favorite story or cartoon characters, it is already a form of fan fiction (9).

Thomas provides a concise definition for fan fiction. He writes that the term refers to "stories produced by fans based on plot lines and characters from either a single source text or else a 'canon' of works; these fan-created narratives often take the pre-existing story world in a new, sometimes bizarre, direction" (1). Rather than passively consuming texts as readers, these fans serve as producer-consumers (or prosumers). They contribute to the ecology of a text through creating their own version of the original work, a far more significant involvement than discussions and reflections in reading groups.

Fifty Shades *as* Twilight *Fan Fiction*

As *Twilight* fan fiction, *Fifty Shades* follows its original work's canon, or the world created by its author. As stated earlier, a story about a high school girl and a 104-year old vampire, and another about a young female in her early twenties with a young billionaire, do not appear to be connected. *Twilight* follows conservative sexual norms, including abstinence, true dedicated love, and sex only as procreation. This is not a surprising characteristic of the series, considering the author's Mormon faith. On the other hand, as the nickname "mommy porn" suggests, *Fifty Shades* is known for its edgy portrayal of sexual acts. Despite these differences, *Fifty Shades* is based on the original characters and canon of *Twilight*.

Erica Mitchell liked the film adaptation of *Twilight* so much that she went on to read the books, beginning in December 2008 (Baelo-Allué 228). As she recalls:

> Just after Christmas, I sat down and read the books, and I escaped for five days. I just loved them…. It's just such a fabulous love story. I read them and reread them and reread them. And on the 15th of January I sat down to write an original book for the first time ever. I finished it in April, and then I started another one. I kind of came to a halt with it 96,000 words later, in August, and then I discovered fan fiction. I thought, "This is interesting." I just wrote one in three weeks. And while I was doing that I had the idea for what would eventually become "Fifty Shades," and I started writing that there and then [Johnson para. 22–23].

As Baelo-Allué noted, Erica Mitchell's characterization of her creative work as "original" is misleading. Her work, initially entitled *Master of the Universe* under the pen name of Snowqueens Icedragon, was fan fiction, rather than an original work. Reading *Twilight*, for her, was, in the words of Roland Barthes, reading that "[cultivated] the desire to write" (qtd. in de Certeau 176). *Master of the Universe* was shared with other fans on a *Twilight* fan fiction website, as well as fanfiction.net, the largest such portal for fan fiction (228).

Master of the Universe became an immediate hit. The story, which at the time still maintained *Twilight* character names as in Edward and Bella, received over fifty thousand comments and established a strong fan base (Baelo-Allué 229). Because there is so much fan fiction available for popular texts like *Twilight*, attaining such wide attention is a major achievement. Thanks to this popularity, the Writers Coffee Shop, a small-sized independent publisher in Australia, published the book for e-readers on an on-demand basis (Balton para. 10; Grinberg para. 9). As the publisher changed the character names to avoid copyright infringement, Edward became Christian, and Bella became Anastasia (Baelo-Allué 229). Erica Mitchell, alias Snowqueens Icedragon, became E. L. James, author of *Fifty Shades of Grey*.

Through blogs and social media, and other informal means, or "word of mouse" as Baelo-Allué calls them, the book's popularity surpassed *Twilight* fan fiction community (229). Eventually, the books sold over 250,000 copies, making *Fifty Shades of Grey* the top *New York Times* e-book fiction best seller (Bosman, "Discreetly Digital" para. 2).

Fan fiction, by definition, follow the canon of the original work. Some fan fiction may read like a sequel or a prequel to an existing story. Imagine a *Fifty Shades* fan writing a story of Christian and Anastasia ten years into their marriage. The story would be an extension of the world in which the original *Fifty Shades* character lived. As for E. L. James's *Fifty Shades*, however, the gap from Meyer's work is much larger. This type of fan fiction, known as alternative universe fan fiction, alters "one aspect of the canon or [answers] 'what if' questions or [involves] more radical changes in place and time" (Baelo-Allué 230). An alternative universe fan fiction is different from fans writing what might have happened before the original story started or after it ended. These fan fiction stories, including the ones that focus on missing scenes from the original work, ask the question of "what else?" (Pugh 47). E. L. James instead asked "what if?" This is how James removed main characters from *Twilight*, maintaining parts of their identities, and then transporting them into a completely new landscape.

When authors of fan fiction negotiate through the process of detaching themselves from the original work while maintaining its canon, a unique combination of similarities and differences arises between the two works. *Twilight* and *Fifty Shades* are no exceptions. Despite the obvious differences, there are numerous similarities. The overall storyline, for example, is quite similar. Both stories are set around Seattle and its vicinity. Bella is uncertain about her appearance. Her parents are no longer together. She quickly falls in love with Edward. The relationship escalates very quickly. Bella marries young, experiences a controversial conception of her baby, gives birth to the baby nonetheless, and lives with Edward happily. Anastasia is also unsure about her appearance. Her parents have been separated. She falls in love with Christian during their very first encounter. Their relationship also develops very fast. Her pregnancy challenges their relationship. But eventually, the baby is born and the couple ends up living together happily.

The main characters in both works have much in common. Both Edward and Christian are Byronic. In other words, they have particular positive characteristics (Myers 154). Edward and Christian are portrayed as handsome, wealthy, physically fit, passionate, and confident. They are also both controlling men. They justify this behavior by their desire to protect their partner. Both also have a secret that is only revealed to their girlfriend. The secret draws Bella and Anastasia into the relationship while Edward and Christian are aware of the danger that their secret poses upon them. Both Bella and Anastasia have a young man—in both cases a minority man—who is romantically interested in them. The stories include a scene in which the female characters face sexual assault close calls from which Edward and Christian rescue them, hence portraying them as heroes. This is a very typical storyline for a romance novel as shown in the discussion on the genre studies in Chapter Two.

Of course, there are differences. Fan fiction writers are active participants in a fan culture. They do much more than consume media. Furthermore, as an alternative universe fan fiction, *Fifty Shades* has its story evolve in a completely different environment. As Baelo-Allué sums up, "*Twilight* is a vampire paranormal romance, whereas *Fifty Shades* is an erotic romance set in realist grounds." She also points out that "*Twilight* builds on the erotics of abstinence, while *Fifty Shades of Grey* builds on the erotics of full sexual exploration" (234). This difference between the two sets of novels also leads to different genre conventions. On the one hand, *Twilight* is not only a romance plot but also a fantasy novel. On the other hand, *Fifty Shades* is a romance plot that is also an erotica. Although the premise of the story—finding a young billionaire right before college graduation, the billionaire turning out to have a dark secret of sexual abuse and BDSM, being involved in a relationship with him and exploring sexuality to the extent Anastasia does, just to list a few—may be as unrealistic as attending a high school with vampires. *Twilight* also shows Bella as someone who has no wish to continue her study past high school and whose only wish is to marry Edward and become a vampire. Anastasia's story is a little more realistic. At least in the book, she wants to work in the publishing industry, although the film adaptation makes no reference to her professional ambitions.

Theoretical Implications

Although there is no question that the Internet and online fan communities helped catapult the popularity of E. L. James's work from an amateur writer's fan fiction to an international megahit in a matter of a few years, as discussed earlier, the digital technology did not start fan cultures or fan fiction. What is nonetheless important about the relationship between fan fiction and the digital culture is the Internet's power of information dissemination, promise to connect people, and potential to affect the traditional idea of ownership and monetization. Such dynamic communities of fan fiction writers identify several important implications.

The aforementioned similarities and differences are not unique to *Twilight* and *Fifty Shades*. Many cultural critics have noted such a pattern that exists in fan fiction. As described earlier, *Fifty Shades of Grey* asks the question of "what if?" rather than "what else?" enabling more detachment from the canon of its original work, *Twilight*. Such alternative universe writing allows fan readers to move beyond their role as "travelers." Michel de Certeau posited that readers are "like nomads poaching their way across a field they did not write" (174). Although James relied on the canon she did not create, she was able to create a new literary ecology of her own.

Readers' creative behaviors as seen in fan fiction stem from their desire for "more of" and "more from" the original text (Pugh 19). Baelo-Allué elaborates that the first kind "would entrain continuation; once the stories stop being published or the main character dies, fans will continue the story because they like it so much they don't want it to end." On the other hand, the "more from" kind of fan fiction "involves readers feeling there is something wanting or missing in the original canon that can be filled with new stories" (231). Pugh introduces several examples of fans not liking certain characters and hence removing them from their fan fiction. or of wanting more character development and realizing it in their creative works (21).

In the binary of "more of" and "more from," *Fifty Shades* belongs to the latter category. E. L. James was not interested in continuing the *Twilight* storyline. Pugh argues that fan fiction is based on the belief that "fictional characters and universes can transcend both their original context and their creator" (222). With this premise, James created an alternative. This writing process challenges the conventional role difference between writers and readers. In other words, authors cannot claim to know everything about the characters or the world of their own story. Pugh argues, "Fan fiction is a genre in which the boundary between readers and writers is shifting and easily crossed. The reader is unusually empowered and may indeed, by dint of playing in the fanfic writer's sandpit, herself before a co-creator" (222).

Such a high-level engagement by readers and fans reflect what Henry Jenkins calls the participatory culture. Among many renowned scholars who have written on the relationship between popular cultural texts and their fans, there are, naturally, some disagreements. For example, although Jenkins uses the word "poacher," he uses it differently than de Certeau. In an interview compiled in the new edition of his 1992 book, Jenkins stated, "Michel de Certeau (1984) believed that readers left few if any visible and tangible traces of their acts of 'poaching' whereas I was arguing that fan culture generated texts that could be shared and exchanged and created a social infrastructure that supported such exchanges" (xxiv).

What happened with *Fifty Shades of Grey* shows that contributions by fans are more visible than de Certeau suggested, not just with the physical presence of the trilogy, but also with the fan-work economy that enabled such a successful fan-work venture to take off. Furthermore, the economy is able to exist not because of Web 2.0. Jenkins correctly discusses that fans have been involved in a participatory culture before the rise of the digital technology enabled participatory culture (xxii). As Busse and Hellekson discuss, the Internet enabled the fan community to move from a face-to-face base structure with fan clubs and conventions to a more dynamic electronic one (13). Parkin cautions that when scholars of fan studies rely heavily on works by Roland Barthes, they "miss the increasing flow of information between authors and fans mediated by the Internet" (64). With the help of the Internet, fan communities and their works became ever more visible and impactful on popular culture in general.

As Brennan and Large surmised, "Fan texts are rarely produced in isolation" (36). *Fifty Shades* was no exception. As any author would know, a text is rarely a work solely by the author whose name appears with such a title. In addition to those who help produce a book, an article, or an essay, there are numerous hands of those who help revise, edit, and rewrite the author's work. In the case of a fan fiction, there are even more people involved in the process. To say the book was written solely by E. L. James is far from the truth. Drawing on Lewis Hyde and Karen Hellekson, Jones states that the concept of the "gift economy" helps explain how fans interact with each other as they produce a fan work.

Cultural and Legal Implications

As a reader and a fan fiction writer, James well reflects the idea of a poacher who lives in a version of Meyer's world. Such a practice of writing is similar to what Don Tapscott and Anthony Williams call "prosumers" (124–150). A few decades before Tapscott and Williams, Alvin Toffler had already discussed the rise of prosumers and the significance of a new economy, which he called the "third wave." Toffler's book, being over thirty years old, makes it clear that critics have been aware of prosumption and its social implications well before the arrival of the digital age. Although Tapscott oftentimes uses prosumption as one of the signature characteristics of youths today, it is not a new practice. *Fifty Shades of Grey* as a fan fiction, from this perspective, is just one of many prosumptive behaviors.

Prosumption is two-fold. On the one hand, it refers to professional consumption (Gunelius para. 4). In the past, consumers were amateurs. Professionals produced products and services that customers who had little experience, if at all, consumed. When such customers engaged in production, they did so as hobbyists. Today, thanks to technological development, availability of free time, and a rise in disposal income among some, such hobbyists are involved in production behaviors similar to those of professionals. A quick trip to hardware stores, cooking ware stores, or camera stores reveals the popularity of professional-grade equipment and appliances among hobbyists. Many of the YouTube and other videos created by hobbyists, including young students, are of professional quality.

Fifty Shades of Grey can be seen through the lens of professional consumption. It is no secret that James's writing skills have been challenged. Bixby wrote, "The novel—it kills us to call it that" (para. 6). Many websites, including The Stranger, mock the novel by listing poorly written lines from the book (Humphrey). Roy Peter Clark, an instructor of writing and author of a writing book, uses *Fifty Shades* to discuss how *not* to write a novel. Even with questions about James's writing skills, with editing, her work met the minimal standard to be published. In addition, technological development allowed a small print shop to produce her work on an on-demand basis. What was originally published was far from what most readers received from a local or online book seller, it nonetheless constitutes the professional consumption culture.

On the other hand, prosumption also refers to the convergence between production and consumption. As has been shown in this chapter, especially in the context of fan fiction, it is not a new tradition. In their work, Ritzer and Jurgenson list numerous examples of other producer/consumer behaviors: pumping one's own gas, calling in a radio show, contributing to Wikipedia, posting reviews on websites, just to name a few. Some examples have been in existence since the mid-twentieth century, while some others developed as Web 2.0 expanded. The authors write, "Prosumption was clearly not invented on Web 2.0, but given the massive involvement in, and popularity of, any of these developments (e.g., social networking sites), it can be argued that it is currently both the most prevalent location of prosumption and its most important facilitator as a 'means of prosumption'" (20).

Fan fiction portals, including fanfiction.net, are a good example of Web 2.0 serving as a "prevalent location" and an "important facilitator" of prosumption (Ritzer and Jurgenson 20). It was originally published as *Master of the Universe* on fan fiction websites. The power of Web 2.0 that blurs the line between production and consumption and its most influential invention, digital social media, enabled James's work to be widely distributed and consumed.

When prosumption opportunities expand and fan fiction writers could potentially make more profit than original writers, various legal questions arise. Meyer once commented, "I haven't read [*Fifty Shades of Grey*], I mean's that's really not my genre, not my thing.... I've heard about it; I haven't really gotten into it that much. Good on her—she's doing well. That's great!" (Prinzivalli para. 3). Although Meyer's comment is encouraging for fan fiction writers, James's work has raised legal concerns.

There is no question that Meyer and her publisher own the exclusive right of the *Twilight* novels. After all, she wrote them and sold the publication right to Little, Brown and Company. The important question, therefore, is how to understand the relationship between *Twilight* and *Master of the Universe*, and ultimately *Fifty Shades of Grey*. Mulligan concisely explains that it was

> originally posted as unauthorized fan fiction online, under the title, *Master of the Universe*. Its main characters, initially, were names Edward and Bella after the primary characters in *Twilight*. *Master of the Universe* explored what Edward and Bella's relationship might look like if, instead of being a celibate vampire, Edward was a decidedly prurient human businessman [para. 4].

When James published the book, she renamed the main characters for copyright reasons (Baelo-Allué 229). However, Mulligan is correct to point out that "she didn't rewrite the book" (para. 5). Although Vintage's claim that *Master of the Universe* and *Fifty Shades of Grey* are two separate novels (Jones 3.3), Jane Little used the Turnitin software to show that the two works are 89 percent the same. Little's study shows that Vintage's claim that *Fifty Shades of Grey* and *Twilight* are very much different because *Fifty Shades* is not the same as *Master of the Universe* is weak. In other words, it is both *Master of the Universe* and *Fifty Shades of Grey* that are fan fiction of *Twilight*.

With this conclusion, two legal questions arise, the first being is *Fifty Shades* a derivative work of *Twilight*? If it is, it would be considered to have violated *Twilight*'s copyrights. David Lizerbram does not think so, stating, "Given that *Fifty Shades* doesn't contain elements of or make reference to the original work of authorship, it shouldn't be considered a derivative work. Of course, we know that *Twilight* was the inspiration, but inspiration alone doesn't create a cause of action for copyright infringement" (para. 9).

The second legal question is about fair use. Referencing the U.S. Copyright Act and *Dhillon v. Does 1–10* (2014), Lizerbram questions, "Did James serve a new purpose by taking the *Twilight* characters and placing them in a new, highly sexualized context?" His answer is in the affirmative. He continues by stating that James "didn't just take the *Twilight* characters and write her own continuing stories about vampires and werewolves and such. Instead, … she used those characters to comment about sexuality and to investigate the underlying adult themes of the original stories" (para. 14). He concludes by writing that "you can safely read or watch *Fifty Shades of Grey* without worrying that you're partaking in a copyright infringement" (para. 16).

Hetgher is not fully convinced that the legality of fan fiction has been settled. He characterizes this issue as "legally interesting" (1872) and argues that "there is no settled fan-fiction case law" (1870). However, many of the authors are sympathetic to fan fiction writers. As an earlier quote suggests, Meyer is one of them. But a user of fanfiction.net, identified as Karen, speculates that "once people start making money from [fan fiction], the authors or the publishing houses might turn around … and say, "Uh uh, no more. Copyright infringement" (Miller para. 5). Another user of the website is quoted as saying, "I personally don't think fan fiction authors should pursue publication…. It's more about integrity than money" (Miller para. 6).

The questions about the validity of fan works—especially the profitable ones—go beyond their legality. It is also a cultural debate. As the history of copyright dates easily back by three centuries ("A Brief Introduction and History," para. 4), recent decades have witnessed the rise of the mash-up culture, remix culture, and most notably, Lawrence Lessig's Creative Commons founded in 2001. This trend argues that certain creative works should remain available for use for free to encourage more creative activities. Much of what fan fiction writers do when they read an original novel and write fan fiction falls under this belief. Mulligan is supportive of this trend by arguing that "courts should permit unauthorized stories that don't merely restate another work but rather build—and effectively comment—on existing characters and settings. Courts have the power to read the derivative work right narrowly and fair use protections broadly, and they should exercise their judgment to do so" (para. 12). This perspective showcases a new way to think about what it means to own an artistic work. Tapscott argues that openness is a new norm. He further discusses that giving up on assets can sometimes bring more benefit. When Tapscott talks about a changing environment and changing emphasis on ownership to sharing, he is indirectly talking about the questions concerning fan fiction as creative works that emphasize more on sharing and collaboration, and less on the conventional model of ownership.

To make matters more complex, U.S. copyright law is not clear about non-economic impact of fan works. In other words, the law tends to acknowledge the importance of protecting economic interests of authors; their non-economic rights are not necessarily protected by the law. Schwabach explains that in the U.S., visual "rights in original works of art are protected by the Visual Artists' Rights Act, but there is no counterpart for works of fiction" (2). Furthermore, as he also discusses, "While fan fiction may infringe on the content owners' copyright and trademark rights, the fans who create and share it are the biggest, and for some genre works very nearly the only, market for the owner's works" (1).

Fan Fiction and Fan Agency

When the cultural and legal validity of fan fiction is recognized, its benefit is more than creative and entertainment opportunities for fan fiction authors. Thomas discussed that "while the activities of fans may take many forms, writing stories deriving from one or more sources' texts has long been the most popular way of concretizing and disseminating their passion for a particular fictional universe" (1). He also argues that the most recent wave of fan fiction scholars has examined the ways in which fan fiction authors have contributed to the development of a larger culture. Thomas writes, "Instead of fans being seen as isolated or marginal, their activities are treated as a fundamental aspect of everyday life" (4). From this perspective, there is little, if any, difference between Meyer, who wrote an original work, and James, who wrote a transformative work based on Meyer's story.

Studying fan fiction also allows scholars to recognize diversity that exists among fans. Although fans have traditionally been seen as monolithically geeky, nerdy, or uncool, fan fiction reveals "why certain kinds of readers are drawn to certain kinds of texts" (Thomas 7). Furthermore, it also shows that readers bring their own experiences, knowledge, background, and other types of context as they consume a text. Such a style of consumption is far more active than a stereotype of passive fans.

In addition, although authors of fan fiction, by definition, maintain the canon of the original work during their creative process, they also assert their own views to determine how much they would deviate from the original work. They may write a prequel or sequel. Or they may write an alternative universe type of work, as James has done. Years after the original work is published, its world may be transformed. Such a practice shows that no work is stable. Even the world of the original work continues to be reinterpreted and reimagined. Fan fiction is a manifestation of active participation by readers and fans.

For some critics, as a later chapter of this book will show, James's writing was less than ideal. Writing in response to Aja Romano's article, Bonnie wrote, "Terrible plot, terrible character development, and terrible writing are what 'Fifty Shades' is, and many of us in the Twi fandom are truly embarrassed that this is the fic that puts us on the map" (para. 2). Another blogger wrote, "I don't like poorly-written stories. I don't like it when poorly-written stories get published. I don't like it when poorly-written stories make millions of dollars." The entry continues to conclude that "*Fifty Shades of Grey* is an insult to fanfic writers and stands a very good chance of damaging fandom as we know it" ("My Problem with," para. 17–18).

Despite such criticisms about James's writing styles and skills—or lack thereof, according to some critics—her trilogy is evidence of fan agency and their resistance to the common label as "mindless consumers" (Jenkins 23). On the one hand, borrowing Lewis Hyde's concept of the "gift economy," Bethan Jones discusses that fans engage in the gift economy in which they interact, and help develop each other's understanding of the canon and fanworks. Fan writing, therefore, is a collaborative and communal, rather than an individual, project.

Interactions that fans have on fan forums, including fanfiction.net, therefore, raises an ethical question about James's trilogy beyond what legal experts may consider. Jones argue that "James ... straddles the line between producer and fans, stealing from commodified culture to create *Master of the Universe* while stealing from fandom to make a success of *Fifty Shades*" (3.8). As noted above, Vintage argues that *Master of the Universe* and *Fifty Shades* are two completely separate novels. However, Turnitin shows that the two works are more identical than different. Such a conflict is just one example of what Toffler might have foreseen as he wrote, "The rise of the prosumer ... will also shift the basis of economic conflict. The competition between worker-producers and manager-producers will no doubt continue. But it will shrink in importance as pro-suming increases and we move farther into Third Wave society. In its place new social conflicts will arise" (300).

Fifty Shades of Fiction

Unlike so-called classical texts, fan fiction is often considered to be of less quality and value. Such an assumption is not difficult to imagine when fandom is frequently looked down on as socially awkward. Further-more, despite the rising quality and quantity of prosumer works, when it comes to fan works, the general public tends to hold them in low esteem. Both fans and non-fans of *Fifty Shades* criticized the quality of James's writing. A part of it was due to the social trend of looking down on women's culture, as noted in Chapter Two of this book. But it was also true that James's work is poorly valued simply because it is fan fiction.

Although personal preferences about James's writing may differ from one to another, examining fan fiction, such as *Fifty Shades of Grey*, enables us to study various social trends. For example, prosumption by fans has long existed but has heretofore been ignored. Both de Certeau and Jenkins, as well as Tofler, have identified a high level of fan engagement well before the Web 2.0 era or *Fifty Shades*. Despite the differences that exist among these intellectuals' perspectives, it is clear that fans are more than just passive consumers. Jenkins, more than de Certeau, advocates the agency that fans exercise in their cultural participation. Fans are not passive con-sumers. They produce popular culture, and what they produce is as good in quality as what is produced by professionals.

In addition to theoretical implications, fan fiction also directs our attention to legal, cultural, and ethical implications. After all, from Lucas Film to Marvel and Disney, many major filmmakers have "licensed pop-ular fanworks ... legitimizing fanart in completely new ways" (Crouch para. 2). As Schwabach argues, "Intellectual property law in general, and copyright in particular, are in a greater state of upheaval and uncertainty than they have been in centuries" (146). He adds that "the Internet changed everything" (13). This is partly because the so-called "gift economy" is now partaken by a greater number of people. The economy has a far larger reach thanks to the technological development. Even fan-based magazines of twenty years ago cannot compare to the reach of a simple fan website.

Furthermore, fan fiction challenges us to reconsider how we approach popular culture in general. Thomas argues:

> While [academic studies] at least try to locate fan fiction alongside literary traditions and conventions, media studies approaches consciously steer clear of any attempt to evaluate fanfiction based on the quality of the writing, the plotting, or the characterization for fear of being seen to be an outsider or "above" the object of study [3].

Thomas is correct in that when academics study popular culture, there is an inherent risk of being elitist. In other words, not just in perception but also in reality, academics may look at popular texts as people with authority. Unless scholars are careful, popular culture can easily be labeled as trifling and meaningless. The history of the popular culture studies is filled with such examples. Instead, scholars of popular culture studies must reject such a hierarchical approach and recognize the agency of popular culture and its producers and consumers.

CHAPTER TWO

Is *Fifty Shades* Romance or Porn?
Defining a Popular Cultural Text

Any popular culture text can be characterized as unique and unprecedented in one way while the very same text can be grouped with other works as belonging to a certain genre in another. Fans may want to argue that their favorite text is different from, or even superior to, anything else, whereas others might point to the fact that it is not as different as they might claim. Although such a debate usually remains highly subjective, contextualizing a text within a genre can show how a story follows particular sets of premises and develops in an expected way. No matter how authors intended to produce a text or how audiences perceive it, comparisons to and grouping with other texts is inevitable because "no text comes to fruition in a social or cultural vacuum wherein the meaning of a book can be reduced to the author's intent alone" (Shachar 148).

Genre studies, as an academic field, has a long history dating back to the Greeks. With its long history and rich scholarship, defining the field or elaborating on its significance in a chapter is not only an impossible task but also unfair to the field. Various scholars have already produced a vast amount of scholarship defining, theorizing, and applying genre studies. The aim of this chapter, therefore, is to use the idea of genre to better understand how the *Fifty Shades* franchise relates to other works. The previous chapter has already revealed that *Fifty Shades* belongs to the tradition of fan fiction. This chapter will reveal how E. L. James's work coexists with other, similar books.

In short, genres are "contracts between a writer and his readers" (Jameson 135). Regis also explains that a genre consists of numerous formulas. In other words, formulas create a genre which serve as a label or an identity of a particular text. Speaking about *Fifty Shades of Grey*, Danny

Elfman, the composer of the movie's score, said that the film belonged to "a genre that didn't exist. There is no genre. There is nothing to look at as a model. And for me, that's heaven" ("Fifty Shades of Grey Featurette"). Such a comment seems to reflect the view that many fans possessed: James's work was a unique one without any precedents. But as noted earlier, no cultural texts exist in a vacuum. Blindly agreeing with Elfman, however, one risks losing sight of a larger literary tradition.

For example, Paul Alpers discussed that genre conventions, as the name suggests, refers to the fact that it is the place where authors of previous texts and the author of the current text meet (470). In other words, conventions enable genres to exist. It is these sets of conventions that allow both writers and readers to identify a text with a particular genre. Even though Alpers admits that such conventions may appear "arbitrary and inflexible" (469), they nonetheless serve as "generic rules" (Fishelov 14). Fishelov discusses that the conventions "stand before the writer as an exemplum, challenge or red flag, they appear to the reader as heuristic 'reading directions'" (14).

Therefore, conventions and genres help both writers and readers. They provide the context, or a playing field. What exactly happens on the field may be unpredictable, but there are also sets of expectations about what may and may not happen. However, these conventions are not static. As Goodrich explains, "Genres are culture-specific and historical" (viii). In other words, as a new text is created as a part of a particular genre using its conventions, the text also reinvents the genre to which it belongs. There are also works that bridge multiple genres by using different genre conventions. Examining *Fifty Shades* from the genre studies' perspective reveals how the trilogy is far from being unique and unprecedented, and it only exists within the confines of the existing conventions.

As already discussed, the book is a fan fiction based on *Twilight*. Although *Fifty Shades* is more realistic than *Twilight* for the simple reason that a billionaire in his late twenties falling in love with a young, sexually inexperienced lady while he is obsessed with BDSM *could* happen, a high school student falling in love with a vampire could not. As a story, however, it is important to remember that *Fifty Shades* nonetheless is an alternative universe fan fiction. These two works share "a similar narrative arc" (Morrissey 10). In addition to being a source of the wildly popular fan fiction, *Twilight* is also a romance novel, more specifically, a paranormal romance novel. As Lee defines, the paranormal romance genre is "a catchall category that includes diverse topics such as time travel, futuristic settings, magic, shape-shifters, supernatural creatures like werewolves and vampires, or other-world-settings" (53). Although it is not a paranormal novel, it still embodies a fairy-tale-like story that is typical of any romance novel.

Readers as well as non-fans have questioned what kind of a story *Fifty Shades* might be. Is it a romance novel? Or is it more like pornography with BDSM? Scholars who study romance novels have, for example, identified certain characteristics that many romance novels have in common with *Fifty Shades*. Similarly, pornography scholars have made various definitions of pornography to distinguish it from romance or erotica. Characterizing a popular culture text to fit an existing category is not always easy. Such categorization may depend on the context in which a text is consumed. It can also depend on the individual who consumes such material.

Therefore, the aim of this chapter is not to seek to which genre *Fifty Shades* belongs. Rather, it aims to focus on the importance of these categories and boundaries they create as manifestations of what readers and societies in general are concerned about. In other words, when the work is characterized as pornography, it is often a part of the argument that pornography is harmful, that *Fifty Shades* is pornographic, therefore *Fifty Shades* is harmful. The problem of such association between E. L. James's work and pornography is that pornography is commonly viewed negatively in the first place and labeling the book as such is used as a way to justify the untested assumption that the trilogy is harmful.

Romance as a Genre

The romance genre is immense. Romance Writers of America reports that the estimated annual sales of romance novels in 2013 were $1.08 billion. The genre occupies 13 percent of the adult fiction market. An estimated 84 percent of buyers are females, and 41 percent of readers are between the ages of thirty and fifty-four ("The Romance Genre: Romance Industry Statistics). Thomas Stewart also wrote that with over $1 billion in sales, the romance genre was the most profitable genre in the publishing industry. The runner-up genre, crime and mystery, makes less than three-quarters of what romance novels make.

On the one hand, the romance genre is not monolithic. Barbara Fuchs called it a "slippery category" (1). The genre follows various storylines. Romance Writers of America explains that the Top 10 most popular tropes are, "friends to lovers," "soul mate/fate," "second chance at love," "secret romance," "first love," "strong hero/heroine," "reunited lovers," "love triangle," "sexy billionaire/millionaire," and "sassy heroine" in the order of popularity. On the other hand, Romance Writers of America also states that there are two basic elements in any romance novel. The first is "a central love story," or that the story revolves around characters falling in love. The second is "an emotionally satisfying and optimistic ending" ("About the Romance Genre"). Romance readers, therefore, can expect a happy ending.

Happy endings are not unique to romance novels, though. Furthermore, the romance genre is not specific to the U.S. There are many prosperous romance communities in the world. But it is also true that culturally, the U.S. tends to prefer a happy ending. Discussing American culture and globalization, Lane Crothers wrote:

> A remarkably consistent feature of most American audiovisual entertainments is the happy ending. On America's televisions and movie screens, problems almost always resolve themselves in the allotted time: the situation comedy ends with a homily about family love; the cop show's bad guy goes to jail; the hero of the action-adventure movie is reunited with his or her child/family/buddies. Even *Titanic*, one of the most popular movies of all time, manages a happy ending amid the horrors of that ship's sinking: the heroine loses her lover to the frigid waters of the North Atlantic, but she is improbably rescued as a sole survivor in a sea of corpses, escapes her hated fiancé, marries for love, and has a wonderful family—all while keeping her ship-borne love in her heart forever [45].

If an American writer wrote *Romeo and Juliet*, the story would have probably ended differently. This preference for a happy ending makes the romance genre even more attractive to many American readers. The genre is about how a man and a woman should behave and how to obtain what they want (Schachar 149). Radway calls this a "fantasy resolution." Life in reality is not as easy, but in a romance novel, stories end happily (Wilson 46).

As noted above, the romance genre is filled with numerous possibilities of how its story might develop, even though an overall expectation is that the story will advance to a happy ending. The wide range of possible story schemes partially explains why Regis characterizes the genre as "confusingly inclusive" (19). Borrowing from the work by Robert Ellrich, Northrop Fyre, and others, Regis expands on the definition of the genre to eventually generate "the eight essential elements of the romance novel" (30). The elements are: "society defined," "the meeting," "the barrier," "the attraction," "the declaration," "point of ritual death," "the recognition," and "the betrothal" (30–38). Regis considered all of these eight elements to be "essential" to a romance novel. They are, according to Regis, different from other common but optional elements in the genre such as the use of scapegoats, and character conversion from bad to good (30). Regis also adds that these eight essential elements do not always appear in the same order. Some of the elements may be more emphasized in a particular story while others might be brief or relatively insignificant for the storyline. The following section will use Regis's eight elements to consider how the *Fifty Shades* trilogy fits the romance genre.

Society Defined

Regis's first element is "society defined." She writes, "Near the beginning of the novel, the society that the heroine and hero will confront in their courtship is defined for the reader. This society is in some way flawed; it may be incomplete, superannuated, or corrupt. It always oppresses the heroine and hero" (31). The fact that the story's environment is presented near the beginning is not surprising regardless of the genre. For any text, it is a necessary process to set the stage. But what's unique about Regis's analysis about romance novels is that the stage is "flawed" and "oppresses the heroine and hero" (31).

In the trilogy, the stage is incomplete for both Christian and Anastasia. Christian, as he admits around the mid-point of the *Fifty Shades of Grey* novel and near the end of the film, acknowledges that he is "fifty shades of fucked up" (267). For Anastasia, the book even begins by her giving up on her own appearance and happy to be "semi-presentable." The story makes a clear contrast between Anastasia and Kate, her roommate, who is supposed to be the beautiful one of the two. James wrote, "Even ill, she looks gamine and gorgeous, strawberry blond hair in place and green eyes bright" (3–4). As for Christian, although it is unclear if "oppressed" is the right word to use to describe what he feels about his own life, he does feel that he has to hide behind a veil in public and carries a scar to hide. Study subjects of Bonomi, Nichols, Carotta, Kiuchi, and Perry "were sympathetic and rationalized Christian's behaviors" for this reason (142).

The condition for Anastasia is more complex. On the one hand, the main culprit of her being oppressed in the story is Christian. As Bonomi, Altenburger, and Walton explain, Anastasia faces intimate partner violence. They write that the novel has "patterns consistent with national definitions of intimate partner violence and associated reactions known to occur in abused women" (741). But it is not just Christian that oppresses

Anastasia in the story. As will be discussed more in detail in other chapters in this book, the story is filled with patriarchy, singular views on female beauty, and other social norms and ideas that are reflective of the society in real life.

Therefore, both Christian and Anastasia are oppressed and restrained in their own ways. Christian has not been able to move forward with his life past his experience as a submissive and an abused child. He admits that his past continues to complicate his life. Anastasia, on the other hand, was originally constrained in her own low self-esteem as demonstrated at the very beginning of the novel. Even though her self-esteem does not remain low soon after, she is still oppressed with Christian's behaviors. The world, for both characters, is not ideal.

The Meeting

The second element is "the meeting." This is when "the heroine and hero meet for the first time," and when "some hint of conflict to come is often introduced" (Regis 31). When Anastasia visits Christian at his office to replace her friend, Kate, she immediately finds herself visually attracted to Christian. But before Anastasia leaves and while she prepares herself to leave his office, Christian sends what Anastasia perceives as "a challenge, or a threat." In addition, when Christian tells Anastasia to drive home safely, she notices his voice is "stern, authoritative" (James *Fifty Shades of Grey*, 15). Early in the story, readers perceive that there will be a conflict between the two main characters.

The most significant conflict for Christian and Anastasia in their story is the power dynamics between the two. In general, Christian gets what he wants while Anastasia struggles to get what she wants from their relationship. Although the *Fifty Shades* movie changed a few details of how their power dynamics worked out—Christian's reaction to the news that Anastasia is a virgin or his proposal to have a date once a week—both the novel and the movie hint at the beginning that power and control will be the source of conflict between the two. Later in the novel, some readers and moviegoers begin to question if Christian feels that he has lost control over his own life, especially as he begins to cater to some of the requests that Anastasia makes. Or, is it a part of his controlling character to show Anastasia a hint of what she could have, such as the glider ride?

Regardless of how one reads the power dynamics between Christian and Anastasia, each character faces something new to him and her. For

Christian, Anastasia is different from past submissives he has had. For Anastasia, a romantic attraction to him alone is already new, let alone Christian's sexual behaviors and preferences. Jean-Michael Ganteau discussed that romance is about "things foreign, foreign in more than just the obvious sense of the term. The foreign … is what is outside the walls of the city, what escapes common experience. It is the realm of the other (226–227). The foreign may be exciting at the moment of the meeting. But it also becomes what Regis calls the barrier.

The Barrier

Regis writes that "a series of scenes often scattered throughout the novel establishes for the reader the reasons that this heroine and hero cannot marry" (32). Anastasia believes that she is not attractive, while Christian is. Her inner dialogue is filled with the idea that she does not think she will be a good match for Christina simply because of her looks. In addition, needless to say, there is an immense gap in class. Anastasia is portrayed as someone stereotypical of a college student. She drives an old car, has a part-time job, and parties at a bar that is not exclusive. Christian's wealth is obvious.

In addition to these external barriers, there are internal barriers, or "[circumstances] that [come] from within either or both" (Regis 32). Christian's past as a subordinate and his fascination and obsession about BDSM are both such barriers. The gap in what Christian is willing to give Anastasia and what Anastasia wants from Christian is, of course, a significant barrier. The presence of Mrs. Robinson is a two-fold barrier. On one level, she is responsible for Christian being the dominant. Although one's dominance in the bedroom normally does not and should not translate to that outside of the sexual context, and for this reason Mrs. Robinson might or might not be responsible for Christian's manipulative tendency outside of the bedroom, she still creates a barrier to their relationship. On another level, Christian's business deal with Mrs. Robinson that is revealed in *Fifty Shades Darker* continues to fuel the hardship for the two.

The barriers are not limited to these examples. In *Fifty Shades Darker*, Leila Williams, one of Christian's former submissives, is involved in the story as she stalks Anastasia. Anastasia does not appreciate the fact that Christian continues to stay in touch with Mrs. Robinson. She even confronts Anastasia after she is engaged to Christian. Christian, on the other hand, sees José as a rival. Even after Christian and Anastasia's marriage, there are barriers to its continuation. Just as Regis suggests and, like many other romance novels, the *Fifty Shades* trilogy is a series of obstacles for Christian and Anastasia to overcome to attain the aforementioned happy ending.

The Attraction

Although a romance novel is filled with reasons and barriers why the two main characters cannot and even should not marry, it also contains "a scene or series of scenes scattered throughout the novel [establishing] for the reader the reason that this couple must marry" (Regis 33). Regis explains that "the attraction keeps the heroine and hero involved long enough to surmount the barrier. Attraction can be based on a combination of sexual chemistry, friendship, shared goals or feelings, society's expectations, and economic issues" (33). The attraction is contrary to what protagonists often feel about themselves. Anastasia does not particularly feel she is good looking. Christian does not have good self-esteem beyond what is substantiated by his wealth. As Schachar discusses, protagonists look into the mirror "expressing a lack of belonging and identity" (151). *Fifty Shades* can be read as a typical romance novel in which main characters seek to find where they belong and who they are by associating themselves with their object of attraction.

The trilogy is filled with cues that could be read as romantic. One website lists eight ways the novel "amps up the romance" ("8 Ways 50 Shades of Grey Amps up the Romance"). The website mentions "generous, thoughtful gifting," including a first-edition copy of a Thomas Hardy novel; "the romancing of Anastasia Steele" with helicopter rides, expensive wine, and gliding; "knight in shining armor ... by saving her from José's unrelenting, unrequited kisses and stepping it up a notch when she needs help fighting her creepo boss Jack Hyde"; having a feeling for Anastasia while Christian had never had such a feeling for other submissives; Anastasia's healing of Christian's broken heart and scars; "fun flirtation" via e-mail; Christian's giving of his heart and flowers to Anastasia; and the two characters being "soul mates" for each other. The study by Bonomi, Nichols, Carotta, Kiuchi, and Perry also noted that some of their subjects identified elements in the *Fifty Shades of Grey* film that they considered romantic (142).

All of these traits that the website lists as "romantic" could be interpreted as manipulative by critics. But it is not just the aforementioned website that identifies the *Fifty Shades* story as romantic. Anne Thompson, reviewing the film for *Thompson on Hollywood*, also listed six reasons why the film is a classic romance. Jaime Dornan, furthermore, also stated that the film's "love story is more important than the BDSM aspect." He continued that the movie is "a love story" (Messer par. 3). The attraction between Christian and Anastasia is undoubtedly there. Its soundness can be challenged, as some social science scholars have analyzed. As a story, however, the characters demonstrate mutual attraction with which they try to overcome a series of barriers they encounter.

The Declaration

In the declaration phase, "The hero declares his love for the heroine, and the heroine her love for the hero" (Regis 34). In the case of *Fifty Shades of Grey*, the declaration of mutual attraction takes place very early in the story. In the book, Christian was immediately interested in Anastasia. She was also mesmerized by his beauty. The first part of the novel is about their mutual attraction that, on the surface level, few would expect to realize because of the vast difference in the two characters' backgrounds. In the film, as soon as Anastasia enters Christian's office, her facial expression reveals her visual attraction to him. If it was not an obvious enough cue, Kate's inquisition back in their apartment shows that Anastasia is interested in Christian. On the other hand, Christian's tight grip on the edge of his office desk and his flirtatious comments to her during the interview also disclose his interest in her.

As Regis notes, these displays of mutual attraction help "create the variety of plots within the set of possibilities open to the romance novel" (34). Sometimes the sense of mutual attraction can lead to conflicts between the two characters. While Christian and Anastasia want each other, they also want different kinds of satisfactions through their relationship. Even the scene of gliding includes the attraction (two characters having a typical romantic time), the barrier (the gliding experience as a date is an exception, not a norm, for Christian, while Anastasia wants it to be the norm), and the declaration (Christian is willing to try something new for Anastasia). The declaration, the attraction, and the barrier are, therefore, all intertwined.

Regis's analysis on the placement of the declaration provides a valuable insight of *Fifty Shades*. She writes,

> Love at first sight is common in hero-centered comedy, where the heroine does not need to be wooed.... Move the declaration to the very end of the novel, and the heroine and hero declare their love for each other after the novel's barrier has been surmounted.... With the heroine in the center of the narrative, it usually becomes a story about the courtship, about the choice of a spouse, with the heroine's declaration scene placed correspondingly late [34].

At first glance, *Fifty Shades* is a heroine-centered story. It is filled with Anastasia's inner-voice. The story is written from her perspective. However, the declaration happens quite early in the story. As noted above, the initial declaration takes place as love-at-first-sight. Even when Anastasia admits to Christian that she has fallen in love with him near the end of the first novel (James *Fifty Shades of Grey*, 509), it is still early in the entire trilogy. The declaration from Christian, on the other hand, does not take place until the trilogy's second book when he proposes to Anastasia and says, "Marry me" (James *Fifty Shades Darker*, 332). But as early as at the end of the first novel, Christian indeed acknowledges that Anastasia is special to him. To respond to Anastasia, Christian says, "You are everything I want you to be" (James *Fifty Shades of Grey*, 509).

What this reading of *Fifty Shades* might suggest is that the story is not romance revolving around "the courtship" or "the choice of a spouse," but rather that around struggles and barriers. Unlike *Pride and Prejudice*, James's work does not reject the love-at-first-sight convention. Rather, it prospers on that promise. Without Christian's obsession with BDSM that affects their relationship outside the bedroom, the story could very well end quickly as a simple love-at-first-sight plot. However, James introduces a substantial gap between the two characters that inflicts emotional pain on Anastasia, and sometimes Christian, to the simple plot and creates a trilogy. Overcoming the differences and trying to make compromises, therefore, become central to the plot of the trilogy as a romance work.

Point of Ritual Death

The point of ritual death is the rock bottom of the romance plot. It is necessary for the plot development and for the excitement of the story. But it is "the moment in the narrative when the union between heroine and hero, the hoped-for resolution, seems absolutely impossible, when it seems that the barrier will remain, more substantial than ever" (Regis 35). A prime example of a point of ritual death is the ending of *Fifty Shades of Grey*. "Is this it?" and "Is this how it ends?" were common reactions in movie theaters at the end of the film.

When Christian shows Anastasia what he is looking for from their relationship by whipping her six times, she calls off the relationship. Anastasia tells Christian, "I can't stay. I know what I want and you can't give it to me, and I can't give you what you need" (James *Fifty Shades of Grey*, 513). The last conversation between them is "Good-bye, Christian," and "Ana, good-bye" (James *Fifty Shades*, 513). In the film version, Christian simply says, "Ana," and Anastasia responds, "Christian." The elevator door closes and the film concludes. The novel version of the story continues a little more, with Taylor, Christian's driver, driving Anastasia home. Once Anastasia gets to her apartment, she regrets her earlier decision by saying to herself, "What have I done?" and cries into Taylor's handkerchief (James *Fifty Shades*, 514).

Although a smart romance reader would know that such a breakup is a part of the overall plot and feel assured that the couple will eventually get back together, Regis's point about that seeming impossibility is present in James's story. The plot has been developed in a way that Anastasia has tried to accommodate to Christian's wants to the best of her ability. Christian has also commented that he was changing for her. But once she realizes how far Christian hopes to eventually take the BDSM behavior, she felt she had no choice but to leave him.

Regis's sharp observation, however, hints that depending on one's experience with romance novels, a reader may respond differently to such a point of ritual death. In other words, a more experienced and sophisticated romance reader "responds to the peril, the mood, and to the repetition of the imagery of death," whereas a less experienced reader "responds to the peril of the situation, or to the darkened mood" (36). In other words, an experienced reader is able to react to the ritual death as a part of a larger storyline while a less experience reader myopically reacts to the shocking nature of the ritual death.

A myopic reaction to the film's end is common in many review sites. For example, Samantha Highfill wrote, "From a storytelling perspective … [the ending] seems like a strange choice—the film spends its entire run time building a relationship, only to tear it apart in the final 20 minutes" (par. 8). Marisa Lascala is more favorable to the ending of the film. She wrote, "I happen to love the ending of the movie…. Regardless, the ending was basically my favorite part…. It ends on a moment of strength for Anastasia. She made the decision to leave. She has agency. It's abrupt, and she stands firm" (par. 6). Despite the obvious difference between

Highfill and Lascala, both writers reacted to the peril of the relationship without paying attention to how the peril interacts with the mood in general and with other instances of metaphorical death.

The Recognition

Another key part of a romance novel is the recognition. Regis discusses that "in a scene or scenes the author represents the new information that will overcome the barrier.... [T]he protagonist is recognized for who he or she truly is, and this recognition fells the barrier and permits the betrothal to go forward" (36). Since the recognition is a way for the couple to overcome barriers, this phase is directly connected to the barriers they have already experienced.

In the *Fifty Shades* franchise, the barriers may include the different needs and wants between Christian and Anastasia, the presence of Mrs. Robinson, and many others. The readers and viewers are not presented with the recognition. The story offers various barriers that ultimately lead to the departure of Anastasia. However, soon after the breakup, Christian asks Anastasia if she was still needing a ride to José's exhibit. Anastasia takes him up on his offer. As they are leaving the gallery, Christian kisses Anastasia. James wrote,

> He looks quickly up and down the street then heads left and suddenly sweeps me into a side alley, abruptly pushing me up against a wall. He grabs my face between his hands, forcing me to look up into his ardent, determined eyes.
> I gasp, and his mouth swoops down. He's kissing me, violently [*Fifty Shades Darker*, 26–27].

Of course, this scene, from the perspective of a healthy romantic relationship, is filled with problems. But James uses it at the beginning of the second novel as a reconciliation to the end of the first book.

The rest of the trilogy has multiple repetitions of Christian and Anastasia fighting and making up. As Jordan Grey wrote, the two characters "like each other, they fight, they make up, they have a lot of kinky sex, they fall in love, the end" (para. 4). Even after they are married, their fights continue to the point that Anastasia is motivated to take time off to see Kate. The history with Mrs. Robinson keeps interfering with the relationship between the two. These ups and downs keep the story moving, and exciting. They also allow readers to be hopeful that even after the point of ritual death, the relationship is alive.

The Betrothal

As the name suggests, this norm is about marriage. Regis explains that "in a scene or scenes the hero asks the heroine to marry him and she accepts" (37). Although she continues to argue that "in the romance novels from the last quarter of the twentieth century marriage is not necessary as long as it is clear that heroine and hero will end up together" (37–38). As for *Fifty Shades*, James made it clear that Christian and Anastasia get married.

At the end of *Fifty Shades Darker*, Christian tells Anastasia, "Anastasia Steele. I love you. I want to love, cherish, and protect you for the rest of my life. Be mine. Always. Share my life with me. Marry me" (530). James, speaking for Anastasia, describes the scene:

> I sob, suddenly overwhelmed with joy, and I join him on my knees, my fingers fisting in his hair as I kiss him, kiss him with all my heart and soul. I kiss this beautiful man, who loves me as I love him; and he wraps his arms around me, his hands moving to my hair, his mouth on mine. I know deep down I will always be his, and he will always be mine. We've come so far together, we have so far to go, but we are made for each other. We are meant to be [531].

At the beginning of *Fifty Shades Freed*, Reverend Walsh announces Christian and Anastasia married (10).

In some romance novels, the story might end with the betrothal. As for *Fifty Shades*, it is just the beginning of the third book. The trilogy ends with Christian and Anastasia having a son named Theodore Raymond Grey, and Anastasia pregnant with a second child, who will be named Phoebe.

Hero and Fifty Shades

Similar to Regis, who identified common characteristics about romance novels, Jameson argues that such works require a hero (139). Fyre calls a romance hero "analogous to the mythical Messiah or deliverer who comes from an upper world" (187). Heroes, just like the romance storylines, also follow a certain pattern. Hume, for example, discusses three stages—equilibrium, struggle, and higher harmony—with which romance writers take its readers through the journey with the hero. For critical readers of the *Fifty Shades* trilogy, it may appear unfathomable to label Christian as a hero. But simply from the perspective of how the story develops, Christian plays the role of the hero who allegedly makes Anastasia happy.

Hume describes the first stage as "the hero at peace" (135). As for

Christian Grey, this phase is very short, between the beginnings of the story until their first date. According to Hume, the hero in this phase "is secure and comfortable within a sheltering world, and whether very young or technically adult, most of his needs are supplied without having to worry or bestir himself" (135). As Anastasia notes during her first encounter, Christian is confident and secure. Although he has a problematic past, he is in control of his professional and personal life. As he repeatedly admits to Anastasia both in the film and in the novel, their relationship is new to him, and Anastasia defies Christian.

The second stage, the struggle, takes the hero away from his comfortable environment. Hume suggests that the struggle is frequently signaled with images of a forest, water, a door, or a trip (136). For Christian, his struggles come from the "more," or in his own words, "hearts and flowers" (James *Fifty Shades of Grey*, 110). In other words, although he wants Anastasia to stay with him, she hopes to have "more" with Christian, which is not what he wants. The gap between what they each want creates the struggle. Furthermore, Christian's relationship with Mrs. Robinson worries Anastasia. Many of these struggles are shown with the cues that Hume discussed. In the film, Christian takes Anastasia to the woods to talk about Mrs. Robinson and to discuss the possibility of pursuing a BDSM relationship. It is after his surprise trip to Georgia that it becomes clear that Christian might want "more." The book version is more explicit about Christian's transformation than the film. In the book, Christian admits to Anastasia that he wants more than a submissive by saying, "I want more, too" (James *Fifty Shades*, 456).

Hume writes, "Whether the forest is merely a wood or an entrapping labyrinth, whether the gate is apparently ordinary or completely magical, whether the water is just a shower or a more ostentatious symbol for the unconscious, and travel in an ordinary ship ... or by means of magic, all of these draw the hero into a new world" (136). Furthermore, that "world is different from the one he has known" (136). This is the world that Christian slowly moves into and that Anastasia hopes to live with him.

Once the hero attains the third sphere, the higher harmony, then he is at peace. Although the harmony appears differently in different novels, it often shows that the hero is at peace in an environment that is different from his original one. Christian's harmony is represented with the presence of Anastasia, who agrees to marry him in the middle of the trilogy. The harmony means that the hero can expect marriage, a significant directional cue for a romance novel, or "a work of prose fiction that tells the story of a courtship and betrothal of one or more heroines" (Regis 19).

Failure of Fifty Shades

Romance novels are often considered to be trifling. Although it is the most popular literary genre in the U.S., it is also the "least respected" (Regis xi). Joan Hollows, for example, explained that "many literary critics [have] regarded romantic fiction as the ultimate example of the trivial" (68). One of the reasons for this discrepancy between the popularity and the respect comes from the fact that the genre is largely for female writers and readers. On the one hand, the majority of writers and readers of romance novels are female. The publishing industry and its relevant business operations, such as book reviews, marketing, and others are predominantly controlled by men. Consequently, the industry is occupied by those who are little exposed to the romance genre. In other words, the public's undervaluing of the romance genre does not reflect its low quality. Rather, it is a result of the society that tends to value what males produce and consume.

Once the romance genre is examined as a locus for female authors' and readers' agency, it begins to have different meanings. Although criticisms about writing styles, sexualizing of female characters, and other issues merit serious examination, it is also true that romance novels can challenge existing biases against women. For example, the novels can position women "as sexually active rather than passive" (Lee 54). In addition, they create "a female *subject* of desire (emphasis in original)" rather than a female object of desire (Lee 54). Such a view on women suggests romance novels can challenge sexual norms and stereotypes. Men do not have to be the ones that "do" and women do not have to be the ones to "be done." If the genre's agency is recognized, a completely different set of evaluations about romance novels become not only possible but also valid (Makinen 42).

Furthermore, as an erotic romance novel, *Fifty Shades* includes depictions of sexual acts that have been considered marginal or have been excluded from the mainstream. Christian's obsession with BDSM, the highly controversial book scene about Anastasia's period, and other examples in the novels and the film also challenge traditional views about human sexuality and sexual norms. As Lee argues, romance novels tend to have explicit sexual depictions (55). James's work is no exception. What is different about *Fifty Shades* from the romance novels which Lee examined is that James did not rely on "a highly coded language" to be explicit, which many critics characterized as James's poor writing skills and style. Despite the quality of writing, romance novels, including *Fifty Shades*, indeed challenge their readers and society to rethink what they consider normal or acceptable. What romance genre scholars suggest is that, as a genre, these novels have a potential to be the vehicle to challenge existing patriarchal and prejudice-ridden narratives by possibly giving female writers, readers, and characters more power.

Even though such power of romance novels is rarely recognized, it is a powerful tool that the genre possesses. Of course, there are numerous romance novels that fail to do so. Romance readers do not pick up a novel with a specific social agenda, either. But because *Fifty Shades* had such a wide reach to its audience, the trilogy could have raised awareness, encouraged discussions, and possibly made a change, even a small one. Unfortunately, *Fifty Shades* failed to take advantage of the genre's potential. Discussing the romance genre, Ann Snitow argues that "when women try to picture excitement, the society offers them one vision, romance. When women try to imagine companionship, the society offers them one vision, male sexual companionship. When women try to fantasize about success, mastery, the society offers them one vision, the power to attract men" (para. 29). In her analysis, she correctly identifies that many of the romance storylines rely on the female achieving success through a male.

Fifty Shades falls under the same category. Anastasia's happiness relies on her heterosexual relationship and marriage. Even though Christian claims that it is Anastasia and not he that is in control of the relationship, Anastasia feels trapped because of her fear of losing him. Even when Anastasia takes initiative with her sexuality, she does so under Christian's influence. Christian continues to emphasize that Anastasia is his. She happily obliges. The hierarchy exists outside the Red Room of Pain. The hierarchy, therefore, is not a fiction confined to their sexual practices, but is a part of the foundation of their relationship. Additionally, as Helen Hazen argues, even if fans claim that sexual "impositions" and violence are "forced onto women by themselves for the sheer sake of enjoyment" (17), based on Hazen's analysis, Quale states that "women are becoming aroused by fantasizing about a violent act against a woman who is portrayed as powerless—empowerment via powerlessness" (19). In *Fifty Shades*, Anastasia is consistently powerless. Even when she defies Christian, their relationship is based on Christian exercising control and power over Anastasia.

Probably one way Anastasia could demonstrate female empowerment was by possessing her own sexuality. It is true that Anastasia chose to stay in the BDSM relationship with Christian. However, as a romance novel, the book positioned Anastasia in a patriarchal and hierarchical environment with significant power disparities. As Quale wrote, her satisfaction came through "heterosexual romance, female domesticity, female submissiveness, female pleasure through male pleasure, and other patriarchal values" (33). Because popular culture reflects who we are, the message of the *Fifty Shades* trilogy should also reflect who we are and what we believe in.

Is Fifty Shades *Pornography?*

One of the most common questions about *Fifty Shades* and its characterization is if it is pornography. On the one hand, many critics who supported censoring *Fifty Shades* or removing the novels from public libraries—as will be noted in Chapter Four—argued that the trilogy was pornographic. On the other hand, many fans claimed that it was a romance novel, or erotica. On the surface level, a romance story follows a certain genre scheme as shown earlier in this chapter, and ends happily. Pornography is different: its focus is on sex. Sex repeats itself, and the story—if it exists at all—is cyclical. Because there exist at least two schools of thought about the genre to which *Fifty Shades* belong, a natural question is, which is it?

Pornography is an immense international industry. It is estimated to be an industry with sales of $15 to $20 billion (Ackman para. 3; Richtel para. 5). Furthermore, with the popularization of high-speed Internet and the increasing availability of high-definition web cameras and other advanced technology, free and amateur pornography prospers online. Therefore, both *Fifty Shades* fans and anti-fans live only a click or two away from explicit pornographic materials that once was unimaginable. Therefore, it is not difficult to imagine that, for many, the publication of *Fifty Shades* generated a sense of panic, or moral panic, for fear that just another sexually explicit work had become available as mainstream literature.

The U.S. Supreme Court Justice Potter Stewart—the justice known for his statement, "I know it when I see it"—is not with us to help identify if *Fifty Shades* is pornography. Historically, attempts to define pornography happened when there was a need to ban or control obscene materials while protecting the freedom of speech. In short, pornography had to be controlled while erotica was to be allowed as a part of one's freedom of speech. Partly because this distinction had to be made, Lindgren argues that a good definition of pornography is the one that separates it from erotica (1155). The Campaign Against Pornography and Censorship also noted that "pornography does not include erotica (defined as sexually explicit materials premised on equality) and it does not include *bona fide* sex education materials, or medical or forensic literature." In addition, the campaign stated that pornography is a depiction of "a combination of the sexual objectification and subordination of women, often including violation and violence" (qtd. in Smith 72).

Although pornography is popular and controversial, defining it is not an easy task. Numerous scholars with various gender political ideas have tried to define the genre. Some were sex-positive feminists, and some others were not. Some argued that pornography was a proof of "men oppressing women" (Salmon 152). For example, according to MacKinnon and Dworkin, pornography can be characterized by three traits: "graphic sexual explicitness," "the subordination of women," and "depictions of any one of a long list of specific sexual acts" (Lindgren 1157). Other feminists, however, questioned if pornography can be a material beneficial to women. Camille Paglia's idea, for example, emphasized that pornography can be positive for women, both politically and sexually. Such a perspective was supported by studies that have shown that countries with more violent pornography do not always have violent crimes against women (Kutchinsky). Combining the views that the pornography could be positive or negative to women, Cass Sustein wrote, "In short, regulable pornography must (a) be sexually explicit, (b) depict women as enjoying or deserving some form of physical abuse, and (c) have the purpose and effect of producing sexual arousal" (592). Because consumers and producers of pornography today are no longer male-dominated, definitions of pornography must address this new industrial environment. Similarly, an increasing availability of gay and lesbian pornography also complicates the simplistic view about male-dominated power assertion.

Some have tried to distinguish pornography from other depictions of sex. For example, obscenity is considered to "[lack] value" while pornography is thought to "[harm] women." (Lindgren 1159). Furthermore, pornography is supposed to carry "the prurient interest element" (Lindgren 1212). Because distinguishing "prurience" defined as "unhealthy lust" from "normal, healthy sexual desires" is difficult, attempts by MacKinnon, Dworkin, Sunstein, and others have often failed to helpfully define pornography. Many of these experts could not agree what kinds of sexual desires are normal and what kinds are not (Lindgren 1212). Applying Sunstein's criteria, for example, Lindgren did not find any depictions of sex to be prurient and none of the works studied were categorized as pornographic (1213). Some other definitions try to distinguish pornography from erotica. *Fifty Shades of Grey*, for example, is sold as erotica by its publisher, even though some critics argue it is pornographic. According to definitions that attempt to separate the two genres, violence is often the key distinction.

Partly because of the violent nature of at least some pornographic materials, Thornton argues that pornography is a way for men to exercise control over women. He wrote, "Rape, sexual molestation, sexual harassment, and pornography make up a set of interconnected practices in and through which men maintain political control over women" (29). For Thornton, erotica "is sexually explicit representation which depicts human beings in such a way as to preserve their human dignity" (32). According to Thornton, there is a clear difference between erotica and pornography. Gail Dines agrees by stating that "pornography is really what men think about women—they hate women" (57). Of course, the idea of patriarchal control as a definition may not work today when inexpensive webcams helped the rise of amateur solo pornography that is created as a form of sheer entertainment of the women producing it.

Even to this day, there is no consensus as to how to define the genre. For example, in 2001, Michael C. Rea wrote an extensive essay defining pornography. His goal was to make a realistic definition that consisted of three parts. Recognizing that there were already too many definitions that failed to truly define the genre, he tried to generate a definition that could be agreed upon. He understood that the same material could be considered pornographic or non-pornographic depending on the context. Therefore, he separated "being pornography" and "treating as pornography." He also recognized that the "communicative content" of a material was the key in defining pornography. He wrote, "Someone who desires and attempts to be aroused by a magazine simply by rubbing up against it, and not by viewing or otherwise attending to its content, is not treating the magazine as pornography even if it is in fact pornography." Last, he argued that with some exceptions, pornography would lack intimacy (135–136).

Rea was not the only one who thought the existing definitions of pornography were insufficient. David Andrews similarly argued that "dominant definitions of pornography have failed to meet some basic empirical standards" (417). Six years after Rea published his work, Jorn Sonderholm also published an essay in disagreement with Rea. Offering counterexamples, he argues that Rea's definition was insufficient. Neither Andrews nor Sonderholm offers an alternative definition. But they show that current definitions fail to address the reality of pornography.

Because pornography has escaped a clear definition, it is close to impossible to definitively argue that *Fifty Shades* is or is not pornography. Across the Atlantic, as British lawmakers try to regulate sexual media content, they were unclear how to define *Fifty Shades* (Attwood and Walters). However, the history of defining pornography is the history of controlling materials that were considered inappropriate for circulation. The history of defining pornography has rarely been a celebration of a genre. What Andrews calls "anti-porn biases" that exist with the question, "Is this pornography?" naturally reflects and underscores the existing value judgment about the text itself. Questioning, "Is *Fifty Shades* pornography?" therefore, is not a neutral question. The question embodies the assumption of those who ask that there is something inappropriate about the material.

Fifty Shades of Romance

Although *Fifty Shades'* massive popularity makes the work stand out because few romance novels in the genre's history has sold as many copies internationally and few become such a major Hollywood phenomenon, the novels are similar to other romance novels in many ways. *Fifty Shades'* base, *Twilight*, is considered by many fans to belong to the romance genre. Mary Anne Moffitt argues that the genre is based on "a happy ending and reconciliation between the heroine and hero … and a promise of love, intense communication, and a vicarious relationship in the affectionate acts of the handsome hero towards the heroine" (239). Behm-Morawitz, Click, and Aubrey also argue that *Twilight'*s storyline fits Moffitt's description. They also argue that fans who enjoyed the relationship between Edward and Bella "were more likely to prefer a romantic relationship in which their partner was protective, possessive, chivalrous, and intensely attracted to them. These fans (both adults and teens) were also less likely to identify as feminist" (151). It is only natural that, as fan fiction, *Fifty Shades of Grey* and its sequels follow a similar storyline that can be categorized in the same genre with *Twilight* and that appeals to similar fans.

James's work also followed Regis's eight essential elements. As Jameson argued, the story has a hero. According to Schachar, romance novels are about self-discovery (149). Both for Christian and Anastasia, the trilogy is about self-discovery. Just like many other romance novels, it contains explicit sexual depictions. All these pieces of evidence, along with many others, support the claim that the *Fifty Shades* trilogy belongs to the romance novel genre.

The romance genre is complex. On the one hand, it is hugely popular. But its popularity tends to be confined within the genre. In other words, romance novel fans read dozens of romance novels a year but there are not many romance novels that appeal to those who are not usually fans of the genre. *Fifty Shades*, from this perspective, was unique. It clearly attracted those who have never read a romance novel before.

Especially because its reach and popularity was vast, it had a potential for social change. Having an opportunity to write fan fiction, to have a large number of followers, and to have one's work published as international bestsellers are empowering experiences. Digital technology enabled James to have that opportunity. Therefore, it is inaccurate to argue that everything about *Fifty Shades* is not empowering for women. James showed what an individual with little experience in writing could possibly achieve. However, the story of *Fifty Shades* that follows a very typical romance novel genre formula and characteristics is probably entertaining and pleasurable, but not empowering, for many fans. The story itself is still patriarchal. Anastasia's happiness depends on Christian. Christian repeats that Anastasia is his. She does not challenge the idea.

Of course, this is not to suggest that readers' involvement and engagement with the trilogy are trifling. As Janice Radway suggested in her canonical work on romance novels, that they are engaged in their own intellectual endeavors. Margaret Marbury, vice president of Harlequin's Mira imprint, commented, "*Fifty Shades* has certainly given a lift to our erotic backlist. It has raised all boats, in that sense" (Deahl, para. 4). She continued, "I don't know how long it will last, but those books have created a new readership. Will those readers start reading historical fiction, or other subgenres of romance? I doubt it. I think right now they're focused on erotica and, even more so, BDSM" (Deahl, para. 4). Her comment shows that no matter how some argue that it is unique, the novel actually is part of a long-existing genre that has dealt with portraying various kinds of relationships. The *Fifty Shades* hype made the genre more visible and allowed women's discussions on sex less taboo.

Because the story is filled with depictions of sex, many labeled the trilogy as pornography. Especially those who attempted to censor James's work from local libraries and bookstores and those who discouraged others from buying or reading the trilogy used this characterization to justify their resistance. Salmon argues that romance and pornography are very different. She writes:

> Although the romance novel has been referred to as pornography for women, it is really in many ways the opposite of male-oriented pornography. The goal of the

romance is never sex for its own sake, much less impersonal sex with strangers. At the heart of the romance novel plot is a love story in which the heroine overcomes obstacles to identify, win the heart of, and ultimately have a long-term relationship (or marriage) with the one man who is the right one for her [153].

Furthermore, she claims that while pornography is about "short-term mating success," romance is about a "long-term mating success" (158). But for McAlister, *Fifty Shades* "fuses the romantic and the pornographic together" (1). McAlister continues to argue that while pornography offers instant gratification and romance novel delayed gratification, the novel is about both (4). Similarly, those who have studied pornography argue that defining pornography is not as easy. It may be possible to pick a sample text and argue for or against the idea that it is pornography. But establishing a definition and applying it to define a text is far more difficult.

Not only is it almost impossible to conclusively demonstrate if *Fifty Shades* should be considered pornography, it is also important to realize that the history of such attempts reflect social bias against materials that were subject to such a question. The value and meaning of the pornography question, therefore, does not exist in its possibility to categorize the story. For *Fifty Shades*, the answer can simply be that it is both romance *and* pornography. As McAlister contests, Christian and Anastasia are "making love and fucking hard" at the same time. With a wide array of sexual preferences, what truly is the difference between the two? (7).

Therefore, what is meaningful about the question, "Is *Fifty Shades* pornography?" is that it helps us see our assumptions and biases about particular texts or genres. Based on what we might have heard or read about a text, we are tempted to categorize it with other so-called questionable, trifling, low-class, or respectable genres to justify our disdains and/or likes. Although genres allow writers to follow a convention to advance a story, and readers to achieve both the thrill of the unexpected and the sense of security about where the story would eventually end up, it also leads to problematic sweeping claims to make certain popular cultural texts marginal.

CHAPTER THREE

My Mom Is Reading It?

Visibility, Technology and Presentist Assumptions

In less than five years, *Fifty Shades of Grey* quickly changed its status from just one of hundreds of thousands of fan fiction based on *Twilight* to an international phenomenon. Even before its initial Hollywood adaptation arrived in February 2015, the literary trilogy itself made a significant impact on many societies. As discussed earlier, popular culture is relevant, reflective, and formative in the society where it is produced and consumed. Examining popular culture reveals information not only about its producers and consumers but also its surrounding environment. The fervor about *Fifty Shades* seems to suggest that it was a unique novel trilogy or film. But is that true? Was it truly so unique that, as Danny Elfman stated, *Fifty Shades* was "unclassifiable" ("50 Shades of Grey," para. 4)?

In reality, E. L. James's trilogy was not as unique or different as many had imagined. It is common for many to assume that they live in a unique period in time. Political speeches, for example, are filled with such exceptionalist views. The same is true with how people talk about recent technological developments. Any period in time is unique in its own sense. Therefore, being unique is not as unique as one might expect.

This chapter will examine what made *Fifty Shades* appear so unique and different from other books and movies. Ultimately, it will not only challenge the notion that the novels were unique and different, but argue that it was far from being so—while there is no question that the public has generally characterized *Fifty Shades* as unique. While reviewing some of the distinctive characteristics of *Fifty Shades*, this chapter will suggest that there is an inherent risk in exceptionalizing *Fifty Shades* and making a rushed presentist claim that the trilogy reflects a major social shift of our time.

Although there may be a temptation among fans to consider E. L. James's work as a revolutionary one that changes social norms and conventional ideas about sexuality, or among the anti–*Fifty Shades* group to label it as the epitome of the social decay in contemporary society, the reality is that the novel is just one of many popular cultural objects that reflect the sentiment of the time. Of course, its popularity is immense. It appealed to a very wide fan base. However, there are many examples of similar literary and film works that surprised the public with their success and that have been characterized as a driver of a major cultural shift. It is, therefore, important to note that *Fifty Shades* is just one cultural object that has the power to contribute to and to mirror the continuous development of social beliefs and values.

On the one hand, *Fifty Shades* is not an exceptional work in literary or cinematographic history as far as its content is concerned. There have been many other works in romance, erotica, and pornography that had similar edginess. What *Fifty Shades* enables us to shed light on is its visibility. The trilogy became visible through merchandising and marketing, as another part of this book discusses. But it was also present because of the viral reactions by young people as characterized by Kiers's tweet, "My mom reads Fifty Shades wtf." This type of reaction, shared virally online through social media, enhanced the visibility of *Fifty Shades*. In other words, talking about the works became as popular as, if not more popular than, actually reading or watching them.

Furthermore, the books were able to attain a high level of visibility thanks to the popularization of e-readers. The publication of the trilogy roughly coincided with the spread of e-readers, such as Amazon's Kindle and Barnes & Noble's Nook. Readers could buy and read *Fifty Shades* in privacy. This enabled the books to attain a strong momentum toward becoming a successful bestseller.

Mainstreaming Fifty Shades

The success of the trilogy is incontestable. The first book, *Fifty Shades of Grey*, published in 2011, and its two sequels, published in 2012, had jointly sold over 100 million copies by early 2014 (Bosman "For 'Fifty Shades,'" para. 1). The books have also been translated into more than fifty languages for the global market (Johnson "*Fifty Shades of Grey*," para. 5). In England, *Fifty Shades of Grey* became the fastest selling book since such record keeping began. Paul Bentley wrote, "The novel, the first instalment

of an X-rated trilogy, has beaten J. K. Rowling and *Da Vinci Code* author
Dan Brown" (para. 3).

This popularity of the book and the trilogy raises a question about
its readership. Paul Bentley's article, for example, characterizes the works
as "mommy porn." Is this really an accurate characterization? After all,
Bentley is not alone in resorting to such labeling. Writing for *Tribune
Business News*, various authors, including Heather Irwin, Steve Johnson,
Jodi Duckett, and Gina Kittner, used the same expression to describe the
trilogy. In addition to popular media, Mary Hastler, the director of Hart-
ford County Public Library in Maryland who decided to ban the books
from its collection, commented, "A lot of the reviews that came out very
publicly and quickly identified these books as 'mommy porn.' Since our
policy is that we don't buy porn, we made the decision not to purchase
the series" ("Fifty Shades of Censorship?" 147). As Chapter Five discusses,
the dismissive tone that exists with the label "mommy porn" sends the
message that *Fifty Shades* was a light novel that bored housewives read
between chores.

Some of the reports about the trilogy's readers seem to support the
idea that the books are popular among "mommies" or middle-aged women
in their thirties, forties, and above. When Steven Johnson attended E. L.
James's book tour in Chicago on May 2, 2012, he talked to one of over four
hundred attendees who had paid $40 to participate in the author event.
Debbie Glickman, a forty-four-year-old female, said to Johnson, "I told
her [E. L. James] she was God's gift to middle age" (para. 14). Similarly,
Jessica Chalvez, general manager of Spice Sensuality Boutique in Rohnert
Park, California, said that her customers who visit her store after reading
Fifty Shades averaged between the ages of thirty-five and fifty-five (Irwin,
para. 6).

In reality, such an emphasis on the popularity among middle-aged
women does not fully describe the impact of the trilogy in the larger society. The "mommy porn" descriptor hints that the books are widely read
by women with a child, or children, at home. The word "mommy" might
even conjure an image of a mother living in a typical suburban home. In
some ways, the group of females that "mommy" refers to may be close to
those who have been described as "soccer moms." According to the
Bowker Study, however, less than 30 percent of sales of the trilogy are by
women with children at home. The report states that "the appeal of the
books has been far more widespread." An estimated 14 percent of purchases were by women over fifty-five years old (para. 1). There were also
many young readers. Catie Briesemeister a twenty-seven-year-old female

in Madison, Wisconsin, shared her positive experience with the trilogy after her co-worker recommended the book to her (Kittner para. 2).

Men also bought and read the books. Even though E. L. James once characterized the books' readership as "women [aged] 17–100," male buyers accounted for about a fifth of purchases ("Men Are Reading" para 6; Bowker para. 1). CBS News humorously reported that "reading on iPads and Kindles or hurriedly picking up the books in stores, some men didn't know about the romance part [of *Fifty Shades of Grey*], thinking the surprise best-sellers by newcomer E. L. James would be more 'American Psycho' than steamy Harlequin" ("Men Are Reading," para 2). The article cited a graduate student and an Iraqi war veteran saying, "People hear about flogging and stuff like that in this book, and they don't get it. I became emotionally invested in the love story, especially from the female's perspective. That was important to me, to put myself in Ana's shoes. It was overwhelming and I'll never forget it" (para. 5).

The popularity of the books also created a general sense of a moral panic among some. The blame put on the trilogy for some of the *Fifty Shades*-inspired incidents was exaggerated. But it nonetheless reflected the fact that high school and college-age readers were present. In addition, *Fifty Shades* books existed at public libraries and college libraries for a wider audience to read. An online news media based in Utah wrote, "Letting your teenager read … 'Fifty Shades of Grey' is a terrible idea" (Lehnardt). Jenn Doll also suggested that the books might negatively impact some children. These concerns reveal that parents and adults were aware that young people were also interested in reading the trilogy.

All these examples suggest that the label "mommy porn" is inaccurate. The readership includes men, older women, younger women, and women without children. As noted earlier, women with children at home do not even account for a third of the sales of the books. Furthermore, calling the books "pornography" is inaccurate. As Chapter Two showed, the genre convention of the romance novel explains much of what happens in the trilogy. Of course, there is no question that there are explicit depictions of sexual acts in *Fifty Shades*. The storyline, however, is more than just pornographic. Therefore, the popularity of the books is far more generalized and widely shared than is commonly characterized.

Many media outlets have noted and speculated if the high level of popularity that *Fifty Shades* had achieved meant that a book or a movie of this kind could now become a part of the mainstream American popular culture. Authors such as Jessica Firger and Karley Sciortino also wondered if *Fifty Shades* made BDSM mainstream. Citing Bianca Jarvis, a sexual health educator, Firger characterized the types of sexual desires depicted in the novels as relatively common in American society. Firger suggested that more people were interested in BDSM activities shown in the trilogy than was commonly believed (para. 3). Sciortino added that even though BDSM might be more common than ordinarily imagined, it was still considered taboo and it actually made BDSM appealing for many (para. 10). BDSM is acceptable but a sufficiently risqué sexual activity for many people. Therefore, they are not happy that BDSM has become a part of the mainstream awareness, compromising the practice's underground nature (para. 10).

Others have talked more generally about the mainstream nature of the books as a cultural object. Leanne Italie argues that *Fifty Shades'* marketing tactics of promoting its powerful soundtrack CD, official stockings, underwear, pajamas, and other merchandise enabled "Fifty Shades of Consumption" (para. 2). Such consumptive behaviors do not only involve sex-related goods. A California-based marketing company for interior decorations had plans to sell kitchen and bath decors inspired by the books. Heather Hill and Marni Harrington also characterize *Fifty Shades of Grey* as a book that has attained "mainstream popularity" (62). These examples show that it was far from being a subculture. It is not just the number of books sold but also how the trilogy was discussed and made visible through a moral panic, productization, and other means that made it a part of major American popular culture.

Presentist Assumptions

Because *Fifty Shades* was such a significant part of popular culture of the early 2010s, it was understandable that social critics paid close attention to why it became so popular. Many of those who examined the backstory of its appeal hastily and erroneously concluded that the so-called *Fifty Shades* phenomenon was because there had been nothing like it as a novel or a film. "*Fifty Shades* is unique" and "*Fifty Shades* is unprecedented" are common perceptions. But this is a presentist assumption, or an assumption that what one experiences at the moment is special and unique compared to what has been available in the past. Privileging what is at hand, as Merricks defined, is a common human behavior (523). Kofi Outlaw wrote in his review of the film that the film had a "unique premise" (para. 1). But this is far from true.

In recent history of popular culture, there are many other examples of books and movies that had generated surprising popularity despite their risqué depictions of sexuality. Grinberg wrote, "Dozens of erotic romance novels by authors such as Eden Bradley, Sylvia Day and Megan Hart have landed on best-seller lists, firmly establishing the genre as a major player in the publishing industry" (para. 7). Writing for *Time*, Belinda Luscombe lists ten examples from the last fifty years: *Valley of the Dolls* (1967), *Last Tango in Paris* (1972), *9½ Weeks* (1986), *Blue Velvet* (1986), *Sex, Lies, and Videotape* (1989), *Henry and June* (1990), *Boogie Nights* (1997), *Eyes Wide Shut* (1999), *Secretary* (2002), and *Brokeback Mountain* (2005). For example, released ten years prior to *Fifty Shades of Grey*, *Brokeback Mountain* was extremely controversial. Critics labeled it as "that gay cowboy movie" (Sewell para. 2). Larry H. Miller, a theater owner in Utah, after learning that the movie included "gay romance," pulled the film from his screen. He commented, "Getting away from the traditional families, which I look at as the fundamental building block of our society, is a very dangerous thing" (Associated Press para. 3). The Catholic Church expressed its "disgust" about the film and classified it as an O-rated film—or "morally offensive" (Sewell para. 2; "USCCB Reclassifies," para. 1). Although the types of sexual activities depicted in these two films are different from each other—gay sex vs. BDSM sex—controversies about movies because of what is considered to be taboo or immoral sexual activities had been prevalent in the history of popular culture. Luscombe shows that *Fifty Shades* was not the first time explicit or controversial sexual depictions appeared in mainstream popular culture.

The film *9½ Weeks* involved the male protagonist's controlling the female protagonist to satisfy his sexual fantasy. Luscombe characterizes it as the film that "made strawberries and blindfolds common bedroom props" (40). In a similar way, Todd Cunningham reports that sex stores sell more blindfolds, thanks to E. L. James. One of the interviewees in Cunningham's article was an owner of a sex store with male customers who visit his store to buy blindfolds because their partners had asked to be tied up (para.13). It is not just Luscombe who compared *9½ Weeks* to *Fifty Shades*. An article in *Telegram & Gazette* reads, "In the end, this will be a 21st-century *9½ Weeks*…. The movie wasn't a success in the United States, but it did make a bundle overseas and became a hot item on video and DVD" ("Fans not Joyous," para. 3). *9½ Weeks*—also featuring an ice cube as a sexual pleasure enhancer just as Christian did in Anastasia's bedroom—was reviewed and critiqued in mainstream newspapers, including the *Wall Street Journal* and the *New York Times*. Similar to John-Henry Westen and Dawn Hawkins, who warned their readers that *Fifty Shades* could "lead to a spike in abuse of women," there was a concern that 9½ *Weeks* was going to negatively impact its audience. The concern became particularly realistic when William Flynn, a sixteen-year-old student in 1991, murdered his teacher's husband, Gregory Smart, in 1990. During the trial, it was revealed that Pamela Smart, the teacher, and Flynn watched the movie and had sexual intercourse multiple times while reenacting a scene from the film ("Teen-ager Tells of Love").

Fifty Shades and *Secretary* are also similar in that both films feature BDSM. Directed by Steven Shainberg and produced by Andrew Fierberg, Amy Hobby, and Shainberg, the movie is based on a short story entitled *Bad Behavior* by Mary Gaitskill. The movie's storyline has two main characters, E. Edward Grey who plays the sexually dominant role and Lee Holloway, Grey's secretary and his submissive. In the film, Grey invites Holloway to engage in a BDSM relationship through which she is awakened to a new kind of sexual pleasure. At the same time, Grey is insecure about himself, leading Holloway to possibly seek a different—more conventional—kind of relationship. By the end of the film, with ups and downs in between, Grey and Holloway marry and continue their dominant-submissive relationship.

Beyond the accidental overlap in names—Edward as in Edward Cullen and Grey as in Christian Grey—and depiction of BDSM sexuality, both movies captured the attention of the mainstream. Of course, *Secretary*, an independent film with the box office of just above $9 million, was less successful than *Fifty Shades*. However, as Margot Weiss describes, it was "one of the more popular small films of the year." The film won the Grand Jury Prize for Originality at Sundance Film Festival. Maggie Gyllenhaal, who played Holloway, was nominated for a Golden Globe and the Independent Spirit Award (112). Similar to Weiss, Belmont also published an academic essay on the film. Journalistic media, such as *San Antonio Current*, *Cincinnati Enquirer*, and *The Independent Weekly*, also published reviews focusing on BDSM depicted in the film.

The comparison to *Secretary* was made soon after the release of *Fifty Shades of Grey*. Writing to *BuzzFeed*, Julia Pugachevsky pointed out numerous similarities between the two films from the hair color of the main female character, the male character's elusiveness, and S&M sex. Pugachevsky, however, argues that *Secretary* has subtler ways to develop a story. She argues that the communication between Christian and Anastasia lacks depth, whereas the dialogue in *Secretary* is more genuine. While James's story is about Christian's desire to touch Anastasia, the relationship between Lee and Edward is better developed. By the end of the film, Anastasia simply realizes Christian is not the person she should be with. Lee, on the other hand, "overcomes self-harm, gains confidence, and challenges Edward as much as she does herself" (para. 17). Similarly, *SundanceTV* wrote that *Secretary* was far better as a movie on S&M. The article states that *Secretary* won an Independent Spirit Award and a Gotham Award, as well as being nominated for a Golden Globe and three Chlotrudis Awards. *Fifty Shades* has a more successful box-office record without any major nomination. *SundanceTV* continues that *Secretary* has a more likeable main character and a realistic storyline. As will be discussed elsewhere in this book, *Fifty Shades of Grey* is filled with product placement whereas *Secretary* stayed away from it. Listing ten reasons *Secretary* ranks higher than *Fifty Shades*, the article concludes that "the 2002 indie film ... blows *Fifty* out of the water" ("Top Ten Reasons," para. 1).

Both *9½ Weeks* and *Secretary* share some of the sexual components of *Fifty Shades*. In addition, they show that *Fifty Shades* was not the first movie to feature such elements in a popular film in the U.S. or elsewhere in the world. However, no other film in history is a better example of an American film challenging the idea of acceptance of, and resistance to, sex talk in public than *Deep Throat* (1972). Written and directed by Gerard Damiano and produced by Lou Perry (Louis Peraino), the pornographic film is a major counterculture product of the mid-twentieth century. It was a big success. Although the film's overall revenue is still uncertain, Michael Hilzik estimates it to be between $300 and $600 million (para. 18).

Deep Throat, unlike *Fifty Shades of Grey* which is labeled as romance or erotica, is pornography. But it nonetheless captured the imagination of many Americans. Luke Ford explains that the film "brought hardcore into popular culture, earning twice as much money as any other porno in history" (49). David Vandor, a worker at the Mayor's Office of Midtown Planning and Development in New York, was quoted in the *New York Times* praising the film as "better than most situation comedies" (Blumenthal 30). Blumenthal continued that United Nations diplomats, police officers, and others also flocked to the theater. Simultaneously, just like *Fifty Shades*, the popularity of *Deep Throat* raised many eyebrows. The year after the film was released, Judge Joel J. Tyler referred to the film as the "feast of carrion and squalor," a "nadir of decadence," and "a Sodom and Gomorrah gone wild before the fire" (para. 8).

In many ways, what *Deep Throat* meant for American society in the early 1970s was far more significant than *Fifty Shades* forty years later. First of all, *Deep Throat* was hardcore pornography while *Fifty Shades* is an erotic romance novel. Although the *Fifty Shades* books and film have explicit depictions of sex and BDSM, it is not to the extent of the 1972 film, which has numerous close-up shots of genitalia. For a movie labeled explicitly as pornography to gain so much attention and popularity is a greater achievement than the records marked by *Fifty Shades of Grey.*

Second, over forty years, social norms have changed. There are more depictions of sex and sexuality in popular culture in the 2010s than in the 1970s. From print media to television shows, popular culture today includes far more sex. Even without explicit reference to sex, more skin is visible. Many of the advertisements, from Arby's and Subway to PETA, use sex as an indirect message to either sell their products or promote their messages. Therefore, for *Deep Throat* to be so popular in the 1970s was culturally more surprising than for *Fifty Shades of Grey* to be popular in the mid–2010s.

The *Fifty Shades* phenomenon was not unique. If anything, with the contemporary society being more accustomed to seeing direct and indirect references to sex than even a few decades ago, it is rather conservative. What makes it worth examining, therefore, is not the trilogy's message or content but the level of visibility it was able to achieve.

Fifty Shades *Seen in Panicking Youth*

As Deller, Harman, and Jones discussed in the introduction to the special issue of *Sexualities* on *Fifty Shades* books, They surrounded many consumers internationally not just as books but also as merchandise, social media topics, music, and so on (859–860). But the high level of visibility was not just about media exposure or consumerism behaviors. *Fifty Shades'* visibility also meant that young people were confronting their parents who were reading and talking about it. For example, soon after *Fifty Shades of Grey* became a bestseller, a countless number of websites, blogs, and social media started to reflect the discomfort felt by youths. A common example might begin with "My grandmother/mother is reading *Fifty Shades of Grey.*" Many people who were writing such comments online, presumably young people who are uncertain how to react to their parent's or grandparent's new book, oftentimes voiced their negative feelings not about the book but about their family member reading it.

On Yahoo! Answers, one young woman wrote, "My mom is reading 50 Shades of Grey? And it's SOOOO gross, and when I tell her that she just laughs and pats me on the head!" She continues, "How would she like it if I read/watched porn? I know what 50 Shades of Grey is about, and it's disgusting me so much! she downloaded it on Kindle for tablet, so I can't arrange for the book to 'disappear' Ideas? Advice?" ("My Mom Is Reading"). The negativity and "disgust" is commonly shared. Megan responds to the initial comment by stating, "My mum is to [sic] she is reading the last one now finished the rest. But it is disgustin and gross" [sic] ("My Mom Is Reading"). Another wrote:

> Why do all the old women keep reading it[?] My mom is 41 going to be 42 and all of her friends keep reading it. Its' [sic] stupid to me. I mean sure they're old now but like um you all have husbands. Does it remind you of when you lost your virginity to your first love and oh how great that was. Also when my mom is with her friends they're like Anastasia comes every time and her friend is all like and mom is like oh no she didn't and I'm will you just STFU [shut the fuck up]! Then my moms' friend was all like its' a good book even better in bed. THE **** DOES THAT MEAN? [emphasis in original; "Why Does My Mom"].

Females in their teenage years and in their twenties often wondered why their parents were reading *Fifty Shades*. On YouTube, a teenaged female, AyeltsHayley, shared her experience of her mother and aunt talking about the book. She explains that her mother had wanted to read the book and her aunt was going to let her borrow a copy from her. However, they would not tell AyeltsHayley what the book was about, aside from her mother simply telling her, "You will not read [it] for a long long, long time." Ayelts-Hayley then went online to check what *Fifty Shades of Grey* was about. As soon as she found the answer, she was shocked to realize what kind of story her mother and aunt were reading. She commented, "My mom reads that? Because it's called 'mommy porn.' My mom reads that? That's just weird" (AyeltsHayley).

Jen, in her mid–twenties, wrote on her personal blog in 2012 an entry entitled, "I Cannot Allow My Mother to Read 50 Shades of Grey." She explains that her blog is about "dating, hating, and everything in between." She writes, "I have been on more bad dates than I have fingers and toes to count on—and I'm only in my early twenties! I laugh when I watch *Sex and the City*, because I've had so many dysfunctional relationships that they might as well have made me their 5th friend" (Jen, "About Jen"). In her blog, she describes her conversation with her mother, who was interested in reading *Fifty Shades*. Her response was she did not want her mother to be reading James's novel. But to this, her mother responded, "But all my friends are reading it!" Jen also shared that she was not alone. Her friends had family members who had read or were reading the book, which they agreed to be "too dirty" for their parents (Jen, "I Cannot").

These entries are significant in that discussions about *Fifty Shades* between children and their parents are a unique kind of "sex talk." This is different from a conversation about using a contraceptive or how a baby is made. Lauren Vino wrote, "Most of us have the sex talk with our mothers as teenagers. We think it'll never have to happen again. And then we find E. L. James's 'Fifty Shades of Grey' next to Mom's pillow. Recently, my mother and I had our second big talk when she was in town for a visit. I'm in my 20s now, but I felt just as uncomfortable as I did a decade ago" (para. 1). Comedically written, Vino's essay suggests that many young people found it awkward to learn that their parents read the books. Of course, despite the label as "mommy porn," *Fifty Shades* was not just for parents with children. But an endless list of anecdotes about such sex talks between a young adult and their middle-aged parent or family member show a unique kind of visibility that the book unintentionally achieved.

Visibility with E-Readers

The collective panicking voice of young people is probably a reflection of coming to terms with reality. For many young people, sexual desires and their own parents remain in two separate spheres. The fact that their parents are drawn to a novel characterized by its sexual content is understandably difficult for them to admit. But young adults, one after another, shared their awkward moments to make a case that *Fifty Shades* was very relevant to their lives, even if they were not particularly interested in it.

In general, sex sells. Amateur blogs assist media content to go viral. *Fifty Shades* was no exception to this rule. But its popularity and visibility were also enhanced by the popularization of e-readers such as Barns & Noble's Nook and Amazon's Kindle, as well as other tablets. The accessibility of e-reading devices lowered the barrier to purchase a book that is risqué enough for some potential reader to shy away from purchasing a copy at a brick-and-mortar store.

Pew Research Center reported in 2014 about the rising popularity of e-reading devices. In 2010, less than 5 percent of American adults over eighteen owned an e-reader or a tablet. The number rose to about 10 percent in 2011, the year the first volume was published. Since then, the number for each device has steadily risen to half of all American adults owning either a tablet or an e-reader (2). Romance Writers of America reported that 39 percent of romance books were purchased as e-books, making them the most popular medium, followed by mass-market paperbacks at 32 percent, as of 2014. This change corresponds to the rising popularity of *Fifty Shades*. Michelle Renaud, a spokesperson for Harlequin, said, "[Romance novel fans] love to consume many novels at once, and e-books are an easy way to carry them around" (Grinberg para. 8).

E-readers did not only help *Fifty Shades* become an international hit but also allowed the book to be recognized in the first place. The novel was not originally published by Vintage Books, but by a small Australian printing house named the Writers Coffee Shop. It released the book for e-readers on an on-demand basis (Balton para. 10; Grinberg para. 9). The low cost of publication associated with e-publishing enables publishers to take more risks and be adventurous with books that may not generate sufficient profit if the only means of publication was print. With so many fan fiction based on *Twilight* available online, there was no guarantee that *Fifty Shades* would be different. It was due to e-publishing that the book became accessible to both *Twilight* fans and romance novel readers who had been known for "their voracious literary appetites" (Grinberg para. 7). It was only after *Fifty Shades* gained enough popularity as an e-book that Vintage became aware of its appeal and decided to invest in the trilogy.

The privacy that e-readers afford their users is another factor in the book's popularity. Dian Hanson, who now identifies herself as the "sexy editor" of Taschen Books, commented that when people bought pornographic magazines, they "had to make an effort to acquire their material. They had to go through the embarrassing experience of buying it and presenting it to a clerk" (Stagg, para. 3, 20). In a similar way, *Fifty Shades* readers did not have to worry about others knowing what they were reading. Neil Richard called this "a victory for reader and intellectual privacy" (para. 2). Lush argues that "many people felt comfortable reading [*Fifty Shades*] on tablets because those devices kept the novels mostly private, unlike a hardcover book" (Lush 3D).

This is not to say that many readers were ashamed of their reading choices, especially after the book became a bestseller. Indeed, many women were seen reading it in public-transit systems. There are numerous book clubs that decided to read the trilogy. Public libraries also carried James's books. But Valerie Hoskins, the agent of E. L. James, stated in 2012 that "women have the ability to read this kind of material without anybody knowing what they're reading, because they can read them on their iPads and Kindles" (Bosman "Discreetly Digital," par 21). Jessica Matthews of George Mason University concurs:

> There are some practical reasons why *Fifty Shades of Grey* became so successful. To me it was this convergence of a wide adoption of the ereader and the maturation of social media, because ereaders made it very easy for women to buy that book

and read it without anyone knowing they were reading it. And I think that whole notion of having to conceal the kind of romance reading that women often do, even if it's not that kind of book, but just the whole sense of being caught on the Metro with a cover ... with the buxom blonde and Fabio and all of that—that kind of thing the ereader totally did away with all of that ["Teaching *Fifty Shades of Grey*," para. 1].

Skurnick wrote that *Fifty Shades of Grey* "may not revolutionize porn, romance, chick-lit, or literature. But this one-click wonder is the future of how we'll read." This is a very accurate assessment. The book, in many ways, is not very different from previous literary works. As the chapter on genre studies compiled in this book shows, the book follows many of the genre conventions. But it was also able to attain mass popularity thanks to the development of mobile e-reading technology. It allowed some to read in many more places. They are able to carry multiple books. But for others, it also meant a little bit more of a sense of privacy about what they were reading.

So Much Hype but Not So Unique

There is no question that *Fifty Shades* was a very successful commercial and entertainment franchise. Its publication records and numbers are more than sufficient to show its explosive success at the time when the publishing industry continues to face various challenges (PR Newswire). Anne Messitte, of Vintage, said, "We're making a statement that [*Fifty Shades*] is bigger than one genre.... The people who are reading this are not only people who read romance. It's gone much broader than that" (Boseman para. 5). But it is also important to properly situate the book in the context of other works. Numerous other romance novels have had similar themes and storylines. A previous chapter has shown that *Fifty Shades* follows the general storyline typical of a romance novel. *9½ Weeks* and *Secretary* had similar controversial portrayals of sex, control, and relationships to *Fifty Shades*, even though these movies had come out decades earlier. More recently, *Brokeback Mountain* connected a popular culture text to the issue of morality. *Deep Throat* was also very visible in American mainstream culture despite the fact that it was explicit pornography and it was released in a more conservative time period.

What made the book worthy of study was its visibility. Vintage's marketing scheme worked well. There were many spinoff products. But *Fifty Shades* also took advantage of recent advancements of social media and mobile technology. Fans talked about the book incessantly. Driven by young people to whom social media and communication technology of the early twenty-first century came as intuitive, *Fifty Shades'* presence was strengthened not just in real life but also in a virtual environment. Even those in their teenage years and in their twenties who were not interested in *Fifty Shades* talked about it with their parents. As noted elsewhere in this book, others discussed why people should read the trilogy to spice up their sex life or why people should not read it. Talking about *Fifty Shades* became as popular as reading it.

Marcee Challener, working for the Tampa-Hillsborough County Public Libraries, characterized the books well by stating, "There's sex and eroticism in many well-written literary novels.... It's part of the human experience." From Shakespeare to more contemporary popular novels, romance and sex appear frequently. Challener also argues that the *Fifty Shades* books were "no different from one of the paranormal romances featuring vampires that have been popular for years" (Bosman, para. 22–23). Despite the hype in the mainstream and finger-pointing by those who are concerned about the moral decay assumed to be represented by the popularity of the trilogy, James's work is not necessarily exceptional. To characterize it as such is to privilege one's experience today. Not much can be learned by attempting to figure out why the work was unique. Rather, *Fifty Shades* allows us to understand how its high visibility was attained *even though* and not *because* its story is far from unprecedented.

CHAPTER FOUR

Ambivalent about Sex
Faith, First Amendment and Censorship

The popularity of the *Fifty Shades* trilogy is not universal. For every fan who bought all three novels, who went to watch the film at a local theater during the Valentine's Day weekend, and who pre-ordered James's latest work, *Grey*, there is an anti–*Fifty Shades* voice to be heard. Even Dakota Johnson—the actress who played the role of Anastasia Steele—admitted, "By the time I read [*Fifty Shades of Grey*], everyone had already read it. So I knew the gist, and I knew, obviously, that it was a sexually explicit book. But part of the reason why I was just so excited about the film like this is because it is controversial. It is something that a lot of people might hate and a lot of people might love" ("Fifty Shades—Dakota Johnson Featurette"). Johnson's prediction turned out to be true.

It was not just concerned parents who resisted James's works because of their assumed negative impact on their children or youths who were uncertain how to comprehend their parent's obsession with the books. It was also bloggers and social commentators in general, public libraries, and academic institutions that decided to resist and sometimes even ban *Fifty Shades*, leading eventually to its being classified as one of the "top ten most frequently challenged books of 2013," according to the American Library Association ("Affirm the Freedom," para. 10). Were these concerns and censoring efforts necessary? What explains this outcry? Is it justified? Ultimately, what is at stake when a popular work like this is banned from public consumption?

Just as it was popular to read and watch *Fifty Shades*, it became as popular to resist and hate the franchise. Numerous individuals and organizations have commented online why they do not and will not read the novels and watch the film. In many instances, these rejections and refusals were not just as opposition to *Fifty Shades* fans but even as superior to them (Harman and Jones 952). In other words, those who rejected *Fifty Shades* sometimes present the image that they know better than those who are mesmerized by the world of Christian Grey. Meg Hunter-Kilmer, suggesting that Mr. Darcy from *Pride and Prejudice* was bad enough for avidly Christian literary fans like herself, stated that Christian Grey had no chance of appealing to her ("Why I Hate"; "Why I Won't"). She writes, "From a Christian perspective, I just don't know how you can excuse [the novel's depiction of sex]" ("Why I Won't," para. 3). Some even went so far as to suggest that others should also boycott the franchise. In a way, hating the books has become a new American pastime.

Many have also argued that E. L. James's writing was simply terrible. Barbara Taylor Bradford, a best-selling author, noted that *Fifty Shades of Grey* was "repetitive," and "terribly badly written" (De Lacey, para. 2). A blogger called the book "fifty shades of yawn" (Somarriba). Another blogger wrote, "I do not understand the wild popularity that surrounds this trash of a story with zero redeeming qualities that relies on nothing but nakedness and emotional manipulation in the Pacific Northwest. This is exactly why I stopped watching *Grey's Anatomy*" (Friedel, para. 12). In short, many reviewers agreed that E. L. James was no Charlotte Bronte, Jane Austin, or Thomas Hardy.

Is Fifty Shades *Against God's Will?*

As all these examples suggest, the reasons to resist *Fifty Shades* vary. But there is a strong voice of rejection for religious and faith reasons. It is not a surprise when one thinks of the franchise's content. Due to the sheer number of websites and blogs that are critical of James's work for religious reasons, it is practically impossible to examine them all. However, examining some of the more popular such sites reveal several common themes.

Jim Denison, for example, calls the film "dangerous" (para. 2) in that "the movie is pornographic in the extreme.... [It] is a porn movie disguised as a romance. According to the *Atlantic*, the film shows at least twenty full minutes of sex" (para. 3). Matt Walsh, an online champion against pornography, made the following observation:

> I've noticed that some of the women who give me a hearty "Amen" every time I write a post condemning pornography, are the same ones gushing frantically about this film. They don't want their husbands watching porn, but they'll not only watch

and read porn themselves—they'll advertise that fact to the entire world. As if the hypocrisy isn't bad enough, they had to add in a touch of public emasculation [para. 10].

For Walsh, such behaviors and mentalities of female readers and viewers of *Fifty Shades* is a problem that needs to be fixed (para. 12).

Not all critics characterize the works as pornography. Dannah Gresh recognizes that *Fifty Shades* is, instead, erotica. Nonetheless, she has a perspective about the trilogy similar to others, based on her religious beliefs. She argues that "reading erotica is sinful" (para. 3). She explains further by stating, "There is only one who should stimulate sexual desires in me: my husband. Since that's God's plan for my sexual desire, anything other than my husband creating arousal in me would be missing the mark of God's intention. (Translation: it is sin)" (para. 3). She goes on: "The Bible has said for thousands of years that lust is hurtful and harmful" (para. 5).

Denison also uses what he considered scientific evidence to emphasize the harm that *Fifty Shades* will bring to society. He references Scott Christian's essay published in *GQ* to support his case. Denison writes, "*GQ*, a magazine not known for biblical morality, recently cited reasons readers should quit watching pornography immediately" (para. 4). Pornography, he avers, "damages the brain," "motivates people to see new sexual partners," and leads to escalation of porn use (para. 4). Denison further argues that "the movie glamorizes and normalizes sexual abuse" (para. 5). Denison accurately summarizes studies on *Fifty Shades* by remarking on the pervasiveness of violence in it and the correlation between its readership and the tendency to have an eating disorder, abusive partners, and other behaviors.

Some admitted that they are afraid of what the book might do to them. Writing for *ThinkChristian*, Caryn Rivadeneira writes, "Truth is: I'm afraid of it. Afraid of liking it, maybe. Afraid of being damaged by it, definitely. Thus, I need to steer clear" (para. 6). Of course, the irony is her writing sounds exactly like what Christian said to Anastasia when they went out for a coffee for the first time after the photo shoot. Christian tells her, "Anastasia, you should steer clear of me. I'm not the man for you" (James 49). It did not stop her: she said she wanted to be enlightened.

Some fear that Christian Grey may become the third person in their bedroom. Melissa Edington writes:

What if we determined that we aren't going to allow anyone into our relationship with our husbands? Not a fictional character in a book, not an actor on the screen? What if we decided that we will no longer allow our minds to invite a third person into our bedroom? What if we chose to close our hearts and minds to the fantasies about other men (who don't comfort us when we cry, who don't faithfully support us, who don't play with our children, who didn't pledge to love us until we die)? What if we gave this gift to our husbands: being fully present in the moment, completely focused on him and all that we love about him during intimate moments? [para. 6].

A similar sense of fear is shared by Hunter-Kilmer, who writes, "I just refuse to put myself in a situation where I'm walking up the aisle to receive communion and a graphic image of bondage sex presents itself to my imagination" (para. 9).

Generally, these readers underscore not only the poor quality of the books, but also (and more significantly) its sinful depictions of sex. Walsh summarizes such opinions very effectively by describing the film as containing "the most abominable, morally and mentally bankrupt ensemble of subpar acting and stilted dialogue ever cobbled together and presented, through any medium, to any audience, anywhere, at any point in history" (para. 7).

Although the voice of anti–*Fifty Shades* is strong, a great majority of them have actually not read the novel, a fact that many bloggers attempt to justify. Hunter-Kilmer argues that she usually does not pass judgment on a book until she reads it (para. 5), but made an exception for *Fifty Shades*. She remarked that by not reading it, "I'm not hiding from anything, I'm protecting myself" (para. 9). Gresh says, "There are many things in this world I need not partake in to discern that they are going to be harmful to me" (para. 8). Bob James, who identifies himself as "an ex–Marine and dad of four grown children," argued that "most people who criticize it haven't read it." Admitting that he has read and enjoyed the trilogy, he continued, "They take things out of context and just pick the sex scenes out. I liked the romance. Ana is drawing [Christian] away from the bondage stuff" ("'Fifty Shades of Grey' Draws," para. 27).

Hunter-Kilmer disagrees. He steadfastly explains that "the more I thought about it, the more I realized that it wasn't enough just not to read the books…. Since I haven't read them, I guess I can't exactly tell you what to do. But I can say that I wouldn't read them for ten thousand dollars and that I really, really hope no Christian women do" (para. 10). Gresh hopes her words will spread widely. She commented, "If your heart resonates with mine, please take a moment today to post these words on Facebook or Twitter: "I'm not reading Fifty Shades of Grey." If you have friends who need help understanding why, send them to this blog. I'd be happy to explain!" (para. 9). Denison concludes: "Please, do not see this movie. And do all you can to encourage others not to see it" (para. 2).

Religious Taste on Fifty Shades *Not* "*Singular*"

Although these faith-based rejections of the book are, in many ways, expected, they also raise interesting questions about the ideas and stereotypes shared by those who penned such essays, especially in the minds of the readers who read and liked the trilogy, or, in some cases, disliked it for other reasons. Of course, I do not aim to undermine their personal opinions and ideas, especially grounded upon their religious faith. But I nonetheless hope to reveal the frame of reference that such authors use to resist James's work for moral and religious reasons.

Denison's aforementioned piece on the film for *Christian Post* is not a surprise within its context. However, its characterization of *Fifty Shades* as "pornographic in the extreme" does not reflect the reality of the pornographic genre. If he considers it to be extreme because of the repetitive portrayals of sex scenes, his essay fails to mention many other sexual depictions that could have been included. The 125-minute film had less than fifteen minutes of sex out of seven sex scenes (Bender and Heigl; Boone). The same is true if he meant the film to be "extreme" (para. 3) because of BDSM, a sexual practice that may be considered taboo by some. Denison also appears to misunderstand the nature of a romance novel. As noted in other parts of this book, some romance novels contain very explicit sexual depictions as the genre's normative practice. When Denison uses the *GQ* article as a source, he clearly has the motivation to bring in messages discussed on what appears to be an independent and non-religious source that frequently features so-called men's interests. Christian's essay referenced by Denison, however, was about pornography addicts, rather than casual readers and viewers, about men (not women) who were the predominant readers of *Fifty Shades*. Denison nonetheless cautions that the book "will spread the plague of porn to even more people. Don't be among them" (para. 4).

Matt Walsh writes:

> Do you know what BDSM is? Bondage, dominance, sadism, and masochism. If you don't know what those words mean, be glad. If you do know, you should understand that the most damaging part of *Fifty Shades of Grey* is that God created sex to be a partnership that's fueled by love and self-giving, not pain and humiliation. It's not just that this book misuses sex, it redefines it into something evil and transgressive as the lead character dominates in a hurtful manner. How woman can enjoy that, I can't understand! But I do have a theory. It seems to me that in our emasculating culture there is a hunger so great for strong men that women will stoop to bondage, dominance, sadism, and masochism for just a taste. Do yourself a favor, don't! [para 7].

Despite the film's risqué reputation, Sam Taylor-Johnson, the film's female director, decided to remove a particularly controversial scene in the novel, the one with Christian pulling out Anastasia's tampon. This deletion was likely a way of avoiding an NC-17 label, which would have undoubtedly hurt the film's box-office take. *Fifty Shades* turned out to be a huge hit, especially during the first few weeks after its release. And, despite the public outcry by some groups protesting the depiction of an abusive, problematic relationship, no studies have proven that the James's work actually leads to those behaviors. Perhaps a more accurate interpretation is that, as an example of popular culture, the movie merely reflects a culture that sensationalizes sex, filling novels and motion pictures with stories about relationship violence, date rape, objectification of women, commodification of sex, and other issues. The film, therefore, is not the problem—it is a popular cultural expression of a problem.

Walsh provides four reasons why readers should avoid *Fifty Shades*:

- because you aren't stupid
- because you don't go for cynical, boring, corporate marketing ploys
- because you're a Christian, and
- because you're a feminist.

These reasons are followed up with his elaborative writing. The problem, however, is that, similar to Denison, Walsh does not understand the differences and overlapping that exist between pornography and romance, as well as the arguments advanced by some feminist scholars. First of all, characterizing the book as pornography is questionable. Extensive portrayals of sex and sexual behaviors do not automatically make a novel or movie pornography. There is no doubt we live in a society inundated by pornography-like images from magazines and advertisements, as well as novels and movies, it does not necessarily mean that we are all consuming pornography.

Second, Walsh seems to believe romance novels are benign literary works as opposed to pornography. Such a belief reveals his lack of knowledge about the romance genre. As discussed elsewhere, romance novels are filled with sexual depictions of various kinds. In addition, not all feminists rejected *Fifty Shades*. Being a feminist does not automatically lead one to abhor James's works. Of course, as Walsh posits, some resist them. They argue that the novel and film are anti-feminist and should be avoided. But other feminists recognize the importance of having such literary and cinematographic works and allowing both men and women to read and watch them. Such a disagreement has existed for a long time, as feminism developed.

Last, Walsh's reference to emasculation unearths his prejudice about men, pornography, and sexuality. He believes that the majority of pornography users are male, and that, when women participate in such a behavior, it is emasculating. In reality, female viewership of pornography is higher than commonly expected, with 8 percent of female online video watchers admitting to have watched adult videos. This number is smaller than that for men, at approximately 25 percent (Pew Research Center, 3). However, labeling pornography as an exclusive form of sexual consumption for males reveals Walsh's prejudices about male and female sexuality.

All these examples of religious and faithful people resisting a book like *Fifty Shades of Grey* makes sense and is understandable. But it is also important to realize that not all religious people reject the trilogy. As Deborah Whitehead's study on Evangelical Christian and Mormon women's responses to it demonstrated, "Conservative religious women and mothers *are* reading *Fifty Shades of Grey* and many are reading the hell out of it" (emphasis in original; 926). Whitehead argues that this fact shows the negotiations between religious rules and individual choice, institutional religious authority and secular social norms, and many other facets in life impact the lives of those religious readers.

Two Opposing Reasons Fifty Shades Never Touched Library Shelves

The fact that *Fifty Shades* sold so well inevitably meant there were many waiting to check out the book from their local public library. Despite the financial difficulties that many small public libraries have been suffering (American Library Association), Marc Bodnick argues that the libraries are relevant to the lives of many. Therefore, it was only natural that many readers were waiting for James's trilogy to be available in their neighborhood library as they have expected the latest works by other authors. The number of people who ended up on the waiting list to get a hold of the book was high at many locations. Even with fifty-one copies of *Fifty Shades of Grey*, L. E. Memorial Public Library, in Eau Claire, Wisconsin, had over six hundred people on the wait list (Vetter, para. 2–3). The Cuyahoga County Public Library, in Ohio, experienced over a thousand holds on *Fifty Shades of Grey* in mid–May 2012, even though the library had bought 539 copies of the book (Bosman, para. 20). The library system in Pinellas County, Florida, carried thirty copies of the book, with 650 people on the wait list (Lush 3D). At these locations, as soon as a book was returned, it was immediately checked out by another patron.

Of course, not all public libraries witnessed a large request for *Fifty Shades*. On the one hand, Calhoun County, Michigan, had only a small number of requests. Rick Hulsey, director of Willard Library, commented, "I don't see a groundswell of support here for it.... We haven't had a bunch of requests for it. Admittedly, it's marginal at best. So we kind of said, eh, let's just pass. I mean, if I had twenty people come in asking for it, we would probably reconsider it" (Kelley, para. 4). On the other hand, the popularity of the books at public libraries was clear in Baltimore County, in Maryland. Keith Meisel reported that "all 396 copies of the sexually-themed book in their library system owns are loaned out" (para. 1). The number of holds for the books was as high as eleven hundred, meaning that as many residents were on the waiting list (Meisel, para. 2). The Hennepin County Public Library, which includes Minneapolis, also saw over two thousand holds on James's first book in mid–May 2012 (Bosman, para. 6). Similarly, Marshall District Library, in Michigan, purchased a copy of each book in 2012. Kelley reported that they had never had a chance to "touch a shelf" because someone was reading it at any point (para. 22).

Libraries in many municipalities, however, decided not to carry the book to cater to the high demand by its residents. After all, the *Fifty Shades* trilogy has attracted much attention while being characterized as erotica, or even pornography. Barbara Jones, executive director of American Library Association's Office of Intellectual Freedom, wrote that some of the public libraries, fearing the backlash if they bought a copy, considered removing the books they had purchased already, or have decided not to buy the books at all (21).

One of the most controversial cases of a public library's ban on *Fifty Shades* took place in Florida. Brevard County Public Libraries' ban "galvanized anti-censorship advocates" and "drew intense media attention" (Kennerly "Residents Want," para. 4). The decision to not allow the work to circulate came only after the libraries had already purchased the books. The call was made by Cathy Schweinsberg, library services director. She explained, "Nobody asked us to take it off the shelves.... But we bought some copies before we realized what it was. We looked at it, because it's been called 'mommy porn' and 'soft porn'" (Clarke, para. 4). Britt Kennerly writes that she read the book and decided to "pull all nineteen copies from circulation" ("Residents Speak up," para. 5).

Schweinsberg concluded that "the library does not 'collect porn' and that the book did not 'meet selection criteria'" (Kennerly "Residents speak up," para. 5). In early May 2012, all the copies of *Fifty Shades* disappeared from the library system. She further justified her decision by stating, "We have to pick the very best titles given our resources ... it become more and more difficult when you have self-published books out there that don't have legitimate reviews attached to them" (Kennerly "Residents speak up," para. 7). This decision was significant because when Schweinsberg decided to remove the books from the library's list, there were about two hundred people on the waiting list. The library had to send out a note to each person on the list to notify them that the library no longer carried *Fifty Shades* (Kelley, para. 14). Such a decision to remove books that had been purchased for patrons and that had been highly popular was going to be a controversial one.

Public reactions immediately followed. Some made public responses to Brevard County's decision. Ron Bartcher, president of the Friends of the Library Mims/Scottsmoore Library Group, stated, "Censorship of popular titles should not be tolerated" (Kennerly "Residents Speak up," para. 9). Furthermore, Schweinsberg used the argument that *Fifty Shades* is a self-published book, thus invalidating it. *Master of the Universe* was a self-published book, of course. *Fifty Shades of Grey*, however, was published by a major firm with an immense sales record. Maria Kayanan, of the American Civil Liberties Union of Florida, also said, "We absolutely think it was a violation of the First Amendment" (Kennerly "Residents Want," para. 5). She continues:

> It's absolutely censorship. It's undemocratic and it's un–American and if people don't want to read it, they shouldn't read it. But once they put it on the shelves, that's it. It's government censorship to then remove it. They had a choice at the beginning to buy it or not buy it ... once they put it out there for people to read, they can't just remove the book from the shelves based on one individual's misguided sense of moral propriety [para. 6].

A resident of Brevard was also concerned that banning the book at a library might spill over to other places. Brianna Gayle tweeted, "What's the difference in a library and a book store? If you take *Fifty Shades of Grey* out of libraries, are you going to ban it from bookstores?" (Varga para. 4). Writing for *Florida Today*, Bob Stover opined that it made sense for libraries to determine what was appropriate to carry and what was not. When Stover interviewed Schweinsberg, one of the reasons given was that the book was not well written. "This is not a classic," he said in an understatement. (para. 12). Not disagreeing with her about the quality of James's writing, Stover nonetheless argues, "But if we let only classics into libraries, the shelves wouldn't be very full and there would be no lines at the library checkout counter. Being well-written isn't a prerequisite for most published work today" (para. 13). Stover also discusses that if Schweinsberg's next claim—*Fifty Shades of Grey* is pornography—is true, then it would require a community standard test. Stover wrote:

> Schweinsberg said she takes that into account, but I would argue it is difficult for one individual to make that judgment. When a book is at the top of every best-seller list in the country, it may mean the community standard has shifted to accommodate it—whether we like it or not; whether we recognize it or not [para. 14].

Kayanan and Stover agree that Schweinsberg's personal objection to the book is not a justifiable reason to remove copies that have already been put on the shelves. Talya Varga also wrote, "Is it just a case of vintage reading? Wait until the book has become a 'classic' and has racked up a couple of years, then the erotic images become invisible and the message changes." (para. 5). Varga is not convinced by Schweinsberg's argument, especially because the library carries *Kama Sutra*, *Fanny Hill*, and *Lolita*.

Residents interviewed by Kennerly also agree that it is important to recognize that the books are best sellers. A resident stated, "How can they say this is what Brevard residents want? How do they determine that? … Why is it Nos. 1, 2 and 3 on best-seller lists if it's not what people want?" (Kennerly "Residents Want," para. 13–14). Just about fifty miles away from Brevard County, library patrons waited for their chance to read *Fifty Shades*. Volusia County's library had over two hundred reservations for its fifteen copies of the trilogy and over a hundred for their electronic copy (Kennerly "Residents Want," para. 24).

The National Coalition Against Censorship and the Association of American Publishers also argued that categorically banning erotica from public libraries was inappropriate. In their written statement, the organizations wrote, "The idea that 'erotica' should be categorically excluded from public libraries has no merit…. A policy that excludes an entire category of works that are protected by the First Amendment is a censorship policy, impermissible in a public library" (Teotonio, para. 10). They also point out that such a policy can raise concerns about moral policing. Their statement read: "The very act of rejecting erotica as a category suitable for public libraries sends an unmistakable message of condemnation that is moralistic in tone, and totally inappropriate in a public institution dedicated to serving the needs and interests of all members of the community" (Bosman, para. 15; Teotonio, para. 11).

Random House also issued a statement against some municipal libraries' censorship efforts. In a written statement, the publishing house "fervently opposes literary censorship and supports the First Amendment rights of readers to make their own reading choices. We believe the Brevard County Public Library System is indulging in an act of censorship, and essentially is saying to library patrons: We will judge what you can read" (Bosman, para. 16).

Despite the controversy in Florida, there are many other municipal libraries that banned *Fifty Shades*. Librarians in Fond du Lac, Wisconsin, did not order books because they argued that it did "not meet the community standards." The Gwinnett County Public Library also did not purchase copies because "the books violated its no-erotica policy (Bosman, para. 10; Teotonio, para. 6). Banning or restricting the circulation of *Fifty Shades* at public libraries was not confined to a few municipal libraries.

Following the controversy of certain public libraries not carrying *Fifty Shades* and rising concerns about censorship, the American Library Association issued a statement. It opened by recognizing the difficult questions about making the best use of limited resources. Its statement read, "The American Library Association supports libraries and librarians across the country, who face difficult decisions every day about how to allocate scarce resources in order to meet the wide-ranging information needs of their communities" (Office of Intellectual Freedom, para. 1). The statement further discussed the general selection processes for libraries:

> To guide decisions about what materials to select for a collection, libraries develop selection policies, which outline the principles and priorities they will follow in selecting items for the library. Libraries also strive to be responsive to the requests of community members in choosing materials. Selection is an inclusive process that seeks out those materials that will best satisfy the community's needs for information, entertainment, and enlightenment [para. 2].

After that, the statement was more specific:

> Recent controversy over the novel "Fifty Shades of Grey" has sparked discussion about the line between selection and censorship in libraries. Where selection decisions are guided by the professional ethics of librarianship—which emphasize inclusion, access, and neutrality—libraries choosing not to purchase materials that fall outside their defined collection policies and needs are not censors. Where partisan disapproval or doctrinal pressure guides libraries' decisions to select or remove materials, then censorship can result [para. 3].

The American Library Association's concluding remark underscores the importance of inclusion, diversity of information, and access to information. It read:

Materials like "Fifty Shades of Grey" challenge libraries' professional ideals of open, equitable, unbiased access to information. They raise important questions about how libraries can best include and reflect the diversity of ideas in our society—even those which some people find objectionable. In all circumstances, ALA encourages libraries making decisions about their collections to keep in mind their basic missions and the core values of intellectual freedom and providing access to information [para. 4].

The ALA did not single out any particular case of *Fifty Shades* bans at public libraries to defend or condemn its decision. Jones, however, encourages an inclusive policy. She writes, "There are many reasons for self-censorship, and one is fear. That is understandable now that library jobs are on the line everywhere" (21). But its fundamental approach of providing maximum access to the widest range of information feasible within budgetary and other constraints is clear. Jones continues, "Many of our country's most distinguished librarians have dealt with challenged books and have been able to keep them on the shelves" (21).

The case in Brevard County was resolved within a few months. On May 28, 2012, the libraries announced that it would bring all nineteen copies back to the shelf. The statement read, "Earlier this month, a decision was made to pull 'Fifty Shades of Grey' from our libraries as a result of published reviews and our own initial analysis of the book and its controversial content. Since then, we have begun a review of our selection criteria and that review continues even as the decision has been made to supply the book in response to requests by county residents" (Clarke, para. 6).

Derek Newton, ACLU spokesperson, welcomed this decision by emphasizing, "We view it as a victory for the First Amendment. We're happy that the county has decided to protect the rights of area residents by making this material available" (Kennerly "Racy Tale," para. 10). A resident with a sixteen-year old daughter who is being homeschooled also stated that this decision was the "ultimate hands-on lesson in civics" (Kennerly "Racy Tale," para. 13). When her local library system banned the trilogy, she began a petition and gathered as many as two thousand signatures (Kennerly "50 Shades," para. 8). She continued, "This is a huge victory for Brevard County; for anybody who believes in freedom of speech and not letting censorship take a front seat in this day and age ... adults can make their own decisions about what they read and don't read" (Kennerly "Racy Tale," para. 14).

Not all public libraries decided to bring the books back to their shelves. While aforementioned residents in Baltimore County could not read the book because there was such a long wait list, residents in Harford

County, Baltimore's neighbor, could not access the book because its libraries did not carry it. While the Baltimore libraries' system's director, Mary Hastler, admitted that it was "one of these tricky issues," the libraries maintained its original decision even after their counterparts in Brevard County had decided to bring the books back (Gallo and Zumer, para. 2). She continued to say, "It's clear that we don't buy pornography for the library" (Gallo and Zumer, para. 13).

Characterizing *Fifty Shades* as pornography and using such a label to justify a decision to resist or ban the popular trilogy is not unique to Hastler. Schweinsberg made the same argument by repeating the fact that it had been characterized as "mommy porn," and stating "the library does not 'collect porn'" (Kennerly "Residents speak up," para. 5). Individuals encouraging others not to read or watch it, as shown earlier in this chapter, have also used a similar approach. In reality, as discussed elsewhere in this book, the book is not pornography and is a fan-fiction-based romance novel that follows the conventions of the genre. Although depictions of various sexual acts might surprise some readers, *Fifty Shades* is not a unique book.

This is why banning *Fifty Shades* raises a valid question about what is different about the trilogy. Joan Bertin, the executive director of the National Coalition Against Censorship, accurately mentioned, "Sexually explicit content is present in literature throughout time and [in] classics. If they followed that rule [of not carrying any sexually-explicit material], they'd leave out an awful lot of stuff" (Gallo and Zumer, para. 38). What is unique is for a book of this type to appeal to a vast audience beyond traditional romance fans. It also led certain decision-makers to read the book while many other similar books went unread. Well-intended interventions by Hastler, Schweinsberg, and others turned out to be what many considered censoring efforts.

Some public libraries decided that because the demand was high enough for them to carry their own copies of the books, they could instead take advantage of interlibrary loans. Through Willard Library in Michigan, patrons can access the *Fifty Shades* trilogy via the Midwest Collaborative for Library Services (MCLS). Kelley reported in May 2012 that for ten copies of the books available, the wait list was almost 650 people (para. 18). Albion District Library in Michigan, another member of the MCLS, also does not stock its own copies of *Fifty Shades* but keeps the books available through the interlibrary services. Cindy Stanczak, a librarian in Albion, stated, "I certainly have no problem buying those for our patrons, but the reality is … that we're just not getting the demand for these as we are for some of the other, more popular authors" (para. 20).

The *Fifty Shades* controversies at public libraries brought back questions regarding censorship and the role of public libraries. On the one hand, libraries' limited financial resources justifies the need to be a selection process before they purchase books. Libraries aim to satisfy the needs of their patrons. It also means that popular books should be purchased so that residents are able to read such books regardless of their genres or reviews. On the other hand, when book selections are made which are not based on the local community's needs but rather on certain individuals' moral value judgments, it risks censorship and potential violation of the First Amendment.

Christian-Based Academic Institutions Ban Fifty Shades

Resistance to *Fifty Shades* took various forms. Faith-based resistance to the trilogy and the film, as well as public libraries' bans were not the only examples. Similar resistance and bans took place at faith-based academic institutions. For example, Stonehill College, a small private Catholic college in Massachusetts, had stopped carrying James's trilogy in its bookstore (Goldstein, para. 1). One of the most prominent cases of banning the trilogy happened at Boston College. The Catholic-based university, located in Chestnut Hill, Massachusetts, removed the trilogy from the shelves of its on-campus bookstore as of March 9, 2015. The student newspaper at Boston College reported that there had been "a complaint … requesting the novels to be taken off the shelves" (Suh, para. 1). The complaint came after the bookstore sold the books for several months. The period, of course, corresponded with the resurgence in the public interests in the trilogy with the film's release.

Suh also hinted that the book was popular in the Boston College community. Quoting Tina Plotegher, the assistant director of the bookstore, she wrote, "The bookstore sold out the first volume, and only two copies of the second and third volumes remain in stock" (para. 4). The resistance to the book tended to be small. Plotegher is also quoted as saying, "They didn't believe the university should be promoting a book that goes against Catholic religion…. They weren't complaining to pull it. They were like, 'Oh wow, they sell that here'" (Suh, para. 9). What made the bookstore pull the books off its shelves was just one e-mail that was sent both to the bookstore and the university. A representative for the university e-mailed the bookstore and it was "decided to pull the book so that they would not offend any customers" (Suh, para. 13).

Fifty Shades of Censorship

Though unintended, *Fifty Shades* generated an ideal opportunity for debates on the First Amendment, censorship, and moral panic. As Harman and Jones wrote, there is much to learn from how anti-fans respond to a text. Numerous individuals resisted the trilogy and film due to their poor quality. But many also resisted them for religious and faith-based reasons. This is not to say that religion and faith necessarily stopped people from reading the novels. The Barna Group, a research group focusing on faith-based groups, reported in its 2013 publication that Christian women were as likely to read *Fifty Shades of Grey* as non–Christian women in general, at the rate of 9 percent (Barna). In many instances, they not only expressed their dissatisfaction and concerns about James's works and their refusal to read or watch *Fifty Shades*, they went on to call for action. Many bloggers encouraged their readers to boycott the books and films. This alone is not unique. For various social reasons, boycotting popular culture is common.

But what made the boycotting efforts more formulated was both public libraries and academic institutions' unwillingness to purchase or carry *Fifty Shades*. Although some used James's low-quality writing as an excuse not to include her work from their collection, a great majority of the debate was about the content. Labeled as "erotica," "mommy porn," and even "pornography," the works became, in a sense, a public enemy. Of course, the *Fifty Shades* trilogy was not the only case of books being threatened for removal from public libraries. The American Library Association, for example, reported that, in 2011, there were 326 attempts "to restrict or remove books" (Kennerly "Residents Want," para. 17). At the top of the list was the *Hunger Games* trilogy. In Brevard, Madonna's book entitled *Sex* (published in 1992) was also banned (Kennerly "Residents Want," para. 8). Although James's books are now back on the shelf for the residents of Brevard, the controversy challenged us to think about the role of public libraries. Furthermore, when Boston College campus bookstore decided to stop selling the books, Boston College's university library kept its electronic copy of the trilogy available for its patrons. This raises the question about the role of bookstores and libraries, especially at a higher education institution that is founded upon a particular faith.

Examining American resistance to *Fifty Shades*, both in religious and non-religious settings, shows that the rejection of the popular trilogy and film was multifaceted. Some simply refused to consume James's work and claimed it was not worth their time and money. Some had religious objections. But many were also simply afraid that they might like the story of Christian and Anastasia. Such a sense of fear hints at the long-held Victorian perspective on sex, even to this day. On the one hand, the U.S. appears to be a culture of sex. Sex sells. Sex is omnipresent. But on the other hand, Americans appear to be quite unsure how to deal with the subject outside their own bedrooms.

The debate on banning the books in a public library fueled the discussion on what it should do when the people it is designed to serve want to have access to controversial books. The American Library Association explained that, in 2012, there were 464 "reports on attempts to remove materials from shelves and school curriculums." The number had fallen to 307 the following year. But the organization also explains that removing "just one book from a library prevents hundreds from having free access to information" (Flood para. 12). In 2013, the Captain Underpants series, *The Bluest Eye* by Toni Morrison, Suzanne Collins's *The Hunger Games*, and others received frequent challenges. Reasons for this included the use of offensive language, violence, religious viewpoints, sexual content, substance use and abuse, and political viewpoints.

When such American experiences are compared to those of other nations it is possible to observe that different norms affect how a popular culture is perceived. Ben Sanderson, of the British Library, explained that it was not up to the organization to judge which books should be stocked and which should be removed. The different ways in which the U.S. and the U.K. libraries handled the *Fifty Shades* controversy "shows the controversial gap between cultures within the two countries" (Varga para. 5). As noted later in this book, the movie version of was subject to censorship in Japan, where two different versions—R-18 and R-15—were released. Japanese film reviewers, almost without fail, mentioned how distracting the censorship effort was, but rarely questioned their need. France, on the other hand, considered the film to be inoffensive. As a whole, these international differences show various cultural norms that affect how a popular culture text is discussed, appreciated, and challenged.

CHAPTER FIVE

Not for Anastasia's Pleasure
The Trilogy's Failure to
Liberate Sexualities

Even for non-readers and non-viewers of *Fifty Shades of Grey*, it is a well-known fact that E. L. James's story revolves around BDSM. While the theme might have driven some to pick up a copy of the novel or to take a trip to a local cineplex, it also discouraged others from following one of the most controversial literary franchises in recent years.

Although *Fifty Shades* can be analyzed without its depictions of BDSM, it ended up as one of the signature labels to describe the trilogy. It is important to note, however, that many BDSM experts and practitioners stated that the trilogy did not accurately reflect the lifestyle. Emily Sarah, in her interview with Anna Smith from the *Guardian*, said, "I don't think E. L. James has had a huge amount of real-life experience; I think these [depicted sex acts] are probably her fantasies. I get the impression she hasn't had much safe, consensual S&M in her life" (Smith "Fifty Shades of Grey," para. 6). Popular culture scholar Catherine Scott even suggested that James might have as well written her books using information about BDSM from Wikipedia (66). This lack of experience was confirmed by James herself, who admitted to an interviewer, "I am fascinated by BDSM, and fascinated as to why anyone would want to be in this lifestyle" ("Interview with Fifty Shades," para. 16).

The fact that James's depiction of BDSM is inaccurate or is based on her fantasy is not, in itself, significant. Many authors have written stories based on their fantasies and stereotypes. *Fifty Shades*, after all, is not a how-to guide to BDSM. Exoticization of the unknown or the less-known is a common practice among best-selling authors. Furthermore, fantasy stories can easily be enriched by the known. However, James's portrayals of the relationship between Christian and Anastasia that is characterized

84

to be based on BDSM can lead to misunderstandings about BDSM that have social and political implications. In other words, *Fifty Shades of Grey*, through its misrepresentation of BDSM, can easily be mistaken as reality. Consequently, the story misrepresents the reality of power dynamics between the participants. Additionally, it portrays the BDSM lifestyle as deviant and, ultimately, problematic and abusive.

The Reality of BDSM

Despite these simple labels of bondage, discipline, sadism, and masochism, there is a wide variety of sexual activities associated with BDSM. Academicians Weinberg, Williams, and Moser characterized that "SM was constituted by a set of five social features which sustained a particular class of fantasies with erotic meanings: dominance and submission, role playing, consensuality, a sexual context, and mutual definition" (380). Will Damon, in his academic treatise on the subject, emphasizes that "safe, sane, and consensual" practices are key to successful BDSM (27). Hébert and Weaver also add that simply splitting the BDSM community into those who want to control and those who want to be controlled is inaccurate; there are many individuals, known as "switchers," who prefer both roles (107). The appearance of a power hierarchy between the dominant and the submissive is, therefore, fluid.

Due to the stigma associated with BDSM it is difficult to estimate exactly how popular that particular sexual practice is. This is not unlike collecting data on homosexuality, another stigmatized sexual preference (Jayson, Luscher, and Grabmann). The BDSM lifestyle is assumed to be contrary to so-called vanilla-sex, further strengthening biases against BDSM as kinky and deviant. Even in the mid–2010s, when Americans' general sentiment toward sexuality is far more liberal than what it once was, BDSM is considered to be a subculture that reflects one's darkest sexual desires. Connolly revealed that more than a half of BDSM practitioners said they felt "uncomfortable or worse" about the possibility of their being "outed." Roughly 10 percent said "they could not disclose their BDSM interests to anyone," and 4 percent said they felt they had to "hide" their preference from others (92). This social atmosphere partly explains the background for a popular blog article that cited Dr. Gloria Brame's description of those who practice BDSM as "regular people who happen to get off that way" (Gueren para. 8). Nonetheless, Gueren wrote, "There is nothing *inherently* wrong or damaged with people if they're into it" (emphasis mine, para. 6).

According to one study, 2.2 percent of men and 1.3 percent of women have engaged in BDSM sexual play in the previous twelve months (Richters et al.). Summarizing various industry studies, Busby explains that about 38 percent of surveyed Brits in 2009 owned handcuffs. An estimated 42 percent had experienced role playing and spanking, and 24 percent had experienced bondage. Older studies have shown that over 60 percent of surveyed Canadians have fantasized about tying up their partner or being tied up themselves (Busby 345). Moser and Kleinplatz estimated about 10 percent of adults practiced BDSM. On the other hand, Eveleth cited a study by Durex that revealed "36 percent of adults in the United States use masks, blindfolds, and bondage tools during sex" (para. 2). Connolly found that 11.2 percent of practitioners said BDSM was the "*only* form of sexual activity" and 32 percent spent less than half of their sexual time engaged in BDSM (91). Hébert and Weaver argue, based on this wide range of figures, that "even though prevalence data are varied, it can be assumed that a substantial number of people engage in BDSM" (107).

The Fifty Shades' *Relationship Is Not BDSM*

Many experts argue that *Fifty Shades* is not a movie about BDSM. Stephanie Marcus characterizes it as "less of a movie about BDSM and more like an average stalker-thriller" (para. 2). On one level, it is true that the books and the film show Christian uses some of the tools and behaviors associated with BDSM. The contract he prepares for Anastasia is also filled with references to BDSM-related toys and activities, as well as the roles of "dominant" and "submissive" (James 165). When Christian shows Anastasia his Red Room of Pain, she asks him if he is a sadist; Christian responds by saying, "I'm a Dominant" (James 100). An iconic image associated with the film, that of Anastasia's naked back and a brown riding crop pressed gently against her neck, also parallels an image of BDSM.

Regardless of common misconceptions about BDSM as a "sickness and illness" (Ortmann and Sprott 5), BDSM is based on a set of rules. For example, Weinberg, Williams, and Moser explained it through five characteristics of BDSM relationships. Damon, similarly, did so with three tenets. When these characteristics are applied to the *Fifty Shades* story, there is a base for it to be considered BDSM-like. However, Christian and Anastasia's relationship falls short of what the framework establishes for its practitioners. On the one hand, Christian and Anastasia understand that "the activities have a sexual meaning" (Weinberg, Williams, and

Moser 381). They also mutually understand that their activities are, at least according to themselves, BDSM. These fit the last two definitions of BDSM as proposed by Weinberg, Williams, and Moser. But much of the relationship that James describes is actually contrary to other definitions of BDSM acts. For example, although Weinberg, Williams, and Moser state that dominance and submission are a primary feature of a BDSM relationship, they also caution that the dynamics between the dominant and the submissive is "an appearance of rule over one partner by another" (380–381). The "appearance" enables BDSM acts to include a master-slave play and other pretend/fantasy plays. The concept of "role play"—the second tenet according to Weinberg, Williams, and Moser—also indicates that the power relationship should not be taken as an absolute system of hierarchy that dictates a romantic relationship. In the case of the *Fifty Shades* relationship, however, the power disparity permeates in various interactions between Christian and Anastasia. Christian's unwelcomed appearances at a hardware store or in Georgia are typical examples of the actual "rule over one partner by another" (Weinberg, Williams, and Moser 380–381). The relationship between Christian and Anastasia is beyond an appearance of power hierarchy. It spills over to their life outside of their bedroom—or, in their particular case, bedrooms, or the Red Room of Pain.

Weinberg, Williams, Moser, and Damon agree that consensuality is an integral part of BDSM. Weinberg, Williams, and Moser elaborate on this by defining the concept as "a voluntary agreement to enter into dominant/submissive 'play' and to honor certain 'limits'" (381). Although Christian repeatedly asks Anastasia to be in a relationship with him and attempts to lure her with his wealth and appearance, it is indeed Anastasia who voluntarily agrees to be his girlfriend. The *Fifty Shades* story is filled with Anastasia's inner ruminations, reflecting her uncertainties and doubts. Similarly, to argue that Anastasia had free will to use her safeword, "red," and that by not doing so she was consenting to be whipped, neglects her intricate psychology.

The BDSM relationship between these two characters must be analyzed more closely and cannot be defined, simplistically, as consensual. Ronald L. H. Elliston, the founder of Submission, or the "world's first fetish dance club," calls the relationship depicted in *Fifty Shades* "very dangerous" (Smith "Fifty Shades of Grey," para. 7, 11). Similarly, Jon Blue, who hosts House of Shadows BDSM events, characterized the film as "an instruction manual for a psychopath" (Smith "Fifty Shades of Grey," para. 15).

Nichi Hodgson, a twenty-eight-year-old journalist with some BDSM experience, found Christian's personal background problematic. She writes, "There are thousands of perfectly well-adjusted members of the BDSM community who simply enjoy kinky sex, with absolutely no underlying neurosis necessary" ("Just How Realistic," para. 7). Research indeed backs up Hodgson's claim. A study that involved over nine hundred BDSM and over four hundred control participants revealed that BDSM practitioners had "a set of balanced, autonomous, and beneficial personality characteristics ... [falsifying] the view that BDSM practitioners are psychologically disturbed or characterized by maladaptive psychological processes or even psychopathology." The study also argues that "it is unlikely that having experienced one or more traumatic (sexual) experiences is a major cause for developing a preference for BDSM activities" (Wismeijer and van Assen 1951). Newmahr also insists that BDSM is a "serious leisure endeavor" and must be separated from violence (329). In *Fifty Shades*, BDSM-like activities are not presented as such. They are shown as evidence of Christian's past that continue to affect him negatively. Even though many of the romance novels revolve around the theme of a heroine curing the hero, thus leading up to a happy ending, Christian's past and his engagement in power-driven violent behaviors in a sexual context are dangerous and not reflective of the BDSM culture.

Questions about Consent

As previous scholars have documented, consensuality is an important part of a healthy BDSM relationship. Barker explains that so-called SSC (safe, sane, and consensual) is also known as "risk aware consensual kink" or RACK (896). Defining what is "consensual," however, is more difficult and complex than it might appear. Many legal experts have debated the meaning of "consent" and what it looks like, especially when someone is involved in an act of BDSM (Busby 349–350). Recently, the issue of consent has been widely debated in the context of sexual violence, especially in cases of date rape. Numerous online posts on Yahoo! Answers and Quora archive questions from heterosexual men who are confused about what women want, sexually. An anonymous writer posed a question, "Why is it, when women say no, they really mean yes?" In response, Claire J. Vannette, wrote, "Assuming you're talking about sex, yes, this happens. Sometimes women say 'No' and they mean 'I want to, but I don't want to admit that'" ("Why Is It," para 2). With such messages flooding both online and offline relationship advice, is there any wonder that, in 2011, fraternity members at Yale University marched across campus yelling, "No means yes! Yes means Anal!" (Mason and Shaw para 3.) More recently, in 2014, the same saying was seen on a banner on campus at Texas Tech University (Kingkade).

In 2015, the state of Michigan introduced a "Yes Means Yes" law to clarify that "silence or indifference aren't consent" and that "only a freely given 'yes' counts" (Friedman para. 1). This law was also invoked when Michigan State University was characterized as "a sexually hostile environment" by the U.S. Department of Education (Feldscher para. 5). The accusation came after a study revealed that about a quarter of MSU's female undergraduate students had been sexually assaulted, and over 10 percent had been victims of "completed or attempted nonconsensual ... rape" (Lawler para. 4). Only a few years prior to the study, two Michigan State University basketball players were accused of sexual assault. The encounters were later characterized as a matter of "he said, she said," even though the female victim's lack of consent was acknowledged, and no charges were filed against the male athletes (Traywick para. 10).

Traywick underscores that "while a man who rapes off-campus could face years in jail for his crime, a man who rapes on-campus is unlikely to even be expelled." In addition, there is a tendency among administrators to view sexual assault as "teachable moments" (para 17–18). In many cases, proving consent alone can be a difficult task. The audience of *Fifty Shades of Grey*, for example, expressed varying views on consensuality between Christian and Anastasia. A focus group interview conducted by Bonomi, Nichols, Carotta, Kiuchi, and Perry, involving college-aged female students, demonstrated that subjects disagreed to what extent Anastasia had consented in the film. From major American universities to research findings, examples suggest that "only yes means yes" may not sufficiently address the important question about what genuinely represents consent.

For example, while Christian is willing to negotiate the terms of his relationship with Anastasia and allows her to accept or decline any part of the BDSM-like activities, it may appear that it is a form of consent building. However, the negotiation is one-way. The non-disclosure agreement prevents Anastasia from discussing her relationship with her roommate, Kate. Anastasia is not allowed to ask questions or seek advice from friends. The contract was given from Christian to Anastasia, who is expected to read it and research it (James 148). Christian buys Anastasia a laptop to conduct said research. The entire process of what passes for consent building is a one-way process.

Through the negotiation, Anastasia only has an option to say yes, or no. She is not given an option to add what *she* wants to add to the list. The only time she expresses her desire is when she seeks a more traditional relationship that involves looking at Christian or touching him. Christian rejects those ideas outright. Even in the movie—the negotiation scene in the film develops differently from the novel—Anastasia does not have an opportunity to add anything to the contract. The film's deviation from the book leads Christian to say, "Can I just say how impressed I am with your commitment to this meeting? And in that spirit, I'm going to throw in a sweetener. How about once a week on a night of your choosing, we go on a date. Just like a regular couple. Dinner, movie, ice skating, whatever you want." Anastasia responds by saying, "Accepted. You're very kind."

The one-way nature of the relationship is illustrated by dialogue following Christian's flogging of Anastasia. She tells him, in no uncertain terms, that she did not like the experience. Christian responds, "You didn't at any time ask me to stop—you didn't use either safeword. You are an adult—you have choices" (James 295). The relationship framework is structured, first and foremost, that Christian sets the boundaries. Second, Anastasia either agrees or disagrees with said boundaries. Because she has agreed to participate in an act, it is her responsibility—or even her fault—if she experiences something to her dislike. This perspective is similar to blaming the victim with such dismissive statements as "But she could have said 'No.'"

If the storyline of *Fifty Shades* is safe, it is because Anastasia allegedly has a choice to get out of her relationship and reject Christian's requests. She is assumed to be able to use a safeword and is in control of her own destiny. But arguing that Anastasia agreed to be in a relationship with Christian and to be subject to his violent sexual behaviors simply because she did not explicitly use her safeword is contrary to the recent social shift from "no means no" to "only yes means yes." As noted above, Christian blames Anastasia for not stopping him when he first spanked her. Anastasia describes, "I have to concentrate to handle this pain.... I cry out on the tenth slap" (James 274). Even when Anastasia cries "Aargh!" Christian simply responds, "I'm just getting warmed up" (James 274). Anastasia continues, "He hits me again ... this is getting harder to take. My face hurts, it's screwed up so tight.... I cry out again" (James 275). Christian, again, simply says, "No one to hear you" (James 275). Even though Anastasia cries out six more times, Christian does not stop. For Christian, the lack of "no" as indicated with a safeword is the equivalent of a "yes."

Considering the fact that *Fifty Shades of Grey* was based on Stephenie

Meyer's *Twilight*, it is understandable that Anastasia is portrayed as an individual who, at least superficially, lacks confidence and individuality. James's book begins with Anastasia's dissatisfaction about her hair: she is jealous that Kate, her roommate, is pretty even when she is sick (1–2). Although some readers and moviegoers argued that Anastasia has exercised more agency than one might expect and that she was more in control of her relationship with Christian (especially near the end of the first book), she is generally portrayed as a submissive character. Self-confidence is not her forté. Parkin wrote that "many *Twilight* readers interpret Bella as an anti-feminist heroine because of her conservative decisions and her complacency in the face of possible bodily harm" (66). The same can be said about Anastasia. This is to say that "definitions of feminism revolve around choice" (Parkin 67). Fans have pointed out that Anastasia rarely made her own choice in her relationship with Christian.

The issue about consensuality in a relationship like that of Christian and Anastasia's also poses a question about individual choice. On the one hand, as discussed above, there is a debate as to whether Anastasia fully consented to being whipped. An argument has been made that she did so by not using a safeword. But studies have found that many victims of sexual abuse feel they cannot say "no," even if they are being victimized (Adams-Curtis and Forbes). On the other hand, claiming Anastasia should have been more assertive about her own wants to avoid physical and emotional pain is also to unfairly overemphasize what an individual can do.

Focusing on individual responsibility and consent is characterized as a "neoliberal" view by both Meg Baker (897) and Angelika Tsaros (875). As Anastasia is more and more involved in her relationship with Christian, she never identifies herself as his submissive. Rather, she constantly challenges him to see if he would be willing to have "hearts and flowers" with her (James 244). Tsaros concludes that Anastasia ends up "understanding [Christian's sexual preference] via pathologizing" (870). Tsaros explains the concept of "pathologizing" by borrowing concepts from Margot Weiss. In other words, Anastasia, who originally found Christian's sexual tendency troubling and confusing, begins to make sense of it by convincing herself that it is a form of pathology. In the process, Anastasia experiences "acceptance by normalization," or "[accepting] representations when they are similar enough to normalized western sexuality" (870). Tsaros continues: "Anastasia's seeming *acceptance* of Christian's desires … turns to mere *understanding*, pathologizing, at which point she leaves" (emphasis in original, 875). Emma Green also agrees that James presents BDSM "as a pathology, not a path to pleasure" (para. 35). James, Anastasia, and *Fifty*

Shades readers and viewers observe Christian as someone with problems. The existence of the problems justifies his obsession with violent and controlling sex. It is a way to make sense of his behaviors, not just for the story's author or the story's female protagonist, but also its audience.

For Anastasia, this is to say that she never truly consented to Christian's sexual acts. She might have been willing to try what he wanted, but when she was pushed beyond her boundaries and questioned if Christian was "trying to mold [her] into something [she is] not," Anastasia was not fully willing to engage in a BDSM relationship (James 229). When she realizes that Christian would spank her, she reminds him, "I haven't signed." He simply responds, "I told you what I'd do. I'm a man of my word. I'm going to spank you, and then I'm going to fuck you very quick and very hard" (James 273). Later Anastasia even sarcastically says to herself, "Like I have a choice" about her relationship, even her own sexuality (James 275).

An argument could be made that Anastasia gave verbal consent. She never signs the contract, but in multiple instances, she willingly joins Christian in his Red Room of Pain. Even in her old apartment, she permits Christian to spank her. When an angry Christian orders Anastasia to the Play Room after she returns from Georgia, she simply complies. However, on countless occasions, Christian pushes her beyond her comfort zone. It is not just the dramatic whipping scene at the end of *Fifty Shades of Grey* that her limits are violated.

Prejudice about Male Sexuality and Female Submissiveness

The trilogy also presents a problematic view of male sexuality. First, Christian "just *knows*" what Anastasia wants and she "isn't expected to say what she wants from sex" (Green para. 38). To be fair to James, this is expected. As Green admits, readers "don't pick up romance novels because they're itching to read multiple pages of mature, sophisticated dialogue about feelings of vulnerability and personal boundaries" (para. 39). Nonetheless, James's descriptions about Christian's and Anastasia's sexuality reflect a problematic stereotyping of each gender. In short, men are sexual and women are the recipients of male sexual desire.

Not only does Christian know what Anastasia wants, he also knows— or is supposed to know—when "no" means "yes." In other words, he knows that she may say that she does not want something but she actually does, albeit subconsciously. Clearly, this speaks to the larger social discussion about what "no" and "yes" mean. It is partly because of this, with "but a few swift strokes, he [Christian] can get her to orgasm—loudly, frequently, in any position and any location—by intuiting what her body wants" (Green para. 38). But this problematic depiction of Christian's behaviors goes beyond this in the Red Room of Pain. He buys her a first-edition copy of *Tess of the d'Urbervilles* by Thomas Hardy, which Justin Ocean estimates to be around $14,000. He also buys her an Audi A3 for graduation—estimated, again by Ocean, to be about $30,000. Anastasia tells Christian that taking his gifts made her "feel cheap" (James 252). But Christian only answers, "I will buy you a lot of things, Anastasia. Get used to it" (252). Aside from these gifts that Anastasia feels uncomfortable receiving, he also shows up at her work before they start dating and, in Georgia, when she felt she had to clear her mind away from him. He knows what Anastasia wants or needs, even when she says otherwise. Both sexually and non-sexually, Christian exercises control over Anastasia.

Christian is taking the power dynamics between the dominant and the submissive outside of the confine of his sexual acts. On the surface level, he says the BDSM play will only be on the days when they see each other, as specified in their contract. Since it indicates that the appearance of power hierarchy spills out of the Red Room of Pain, it is already against what is described by experts to be the common BDSM framework. From gifts to constant check-ins, the unequal power dynamics exist outside of their agreed-upon days, let alone sexual encounters. Tsaros writes, "Christian assures Anastasia that her submission will be limited to negotiated time periods, clearly oblivious to the fact that already the seemingly small step of hormonal interference cannot be limited as such and thus unintentionally expanding his control over her body indefinitely" (872).

Contrary to Christian's 24/7 power hierarchical relationship, Jon Blue points out that "a 24/7 BDSM relationship is very, very rare" (Smith "Fifty Shades of Grey," para. 15). He discusses that such power dynamics are very risky in a relationship and it requires much time to establish a sense of trust to make it possible. In *Fifty Shades of Grey*, the relationship develops very fast. Blue comments, "It would take years to build up that level of trust with someone, otherwise it's abuse" (Smith "Fifty Shades of Grey," para. 15). Jon Mietus also problematizes James's depiction of the *Fifty Shades* relationship that is male-dominated. Referencing the quote from the movie, "Mr. Grey will see you now," Mietus writes:

> Nowhere is her continuing education mentioned she supposedly attends college, but graduate school is but a distraction on her road towards voluntary, total sub-

mission. In a world where women currently hold only 4.6 percent of CEO positions at S&P 500 companies, represent just 18–20 percent of all engineering students and make up 24.2 percent of all state legislators nationwide, it's clear romanticizing subservience will only worsen the problem of a male-dominated world [para. 9].

As quoted earlier, Green makes a convincing point that a romance novel is not expected to discuss sophisticated discussions about one's feelings. Similarly, it is not expected to help increase the number of female students in the STEM fields or to encourage more women to be political or take on business leadership roles. That is not the purpose of romance novels. Therefore, Mietus's expectation may not be fair to James. Nevertheless, Mietus makes a good point when he writes, "Every single woman who believes Ana's life is an adventurous, exciting and ultimately pleasurable one will forever conclude they must totally and completely submit to men to achieve satisfaction" (para. 11). Researchers who conducted focus group interviews reported that their college-age subjects were able to list several things that were appealing about Christian and Anastasia's relationship (Bonomi et al.). Of course, *Fifty Shades* does not teach its audience what kind of relationship they should seek. But it exists in the society where its audience can easily identify numerous positives. Therefore, the trilogy, along with other popular cultural texts, helps normalize power inequality that exists between a man and a woman in a relationship.

On the flip side of male dominance is the idea of rape fantasy. The fantasy—it is important to note that the fantasy myth has been debunked as nothing but a myth—is an extreme form of wanting to be dominated or controlled (Arndt, et al). James's works could be used to justify the idea that even someone like Anastasia—a virgin who seeks "hearts and flowers" and who is a romantic type indulging herself in classic novels—has an unconscious desire to be overpowered, controlled—and even raped. Critelli and Bivona report that between 9 and 17 percent of women have rape fantasies (61).

Re-examining if the rape fantasy is valid—or even discussing if the name "rape fantasy" accurately reflects what those who reportedly hold such a fantasy—is not within the scope of this chapter. However, as we discuss power, individual choice, and the depictions of BDSM, it is appropriate to examine how the rape fantasy—or whatever one prefers to call it—is portrayed in James's work. Hawley and Hensley, for example, argue that so many stories aside from *Fifty Shades* follow the storyline of women being dominated. Many romance novels have a female protagonist who wishes to be overwhelmed by the love of her Prince Charming. Just like TV commercials, advertisements, and other popular culture images tend to show women as the dominated, *Fifty Shades* shows Anastasia being controlled, dominated, and subjugated. An implication of such a portrayal, however, is not limited to the potentially negative impact on women's self-esteem. It is also beyond the way in which someone might use those images as a justification to claim that "no" does not always mean "no."

In addition to these risks and implications, Hawley and Hensley argue that the rape fantasy runs the risk of "[overlooking] important intra-gender variability" (582). This is to say that subscribing to such a fantasy as a prototypical female desire can ignore what "alpha females" look for sexually (582). Although it is unfair and unwarranted to expect a particular popular culture work, be it this one or something else, to be socially responsible and reflect the intra-gender diversity, it is nonetheless true that *Fifty Shades* is just another work that fuels the myth and makes the female subordination appear normative. It relies on and perpetuates gender norms and erases diversity within a particular gender group.

Fifty Shades of Inaccuracy

As discussed elsewhere in this book, a moral panic caused by popular culture is common. It is frequently very difficult, even impossible, to accurately demonstrate how popular culture impacts its audience or surrounding society. No matter how many times the question, "Do violent video games make people violent?" is asked, and no matter how many attempts are made to answer this, the result is mixed. Nonetheless, popular culture is, more often than not, used as a scapegoat for what a particular segment of society deems as unwanted behaviors. Therefore, arguing that *Fifty Shades* makes its audience become sexually violent is a claim that cannot be supported. But it is still fair to say that it inaccurately portrays BDSM. Although not rare, it is still a lesser-practiced form of sexuality. Consequently, non-practitioners assumed that James's version of it was accurate, even though she admitted that she has little first-hand experience.

Studies have shown that BDSM might be more popular than one might imagine. From a casual tight grabbing of a partner's body part to "being on top," many engage in sexual practices that have the appearance of power differentials. Practitioners of BDSM, however, underscore the importance of "safe, sane, and consensual." Furthermore, Wismeijer and van Assen argued in their work that practitioners tended to be healthier mentally than non–practitioners. The typical BDSM relationship they describe is different from the one depicted in the novels. True BDSM is confined to the bedroom; the *Fifty Shades* version is not. It is role play, with limitations; again, the *Fifty Shades* version is not. This is why Stephanie Marcus aptly entitled her essay, "*Fifty Shades of Grey* Isn't a Movie About BDSM, and That's a Problem."

Anastasia says to herself, "*He likes to hurt women.* The thought depresses me" (emphasis in original, James 100). Still, she jumps into the relationship with him. Marcus argues, "It's only Christian's extreme wealth and the romanticized notion of his overarching dominant persona that barely mask what's really just completely creepy behavior. In any other movie, a man or woman who tracks down another person at their job, local bar, home and, oh, their *mother's home* in Georgia, a plane ride away, would probably end up in back of a police car" (emphasis in original, para 3). What if Christian were poor? What if he lived in a trailer home? Many of the memes inspired by the book asked the question if Anastasia would have acted the same way.

Amy Adler, a law professor at New York University, commented, "There's an interesting tension right now between the mainstreaming of S&M that *Fifty Shades* represents and also the mainstream horror at rape culture…. There's an increasing vigilance against rape culture on the one hand and the easy acceptance of pornographic S&M" (Green para. 40). Adler continues that the rape culture that we have been witnessing in our society is "a product of books and movies like *Fifty Shades of Grey*" (Green para. 44). Adler, clearly, does not believe that James's work is used as a scapegoat. She does not believe that the negative reaction and resistance to it is a moral panic. Whether or not such a view is appropriate is discussed in another chapter of the book. Regardless of the answer, it is still important that the novels speak to concerns many people have.

Buxton sympathetically adds that it is difficult to depict the emotional aspect of a BDSM relationship in popular culture. He cites Hodgeson, arguing, "It always has to do with costumes and not really [deal] with the relationships or the depth of emotional intensity or the experience…. We're always kind of reducing it to its very simple performative level" (Buxton para. 3). Although it is not James's responsibility to depict the intricacies of the BDSM relationship, it is also important to note that her work is not about BDSM but about a unique type of relationship that involves violence and the pathologizing of a particular type of sexual behavior. BDSM is shown as deviant. Both men and women are confined to long-held stereotypes. As Busby argues, sexual minorities—in the case of *Fifty Shades*, it is those who enjoy BDSM—are depicted in a way that their criminal actions are justified (347). Because of this, the trilogy fails to help liberate various sexual identities or expressions.

CHAPTER SIX

Masking the Real Problems
Moral Panic and
Fifty Shades–*Inspired Crimes*

This chapter borrows from the concept of moral panic, most famously popularized by Stanley Cohen. The moral panic that uses *Fifty Shades* as a scapegoat for serious criminal cases, including rapes and kidnappings, masks the true cause of the problem, namely a social environment in which certain sexual norms, such as controlling masculinity, are celebrated. Victims are both silenced and blamed, and few effective countermeasures to correct the problems are implemented.

It is clear that the trilogy attracted much hype internationally, contributing to a high level of fan excitement well before the *Fifty Shades of Grey* movie came out in time for Valentine's Day of 2015 (Its sequel, *Fifty Shades Darker*, was a Valentine's Day release as well, in 2017). On the one hand, many fans found E. L. James's work to be entertaining, romantic, and pleasurable to read. Some felt it was a liberating story; others felt it was sensual. But it is just as common (perhaps even more so) for many to protest the work as a motivator of rape, of violence against a sexual partner, or to experiment sexually in a dangerous, demeaning manner. Such views appeared silly and ungrounded for many, but not all. For some, these were serious and legitimate concerns.

Chapter Four has already described how anti–*Fifty Shades* voices reflected both religious and non-religious concerns, as well as ethnical questions about consuming what could be considered pornography. Chapter Five discussed what the books said about BDSM, both what it got wrong and what it got right. As Chapter Three briefly mentioned, sexual norms are nothing but socially constructed. To call BDSM subcultural is simply a reflection of socially concocted expectations, and nothing more. Therefore, claiming that certain individuals were driven, because of the trilogy, to BDSM and eventually to criminal behaviors, cannot be substantiated. There is no legitimate way to criminalize BDSM behaviors conducted as sexual activities.

However, after the publication of the trilogy and the release of the movie, multiple criminal cases were reported in connection to James's works. It is, therefore, understandable for casual critics to wonder if *Fifty Shades* could encourage its fans to problematic behaviors. Parents today argue that popular culture consumed by their children is making them lazy, anti-social, even stupid. But parents of twenty years ago had similar concerns about their children who are today assuming the parental role. The same can be said for previous generations. Concerns about *Fifty Shades*, therefore, are nothing new.

What Is a Moral Panic?

Moral panic, as a concept, dates back at least two centuries. A religious publication called *The Millennial Harbinger* had cited a sermon given by Dr. Cox in 1830, in which he stated, "To paralyze the soul, or to strike it through with a moral panic, is not regeneration" ("Dr. Cox on," 546). In modern academia, Stanley Cohen is credited with popularizing the concept. He writes that a moral panic occurs when

a condition, episode, person or group of persons emerges to become defined as a threat to societal values and interests; its nature is presented in a stylized and stereotypical fashion by the mass media; the moral barricades are manned by editors, bishops, politicians and other right-thinking people; socially accredited experts pronounce their diagnosis and solutions; ways of coping are evolved or (more often) resorted to; the condition then disappears, submerges or deteriorates and becomes more visible [1].

Erich Good and Nachman Ben-Yehuda put it in simpler terms: a moral panic often happens when individuals say "X is a social problem in this society" (151). From our over-dependency on mobile technology to an increase of obesity, the so-called "social problems" that can fill in the "X" blank seem almost endless. Therefore, Good and Ben-Yehuda wonder

if public concern is a logical, almost inevitable, product of impending or concrete, inflicted harm, then that concern is not problematic, not a phenomenon necessitating an explanation. If, on the other hand, objective harm and public concern vary in large measure independently of one another, then this concern demands an explanation. How do definitions of social problems come about? Why is a social problem "discovered" in one period rather than another? … Who wins, and who loses, if a given condition is recognized as a social problem? How do groups, classes, or segments of the society struggle to establish their own definition of social problems? How is problemhood established? And by whom? [152].

These questions are relevant to the way in which *Fifty Shades* has been discussed in the media. As detailed later in this chapter, there have been reported criminal cases connected to the trilogy. Does that mean the overall negative attitudes toward James's work is valid? There is no denying that many societies have witnessed problematic relationships both between friends and acquaintances, and strangers. But is it justifiable to put a partial blame on *Fifty Shades*? Or is it more scapegoating than truly identifying an underlying problem? To help answer these questions, consider Goode and Ben-Yehuda's five characteristics of moral panic: (1) concern, (2) hostility, (3) consensus, (4) disproportionality, and (5) volatility.

First, a moral panic begins with "a heightened level of concern over the behavior (or supposed behavior)" (156). *Fifty Shades* met an increased level of concern. As noted elsewhere in this book, it was not just the religious groups but also parents, educators, and the public in general that expressed their concerns about James's work, both online and off. It was not just about the quality of James's writing or the story's value (or lack thereof) as literature that fueled the concerns. There were also organized efforts to express concerns about reading or watching *Fifty Shades*. Natalie Collins and Emma Tofi, for example, started the online "50 Shades of Abuse" campaign to argue that the work "[depicts] the reality of domestic abuse" ("50 Shades of Domestic," para. 3). Clare Wiley also interviewed those who protested against the film and reported her findings in *Vice*: "[The campaign] has riled a number of women who are now planning to boycott the film, furious at what they believe to be a glamorization of violence" (para. 2). These examples (and many others) meet the criteria for concern as the first tenet of a moral panic.

Second, the behavior is subject to hostility, creating "a dichotomization between 'them' and 'us'" (Goode and Ben-Yehuda 157). On a surface level, the dichotomization around *Fifty Shades* is simply between fans and anti-fans. But, eventually, it led to a more pronounced gap between "them" and "us." Some of the online posts vehemently denied the perspectives of those who expressed their concerns. Those who were opposed to it discourage others from reading the books or watching the films. Some used religious terms, such as "sinful" and "immoral," or even "a mortal sin" ("Is It a Mortal Sin," para. 7). It also created a dichotomy between fans and anti-fans, both of whom were highly committed to support or resist E. L. James's work.

Third, there is a consensus that the group, labeled as "them," poses a legitimate threat. It is a "fairly widespread" sentiment that may or may not be shared by the majority of the population (157). This was also true concerning *Fifty Shades*. Reasons to resist the books and films vary, from religious to ethical to health-related perspectives. Additionally, the fact that major media outlets, from the *Washington Post* to the *Atlantic* to *Psychology Today*, discussed these views in depth show that these sentiments were at least widely recognized, if not shared.

The fourth tenet is that "the concern is out of proportion to the nature of the threat, that it is, in fact, considerably greater than that which a sober empirical evaluation could support" (Goode and Ben-Yehuda 158). Recent moral panics provide numerous cases of conflated fears. When anti-immigration political candidates argued that illegal immigrants use so-called anchor babies to remain in the U.S., for example, Janell Ross, of the *Washington Post*, immediately explained that it was "a largely mythical idea" (para. 4). Other cases, including so-called "welfare queens," to race- and religion-based examples such as building a mosque at Ground Zero and crack babies of the 1980s, proved to be spurious. The same was true with *Fifty Shades*.

The final tenet of moral panics is that they "erupt fairly suddenly ... and, nearly as suddenly, they subside" (Goode and Ben-Yehuda 158). For *Fifty Shades*, a voluminous voice of resistance was heard in 2012 and 2013 when the trilogy was still new. But, by 2014, much of the discussion—far less intense in nature—dealt with who would play the role of Christian Grey and Anastasia Steele in the film adaptation. Fans wondered why Charlie Hunnam, who was originally cast to play Christian, was dropped. They also wondered why Ryan Gosling, whom E. L. James had in mind as a model for Christian, refused the part (Weisman). Anti-fans were relatively quiet during this period. In 2015, once the movie came out, the aforementioned dichotomy was virulently reborn. Within half a year, though, the outcries subsided. When James published *Grey* to retell the story from Christian's perspective, a small number of people repeated their concerns, although most were simply criticizing the book as a way for James to capitalize on its brand even further. Questions concerning morality disappeared very quickly.

This is to show that, out of Goode and Ben-Yehuda's five criteria, four are clearly met. One last question, however—Was the level of public concern valid?—was answered in *Plus Media Solutions*: "James' series has been heavily criticized by some for its glorification of an abusive relationship, [and] scorned by BDMS members for its misrepresentation of their community" ("Washington," para. 7).

Crimes Associated with Fifty Shades

One of the highest-profile criminal charges associated with *Fifty Shades* took place on February 21, 2015, about a week after the release of the film. Writing for the *Chicago Tribune*, Steve Schmadeke reported that Mahammad Hossain, a nineteen-year-old freshman at the University of Illinois at Chicago, was charged with sexual assault of a fellow student ("Prosecutors"). The two students, Schmadeke wrote, were not a couple, even though they had had consensual sexual encounters "four or five times" ("Student Accused of").

The report in the *Chicago Tribune* stated that the young man and woman consensually went to Hossain's dorm room one evening. Schmadeke quotes Assistant State's Attorney Sarah Karr, who recapped the event as follows: "Hossain allegedly asked the woman to remove her clothing and she did, keeping on her bra and underwear.... He then bound her hands above her head to a bed with a belt, used another belt to bind her legs and stuffed a necktie into her mouth" ("Prosecutors," para. 7). Hossain then "used a knit cap to cover the woman's eyes ... and removed the woman's bra and underwear. He then began striking the woman with a belt. After hitting her several times, the woman told Hossain he was hurting her, [and] told him to stop" ("Prosecutors," para. 8). Hossain, however, did not stop. He continued to hit the woman using his fists. Karr stated that after the woman managed to free her arms. Hossain then "held her arms behind her back and sexually assaulted her as she continued to plead for him to stop" (Schmadeke, "Prosecutors," para. 9). After the female victim left Hossain's dorm, she reported the encounter, and the campus police arrested him ("Tying up Classmate"). Hossain admitted that he had done "something wrong" (Hicks para. 6), but he also explained that he was simply "recreating scenes from *Fifty Shades*" (Gajewski para. 4). He was later charged with aggravated criminal sexual assault and his bail was set at $500,000.

The description of the incident does indeed share some similarities to the film. Christian Grey covers Anastasia Steele's eyes, ties her hands above her head, and restricts her movement multiple times. He hits her in various ways using his palm, a whip, and his belt. According to his attorney, Hossain insists that that the sexual acts were consensual ("Washington"). The female accuser agreed that the interaction with Hossain on February 21 was consensual—at first. On that day, the female student had watched *Fifty Shades of Grey*, alone, in Chicago. After the film, she received a text message from Hossain, who asked her if she "wanted to do something dangerous" (Schmadeke "Judge," para. 19). Since Hossain did not tell her what he had in mind, she said, "It depends on what it is" (Demarest para. 11). She imagined what Hossain had in mind to be one of the "adventures" the two would periodically go on, exploring the city. She recalled that, on one occasion, she and Hossain talked all night while sitting on the campus building ledge twenty feet off the ground" (Schmadeke "Judge," para. 20).

The female student testified that all of the activities, from having her ankles tied and having her mouth gagged with a necktie, were consensual (Schmadeke "Judge"). She continued to explain that Hossain had told her that "he wanted her to resist and struck her so hard it hurt.... And she began to tell him no, to shake her head, to tell him he was hurting her" (Schmadeke "Judge," para. 22). Cook County Circuit Judge Peggy Chiampas asked her, during the hearing, if she "had said anything to Hossain when he bound her wrists or while he allegedly sexually assaulted her" (Schmadeke "Judge," para. 9). Her answer was "no." However, Schmadeke reported that the student had "denied they were re-enacting scenes from 'Fifty Shades'" and said she didn't know what Hossain meant when he told her he wanted her to resist" ("Judge," para. 24). In other words, when she resisted Hossain's sexual advances, it was genuine, and not a part of the roleplay. Eventually, Hossain was cleared by Chiampas on March 19, 2015, for not having sufficient evidence in the case ("Student Accused of"). Although he was originally banned from UIC, after the case was dismissed, he was allowed back on campus ("Student Accused of").

Other Controversial Cases

In another instance of life imitating art, a therapist shared on BBC's *Radio Five Live* that one of his clients had confessed to him that he had re-enacted scenes from *Fifty Shades of Grey*. He told his interviewer, Rachel Burden, "To be blunt, we have had nightmares over the effects of *Fifty Shades of Grey* and what children now think is normal adult sexual behavior. Within the last twenty-four hours I have worked with a young man, a twelve-year-old, who thought that *Fifty Shades of Grey* was a normal part of sexual behavior with a young girl" ("*Fifty Shades of Grey*," para. 4–5).

In another case, Steven Lock, a gardener in England, had "master and slave" sex with a woman in her forties whom he had met online (Rojas para. 2). The prosecutor, Duncan O'Donnell, stated, "She went there expecting a fantasy when Mr. Lock wanted reality. She may have expected some playful spanking, to be hit lightly perhaps, but she received a lashing with a rope" (Rojas para. 4). Lock, however, argued that the act was consensual. According to his testimony, he "put a rope around the woman's neck and pulled it tight before padlocking her wrist to a chain fastened to his bedroom floor…. He then allegedly ordered her to bend over the bed and struck her fourteen times with the rope, causing fourteen-centimeter-long bruises to her buttocks (Rojas para. 11–12). Asked about the relationship to *Fifty Shades of Grey*, he answered, "That's where we got the idea from" (Rojas para. 10).

Another case in Europe involved a wealthy forty-one-year-old banker who purchased a copy of *Fifty Shades of Grey* to spice up her sexual relationship with her husband. To her dismay, her husband refused to re-enact any scenes from the book. As a result, she filed for divorce. A newspaper report wrote, "The wife refers to the book and her husband's lack of sexual adventure in her grounds for divorce" ("Sex Just Not," para. 4).

There was even a tragedy in which a victim died from an encounter inspired by the book. The case involved a thirty-one-year-old Swedish man and a twenty-eight-year-old German woman. The woman, an exchange student in Sweden, paid a visit to her boyfriend, whom she had met online. According to a report: "The incident occurred in October [2012] when they were playing a violent sex game and she suddenly stopped breathing. The man attempted to revive her before the ambulance arrived…. She was in the hospital for two days before her life support machines were turned off. Her death was caused by brain damage due to her airways being restricted" ("Man Stands Trial," para. 6–8). Authorities also revealed that, before her death, the victim had been "taking a cocaine substitute and drinking alcohol" ("Man Stands Trial," para. 11).

Fifty Shades of Disproportionality

Indeed, websites and popular magazines are filled with articles on how to make one's sex life more exciting with the help of *Fifty Shades*. Kristen Sollee wrote, "Ever since the *Fifty Shades of Grey* series burst onto the scene in 2011, people have been buying sex toys in record numbers to get their kink on" (para. 1). She continued,

> Whether you're into it or not, it's hard to deny that kink has become way more widespread and more acceptable since the books came out, and if that inspires women to feel more sexually confident, then that's awesome…. If you read this

article with a resounding "Um, YES!" then you'll definitely want to check out these tips for having the bad girl sex of your dreams. But either way, for these people, *Fifty Shades* served as a contemporary version of the Kama Sutra [para. 5-6].

Jamie Dornan, the actor who played Christian Grey, was also quoted saying, "I'd be delighted if *Fifty Shades of Grey* would have an actual impact on people's sex lives" (Fowler, para. 2). A twenty-two-year-old viewer of the *Fifty Shades* film was quoted in *People* magazine, "[Christian Grey] incorporates everything a girl can dream of: power, passion, desire, sex and last but not least this special kind of mastery!" (Fowler, para. 4). To respond to the desires of men, women, and couples that hope to use the works to "change [their] sex from vanilla to *Fifty Shades of Grey* sex," Trina lists twenty wants to realize the dream. The list includes the use of rope, long and short whips, a corset, a riding crop, edible underwear, a paddle, a leash and collar, and other such items (para. 3).

The inherent excitement regarding *Fifty Shades* is just one set of examples that constitute general overreactions to E. L. James's work. But the way in which fans and anti-fans overreacted to the series was not monolithic. Sometimes, overreaction took place as a massive number of people flocked to bookstores and movie theaters. The trilogy helped both the publishing and film industries. There were numerous articles in magazines on how to use fiction to spice up one's sex life. Expecting what one sees in media from the body shape of a magazine cover model to sex in pornography to be realistic is common. *Fifty Shades* fervor was no exception.

Simultaneously, *Fifty Shades* became a convenient scapegoat because of its massive appeal to many fans. When readers and viewers of it engage in a troublesome, sometimes criminal, behavior, many were quick to blame James's work without examining what truly led individuals to conduct themselves in such a way. First of all, few were careful enough to question what "normal" sexuality was supposed to mean. As discussed in Chapter Three, the idea of "normal" sexual activity or what sex "should" entail is highly subjective and contextual. But much of the scapegoating was based on labeling the sex to be deviant, or even criminal. Second, few connected the works to larger social issues around relationship violence. In other words, the cause of the problematic behavior by a *Fifty Shades* audience was assumed to be attributable to a specific popular cultural object.

For example, even when Hossain's abuse was revealed, few questioned if there were factors other than *Fifty Shades* that might have led to the incident. Both media and legal experts were quick to blame the movie.

During the hearing, Hossain's lawyer, Sandra Bennewitz, mentioned that Hossain was "involved with several UIC leadership programs, was a student ambassador to the alumni association and was on the triathlon team" (Saul para. 7). When presented with Hossain's various engagements at the university, Judge Adam Bourgeois asked, "How can someone involved in all that let a movie persuade him to do something like this?" (Holley para. 5; McSpadden; Saul para. 8). The attorney for Hossain also stated, "This kid is a star.... He's a top-notch student. He graduated with a 4.6 [GPA] from high school. He's a triathlete. He's what they call a UIC alumni ambassador.... This is not a rapist" (Schmadeke "In 'Fifty,'" para. 9). Although his achievements are laudable, these statements are troubling because such a view excuses individuals for their behaviors and tries to use popular culture as a scapegoat without appropriately showing the linkage between a popular cultural work and the behavior in question. It is important to note that Hossain, three months after the original incident, was brought back into court because he was allegedly involved in sexting with pictures from the March case (Jalabi).

When a couple was caught having sex in a museum in March 2015 and the pictures of the incident taken by a closed-circuit security TV were released, the behavior was attributed to the film ("Fifty Shades of Grey: CCTV"). Although the couple had attended an event celebrating the *Fifty Shades* release in Las Vegas earlier in the day, it is important to note that the article only makes a superficial connection between the couple's behavior and the film without discussing what truly drove these individuals to engage in sex in public.

Similarly, in China, a parallel was made between a crime and the trilogy. In this incident, a businessman was imprisoned for kidnapping and sexually abusing a woman. Ma Yujia reported, "The man, surnamed Li, locked the young woman in his rented room, beat her and forced her to play sadomasochistic games with him, paralleling the plot of the erotic novel and film 'Fifty Shades of Grey'" (Yujia para. 1). Yujia wrote that the victim, a prostitute, was locked in Li's house for over forty hours. She was "beaten and sexually abused in bizarre ways several times" (Yujia para. 5). It was only because the victim's co-workers began to worry about her absence that they called the police. The police found many pornographic materials at the scene, some of which had sadomasochistic content. The problem with the report is that nothing truly connects the man and the trilogy; Yujia does not even discuss if the man had ever read it.

Scapegoating *Fifty Shades* is not limited to these violent cases. When middle school students in Pennsylvania were discovered to be in possession of a *Fifty Shades of Grey* crossword puzzle, it was hastily concluded that the film was to be blamed. Parental responsibilities, the accessibility of such materials to middle school students, or social hype about the trilogy in general were not considered as a possible contributor to the incident. In another case, a man sprayed a bottle of sauce over his girlfriend when she refused to read *Fifty Shades of Grey*. The man's behavior, once again, was attributed only to the book and not to his personality or disposition (Angelowicz).

What these examples suggest is that a behavior observed or reported in the media was simply similar to what was seen in *Fifty Shades*. Furthermore, the similarity tended to be that the sexual behavior involved a form of BDSM or abuse, neither of which was invented by E. L. James. An aforementioned therapist, Dr. Steve Pope, stated, "In my day a bottle of cider in the local park was the great experiment. These days you have things like this happening because porn normalizes taboo behavior. What we are moving into is long-term effects of what they think is normal behavior" (*"Fifty Shades of Grey,"* para. 7–9). It is understandable that Pope, like many others, is perplexed about yet another problematic behavior in contemporary society.

But as was mentioned above, every generation faces new types of social concerns. Unfamiliarity helps make the concern more significant than reality. Of course, the seriousness of criminal cases allegedly inspired by James's works should not be downplayed. These cases cannot be excused, regardless of the reason. In order to address the seriousness of these issues, however, it is not only insufficient but also incorrect to blindly blame popular culture—an easy scapegoat. But in a society where about 0.1 percent of the population over the age of twelve experiences rape or sexual assault every year (U.S. Department of Justice 5), scapegoating is unlikely to identify the true cause of the problem. After all, popular culture exists simply because there is a society that creates it. Popular culture can influence how people behave, but it also reflects what they believe and want. *Fifty Shades of Grey* simply reflects the values and sentiments of our society in which a female water polo player is sexually assaulted during a game (Briscoe and Keilman), student-athletes at Vanderbilt, Florida State, Brown, New Mexico, Baylor, and numerous other universities have allegedly assaulted women, and what Karen Boyle calls "everyday pornography" remains popular because, in short, sex sells.

CHAPTER SEVEN

Extending the World
of the Novel

Fan Fiction, Book Clubs,
Parodies and Beyond

Production and consumption of popular culture is complex. We no longer live in a period when popular culture was produced by a limited few, who identified themselves as producers, for the masses, who identified themselves as consumers. This is partly due to the advancement in technology that enable user-generated content and its exchange with social media. But it is also due to the fact that we now recognize the value of contributions made by popular culture consumers to be more than just trifling or silly. This is to say that even before the turn of the twentieth century, fans of popular culture generated their own content—a notable example would be fan magazines—albeit far smaller in distribution size compared to today's equivalent. The history of the twentieth century is filled with examples of popular culture fan engagements that remained undocumented by scholars and unvalued by so-called professional producers until the end of the century. Therefore, the blurred line between producers and consumers is not a new phenomenon. It is, however, also true that the line has become even blurrier. Furthermore, consumers today may produce a version of the original work for a new set of consumers, as was seen with the proliferation of fan fiction. Readers of this genre may prefer fan fiction to the original work.

This intricate relationship between producers and consumers makes the world of popular culture dynamic. It also attests to the fact that a single popular cultural object can be extremely far-reaching. For example, *Twilight* had its own immense fan base. But once E. L. James wrote *Fifty Shades*, *Twilight* indirectly reached out to a substantially different set of fans. It also entered the minds of so many more who continue to be unaware that they are fans of a story remotely (but nonetheless) based on *Twilight*. This dynamism reflects the popularity of popular culture. For example, one way to explain the popularity of the *Fifty Shades* trilogy may be the vast number of times E. L. James's work has been referenced or adapted in a different context. Just like James wrote her novel based on Stephenie Myers's *Twilight*, many *Fifty Shades* fans wrote their own versions. Additionally, once the first movie came out in February 2015, it contributed to a surge in popular cultural references on various media from user-generated contents on YouTube to more mass-targeting programs, including late-night comedy shows. Just as examining *Fifty Shades* as fan fiction reveals how James extrapolated the world of Edward and Bella for Christian and Anastasia, studying how fans—and sometimes anti-fans—referenced the work shows the ways in which they actively engaged with James's works.

Although it is easy to conclude that Jamie Dornan or Dakota Johnson appearing on TV talk shows to promote the movie, or that "Fifty Shades of Peter Griffin," included in the *Best of Family Guy* DVD, is meaningless, these examples make up a part of how people experienced the *Fifty Shades* trilogy and feature films. Popular culture, as a dynamic entity, keeps changing, with new meanings added and new contexts created.

Some *Fifty Shades* fan fiction deals with the time period between books, one not elaborated on by James. Others were so-called alternative-universe stories in which, for example, Christian is a woman, or Anastasia works for the FBI. There is also fan fiction written from Christian's perspective, some of which foreshadow James's 2015 sequel, *Grey*. Whereas a minority of fans wrote fiction based on the franchise, many other women (and perhaps some men as well) consumed the trilogy as a collective reading exercise, namely in book clubs, both on and offline. Lists of questions compiled by and for these book club members shed light on how the book was discussed. The answers to those questions reveals much regarding stereotypes and prejudices that our society continues to have toward book clubs in general, and women discussing sexuality specifically.

Some *Fifty Shades* adaptations were comic essays, not fan fiction. Some were cookbooks. There are also online memes, some of which poked fun at the franchise. Others made social criticisms, for example, about the dangerous dynamic between Anastasia and Christian. Although many of these self-published offerings can be characterized as inconsequential, they show the complex nature of how popular culture is consumed and reproduced.

Fan Fiction

From Wattpad to Archive of Our Own, numerous fan fiction portal websites feature offerings based on *Fifty Shades*. Despite their amateurish nature, these stories have been widely read. Wattpad, for example, boasts over 40 million users every month, and over 100 million stories (McCromick). Hearing about the popularity of her own work among these fan fiction writers, James commented that she "was flattered" and considered it "a huge compliment" (Alter para 11–12). Although most of these fan stories are short—in some cases fewer than one hundred words, and generally do not exceed a few thousand words—there are some aspiring novelists who have written far more words than James herself.

On the subject of "what if?" ThisAngelCanFly, for example, asked, "What if Ana hadn't met Christian through an interview?" and "What if Anastasia was the perfect submissive?" ("Fifty Shades," para. 1). These questions completely undermine the premise of James's world. Instead of being a virgin college student who resists being Christian's submissive, Anastasia, in this version, had already lived with her dominant, Master Damien, for three years, until their relationship collapsed. In the meantime, Christian was looking for a new submissive. The story maintains some of the key phrases from the original novel, including "Mr. Grey will see you now" (ThisAngelCanFly "Anastasia," para. 5). But Anastasia meets Christian for coffee for the first time to discuss arrangements for their dominant/submissive relationship. ThisAngelCanFly asks, "Can Ana change Christian's mindset about love? Can Christian help put back the pieces of Ana's heart?" ("Fifty Shades," para. 4). annloveswriting's story, entitled "Professor Grey," which was posted online in April 2013, also imagines what it would be like had Christian and Anastasia met in a different way. This story begins with Dr. Flynn unable to give a lecture in his business psychology class in which both Anastasia and Kate are enrolled. Dr. Flynn then asks Christian to step in to cover for him. The narrative continues:

> The two girls are late to Christian's first class and Ana is forced to sit right up [at] the very front. Intoxicated by his good looks, Ana texts Kate but soon realizes that Christian has seen her and he takes her phone out of her hand, ready to make an example out of her and embarrass her in front of the class, and in the process reads her and Kate's conversation, which he laughs at [para. 14].

When Christian returns her phone later, in "a panic [Anastasia] offers to kiss him in return for the phone" (Faherty para. 27). After the first kiss, Christian asks for another kiss, this time over dinner. Anastasia tries to decline the invitation, but finally acquiesces. annloveswriting's fiction ends here, leaving its readers to imagine what might have happened during dinner and how the story would have developed further. In "A Different Story," by ExpectingAmnesia, Anastasia and Christian had already met each other twenty years prior to their recent encounter. crispparsley's "Young and Willing to Try," set in England, starts with the two main characters meeting in a pub as Anastasia celebrates her graduation from school. lanieloveu added a novel twist to the beginning of the story. In her eighty-thousand-word novel "Addicted to Love," Anastasia has a boyfriend named Jacob Riley. Jacob is madly in love and is ready to propose to her. Anastasia, however, is not sexually satisfied and is interested in someone else, namely Christian, who has enabled her to sexually explore. In "Moving On," by robsessd73, Anastasia, at age sixteen, suffered the loss of her parents. She then started to live with her godparents, Grace and Carrick Grey. Christian, it seems, is her de-facto brother.

Other would-be novelists wrote what might have happened after Anastasia left Christian at the end of the first book. KeepSaying's "Another First," told from Christian's perspective, begins with his waking from a bad dream, a repeated theme in the original books. Desperate to win Anastasia back, he sends her an e-mail, offering a ride to José's gallery opening. Dr. Flynn also realizes that Anastasia is different from other submissives with whom Christian has been involved. It is clear that Anastasia is special. The novel serves as a bridge between the first and second novels. "This Is It," by LiveHappy247, also covers this undefined period right after the breakup, told from Anastasia's perspective. She shares the story— although not all of it—with Kate of how her relationship with Christian had ended. Kate tries to make Anastasia feel better by taking her out to a club. Anastasia dances with Ethan, Kate's brother, only to realize Christian is staring at her. It continues:

> Instructing Ethan not to stop dancing and the two take it up a notch bumping and grinding, making Mr. Grey more and more jealous. After finishing the dance, Ana goes outside for some fresh air, eager to avoid Mr. Grey, however as the door closes she realizes she's alone with a man who has some horrible intentions. Thankfully Christian arrives just in the nick of time, and the man is left on the ground and Ana unharmed [para. 20].

These two stories fill the gap between *Fifty Shades of Grey* and *Fifty Shades Darker*, during which Christian and Anastasia spent time alone, away from each other. It is a rather short period, but, for avid fans it is long enough to create their own stories.

One element fans chose to elaborate on is the sometimes-argumentative nature of Christian and Anastasia's relationship. Posted on the Archive of Our Own site, for example, is chrrishish's "I'm Fine," which takes place during the period described in *Fifty Shades Darker*. The story's main question is if Anastasia, because of her most recent heated argument with Christian, will be alone or if he will decide to come around. Similarly, Fannieforever15's "Not Simple as Black and White," focuses on the couple's discord. In Daredevil_Fangirl's "Fifty Shades of Mind Blowing Misunderstandings," Anastasia suspects Christian of having an affair. According to the original novel by James, the two main characters have arguments, but they never last long. In Niftynickis's "Fifty Shades Later," their separation lasts for over twenty years. Then, one day, Anastasia hears someone knocking at her door. She opens the door, only to find Christian standing there. This is a major departure from James's storyline.

"The Final Goodbye," by marpuri, is a very different kind of a story. Unlike "26.2 Shades of Anastasia," in which a major theme is cheating, marpuri's work is about long-lasting love. Christian and Anastasia have been married for sixty-five years and are still deeply in love. In their old age, a dying Anastasia is undergoing hospice care. Christian, already in his mid–nineties, has also become frail. The two fall asleep in each other's arms one night, only for Christian to wake up to find that his love has passed away. Christian "cries and then gently kisses her, and falls back to sleep with her in his arms. The two are found by care aids later in the morning, Christian having died just one hour after Ana" (Faherty para. 15).

Some fans made even greater changes to the *Fifty Shades* world. ChloeMagea's work, entitled "Wicked Deeds," features Christian Grey, but not Anastasia Steele. Instead, ChloeMagea writes about Madaline Barns, who is not Christian's type. However, Christian decides to go after her simply because she is indifferent to him. Christian switches genders in cinnamonandstrawberries's "Fifty Shades of Red," in which he is depicted as a dominatrix. Or, iscalox's work, written in Russian, starts with the premise that Anastasia had killed Christian's lawyer. In Viola Valentin's "Fifty Shades of Sanity," Anastasia is an FBI forensic psychologist whose work is to assess Christian's psychological condition. In angelus2hot's 100-word-long squib, "Skinny Dipping," Anastasia—as the title suggests—takes a swim in the nude. In GreyCanSuckMyDeathStart's 300-word story, "The Escape Project," Taylor is portrayed as the hero. After seeing Anastasia suffer in her marriage with Christian, he intervenes, saving her from her abusive husband.

Many of the essays cited above are short, and most have been read by a very limited number of viewers. A great majority of the writers are amateurs, pleased to have an outlet for writing alternative plots to their favorite franchise. One especially popular site, fanfiction.net, archives nearly 2,500 examples of *Fifty Shades* derivations (Alter para. 10). Although a great majority of these stories are short, some are lengthy and elaborate. LucindaRemyJohnson's "Claiming Anastasia" contains close to 120,000 words; "Fifty Shades-Average Joe," by khillintessier, has over 140,000 words. The quality of these novels vary, but rarely rise to the level of good writing. But these authors demonstrate different ways in which fellow fans can engage with the original literary work and even advance the storyline.

Fans Outperform E. L. James

Because the maiden book in the trilogy was told from Anastasia's perspective, many fans were curious as to how Christian would narrate the story. So, when the sequel, *Grey*, was announced, an estimated 1.5 million copies were pre-ordered on Amazon, making it one of the most anticipated books of 2015 (Alter para. 15). As stated earlier, James was not the first to publish a novel based on Christian's point of view. One of the most prominent fan fiction examples of this concept was penned by Gillian Griffin, a British mother of three (Alter). Griffin's work, entitled "Meet Fifty Shades," represents a year's worth of writing, and has been viewed over eight million times on her blog (Alter para. 6). For Griffin, it was not her first fan fiction: she had also written one for *Downton Abbey*. But this time, she was able to compare her work with the original author. In an interview with Alter, Griffin stated, "I'm very curious to see how [James's] story is different from mine…. It's a little bit weird, because it's her story, her work, her characters. I was just borrowing them for a bit of fun" (para. 7).

Similarly, Emine Fougner, a resident of Arizona in her forties, also wrote a version of the story from Christian's perspective well before James did. She remembers that she and her friends agreed that "Christian was the darker, more interesting character" and that they did not "really care about Ana; [they wanted] to hear what he [thought]" (Alter para. 19). Fougner's completed work, containing 3,500 words, was posted on her blog, A Walk in the Clouds. Her magnum opus was viewed more than 14 million times, in 186 countries. Alter explains that six volunteers translated the story into six different languages.

By the time *Grey* came out, in mid–2015, a *Fifty Shades* story told from Christian's viewpoint was not a new concept at all. For many fans, it had been written numerous times, with some versions attracting millions of readers. *Grey* had a potential to be successful: the high number of pre-orders suggested this. But, once the book came out, even avid fans made critical comments. One Amazon review reads, "All I got out of this book was a repeat of the original." Another wrote, "This book is just an attempt for the author to squeeze every last drop of $$ she can get from this franchise" (Alter para. 16). For those who had not read any *Fifty Shades* fan fiction, *Grey* was new. But for those who constituted core fan groups, critical perceptions were common.

When fans write an established character's story before the original author does, it creates an intricate relationship between author and readers. In a way, fans have already established the worldview that the original author was supposed to create. The author is put in an awkward position in which her new work does not appear new or original. Indeed, fans had decidedly mixed reactions to *Grey* and those fan fiction novels narrated by Christian that predated James's work. Penny Bruggemann, a reader in Illinois, stated that she liked Fougner's work better than James's. She says, "I prefer her writing to E. L. James's writing…. I don't think anything can compare" (Alter para. 21). Agreeing with Bruggemann, Krystal Shores Bailey, from Alabama, is was clearly skeptical about James's forthcoming sequel; she wrote: "I know *Grey*'s going to be a letdown for me. I've already read it through Emine's eyes, and I honestly don't think E. L. James can touch her version of Christian" (para. 22–23). *Grey*, and other versions of similar fan fiction, challenge the concept of who truly owns the power to write such a novel, and if any one version is the most authentic.

Reading the Fans

Book reading is said to be declining. Even though the U.S. in the last decade or so has seen numerous best sellers, from *Harry Potter* to *Twilight* to *Fifty Shades of Grey*, a common lament in this increasingly technological world is "People are no longer reading." In 2004, Raksha Shetty, reporting on behalf of CBS News, that between 1992 and 2002, there was a 7 percent decline in sales of adult literature. During the same period, there was a 4 percent decline of adults who read any book at all. A more recent study, by Pew Research Center, also contends that fewer Americans are reading print books (Raine and Perrin). But the decline is marginal. Another Pew study, written by Kathryn Zickuhr and Lee Raine, states:

Though e-books are rising in popularity, print remains the foundation of Americans' reading habits: Among adults who read at least one book in the past year, just 5 percent said they read an e-book in the last year without also reading a print book.

In general, the vast majority of those who read e-books and [listen to] audiobooks also read print books [para. 5–6].

As noted in Chapter Three, more Americans are reading digital books. Furthermore, contrary to popular belief, young adults are more likely to read than older adults (Raine and Perrin). Reading, therefore, continues to be a popular activity among many Americans.

While readers choose books for various reasons, in different contexts, and on different media, one of the popular collective reading activities is participating in a book club. From well-organized "One Book, One Community" programs to more casual discussions over coffee or beer, book clubs are gaining in popularity. Writing for the *New York Times*, James Atlas estimated that "five million Americans gather every few weeks in someone's living room or in a bar or bookstore or local library to discuss the finer points of Middlemarch or 'The Brothers Karamozov'" (para. 2). Similarly, JSTOR Daily reports that over half of American women who read at least a book per month belonged to a book club, most of which meet in person (Burger para. 5).

Because of the popularity of the *Fifty Shades* trilogy, it is no surprise that some book clubs decided to turn their attention to James's works. For example, LitLovers listed fifteen questions for its online book club members.

1. How would you describe this book: as erotica, porn, soft porn, romantic fiction, comedy ... or something else?
2. How do you feel about the portrayal of sex, particularly Christian's predilection for sadomasochism: do you find it overly graphic, refreshingly frank, disturbing, amusing, offensive, arousing?
3. Does this book place women in a degrading light, as some have claimed?
4. Are you surprised that a woman would/could write about submissive-dominant relationships so openly? Does her feminine perspective bring a different view on sexuality than a male writer's might?
5. What about the characters, Anastasia and Christian? Are they fully developed as three-dimensional characters, complete with emotional and psychological complexity—or are they flat and one-dimensional? Are you able to see beyond the sexual encounters to become sympathetically engaged with the two? Do you come to think of them as real people?

6. Why are Ana and Christian drawn to one another in the first place?

7. As more of his character and background are revealed, does your attitude toward Christian change?

8. Is Ana the submissive partner in the relationship, sexual or otherwise? Would you say she's an equal partner ... or is she dominated by the older, more powerful Christian?

9. What about Ana's mother? What role does she play in all this? What role should she have played? What about some of the other secondary characters—do you have a favorite?

10. What is the metaphorical significance of the see-saw? How might it suggest the book's resolution?

11. What does the title refer to?

12. Many have described the book as a page turner—did you have trouble putting it down? What do you think explains the runaway success of *Fifty Shades*, first published as an e-book? What is the audience (aside from you!), and who should, or should not, read the book?

13. What do you think of the author's writing—E. L. James's frequent use of Adonis to describe Christian, the way Christian continually flashes his gray eyes, or Ana's numerous references to her inner goddess? Does the style engage you, amuse you, put you off, help delineate character...?

14. Do you plan on reading the other two installments of the Fifty Shades Trilogy? Have you read other books similar to *Fifty Shades of Grey*?

15. Who would you like to see play the lead roles in the film version? ("Fifty Shades of Grey [James]")

Similarly, PrincetonBookReview generated twelve guiding questions:

1. Talk about the genre of erotica fiction and the straightforward and graphic descriptions of sex in this book. What effect did the writing style and playful tone of the book have on these scenes?

2. Discuss the feelings that surfaced as your read about submissive/dominant relationships. Did it pique your curiosity? Did anything shock or offend you?

3. The book is marketed as "steamy erotica for suburban housewives." Is this accurate? Do you think reading about intense sexual encounters enhances the sexual experience? Of the many sex scenes, discuss your favorite or least favorite?

4. Discuss the meaning and significance of the book's title. What do you think accounts for the overwhelming popularity of this book?

5. For the majority of people, the sex described pushes the limits of normal. With this in mind, were you able to relate to the human condition underlying the experiences? For example, did you understand the desire for this kind of experience and why each character was drawn to this?

6. Anastasia was surprised when she enjoyed and wanted more of the kinky sex. Discuss the implications of this? Do you think guilt or her lack of experience played into these feelings?

7. Did you feel a strong connection to either Christian or Anastasia? Did you find yourself siding with one more than the other?

8. What was your initial impression of Christian? As more of his background and personality was revealed, did your opinion of him change? Did his actions in any way surprise you? What is your favorite Christian phrase?

9. The author does an excellent job of weaving family drama into the story. For example, Anastasia has a strong bond with her stepfather, and Christian is strongly attached to Mia and his parents. How important do you think this is to the story in general? How important were these bonds to Anastasia and Christian's ability to form relationships?

10. Discuss the relationship Anastasia had with her mother? Did her mother offer enough of what is considered traditional motherly support? Was her influence on Anastasia more positive than negative? How do you think her mother felt about Anastasia's relationship with Ray? Do you think either Anastasia or her mother had any regrets about the way things turned out?

11. There was a wonderful cast of supporting characters in this book. Who was your favorite, and why?

12. What actors do you see playing the roles of Christian and Ana? ("Fifty Shades of Grey by")

These questions reflect a wide range of topics that could be discussed in relation to the first book of the trilogy. Some deal with individual feelings about particular kinds of sexual activities, e.g., question four by LitLovers, and question five by PrincetonBookReview. These lists direct members' attention to the issues of women and their depictions, such as with LitLover's third question. Other questions dealt with the novel's secondary characters.

What is more significant than the specific questions is what they revealed about common assumptions regarding book clubs and reading. Of course, book clubs have a long history of popularity. Book lovers getting together to discuss their books—erotica or romance, depending on how one defines *Fifty Shades*—is not new, either. But many popular media outlets and articles missed this rich history of book readership that Janice Radway, for example, had revealed in her study, more than thirty years ago.

Casilda Grigg's article in the *Telegraph* suggests that "some 20 professional women, ranging in age from 25 to 45" reading and discussing the books "reflects a wider change in social attitudes" (para. 2–3). Christy Craig also noted that discussing *Fifty Shades* in a book club enabled them to see "possibility for empowerment as they felt more comfortable openly reading about sex and sexuality" ("American Women Use," para. 10). Grigg fails to realize that book clubs have long dealt with romance books or those with explicit depictions of sex. Craig's point also reflects the assumption that discussing sex and sexuality had been rare among women. Although it is true that *Fifty Shades* "opened up the dialogue for a lot of people to say, hey, I'm kind of curious about that" (Adams para. 3), book club members discussing sex and sexuality after reading a romance novel was unknown to only non-participants. It is not news for Radway or others who have studied or who have partaken in book clubs.

Of course, not all book clubs embraced it. One of the most popular book clubs, Oprah Winfrey's, decided not to feature *Fifty Shades of Grey* even though Oprah has commented, "Oh, I've got all the *Shades*, for the time I can take some guilty pleasure and just read. But I'm thinking, Stop with the story, get to the juicy part!" (Miller para. 1). Chapter Four of this book has also studied various cases of resistance to reading the book by individuals and groups, especially religious literary fans. But clear evidence of active discussions among book club members exists. More importantly, the way these discussions were reported and discussed reveals certain prejudices and even ignorance about book clubs. Even though book clubs continue to be popular in the U.S. today, for outsiders, it is a marginal culture. Combined with analyses on prejudices against women's work and culture discussed in Chapter Five, these examples show that many women's involvement in book clubs are undervalued, or not valued at all. Such a practice risks missing important socializing and self-reflective experiences of millions of book club participants.

Fifty Shades *Parody Books*

While *Fifty Shades* fan fiction and book clubs are primarily for fans, various parodies made the trilogy more visible even to anti-fans and uninterested members of the public in general. From *Fifty Shades* parody books to so-called Internet memes, fan fervor generated an intricate system that challenges the idea that a popular cultural text belongs to its author.

Parody books are different from fan fiction. While fan fiction embody the love and passion fans have for a particular franchise, parody books are, at best, playful. They often make fun of the quality of the novel or its storyline. The same can be said about online memes. Although many of them are created simply for fun, they also show that a popular cultural text can be hijacked and used for a completely different purpose and context.

50 Shades of Earl Grey is a brand of tea available from adagio.com. *Fifty Shames of Earl Grey*, however, is a parody novel by Andrew Shaffer (under the penname Fanny Merkin) that involves a romantic story between Bill Gates's adopted son and Anna Steal. Shaffer is a well-known satirist who has written other creative works, including an essay in *The Atheist's Guide to Christmas*, as well as *How to Survive a Sharknado and Other Unnatural Disasters*. Anna, in *Fifty Shames of Earl Grey*, is innocent but experienced. She has never been on an elevator and does not even know how one works. Earl Grey, on the other hand, thinks BDSM stands for "Bards, Dragons, Sorcery, and Magick. Shaffer explained, "[Christian] is like, 'I like to spank girls" … and she's like: 'Really? That's it?'" (Considine para. 11). Andy Lewis writes that the book which took Shaffer eleven days to write, unlike many similar ones, is "a complete book from a traditional publisher. This is a full-length and thought-out piece of work" (para. 3).

Shaffer's book can be seen as a form of fan fiction, although he labels it more as a parody. Nonetheless, he commented, "Once you get past some of the grammatical and technical issues [of *Fifty Shades of Grey*], I still didn't get it—Ana is such a weak character. There wasn't much about her that interested me" (Wells para. 18). After the parody was published in August 2012, the book immediately went into its third printing, with twenty thousand copies in print (Wells para. 24). Although he comically admits that his favorite part of *Fifty Shames of Earl Grey* is the section in which Earl and Ana have sex on a dinosaur's back, he simultaneously claims that the book is supposed to show his message that "you should feel comfortable in your own skin. No one should be ashamed of their personal taste, whether it's for BDSM or Nickelback" (Wells para. 26). He continues, "Christian Grey was ashamed of his sexual proclivities in *Fifty Shades of Grey*—BDSM was treated as something dark and mysterious, and a lot of the plot revolved around Ana trying to 'cure' him of his 'deviant' tastes" (Wells para. 25).

There have been other parody books on *Fifty Shades*, but none have been as successful as Shaffer's. A novella of thirty-four pages, by N. J. Sanderson, is titled *Fifty Shades of Shite*. Sanderson explains that the book is "for readers who thought *Fifty Shades of Grey* was excrement." Sanderson continues, "When Bex Lax meets entrepreneur Christian Brown their explosive affair plumbs new depths in romantic fiction. Can she open her mind and her bowels and satisfy his strange tastes?" (Sanderson para. 1–4). E. L. Jamesbergstein also published a parody book, this one 160-pages in length, called *Fifty Shades of Oy Vey: A Parody*. The story involves Chaim Silver and Anatevka Stein. Their relationship is characterized by unorthodox sexual play, mostly dealing with Jewish food and events. Reid Mockery's version, *Fifty Shades of Beige*, is a longer work, close to 350 pages. Christian Grey is replaced by Bobby Beige, a billionaire in Pittsburgh. Anastasia Steel is replaced by Annis Thesia, who is not as beautiful as Ana. Impressively, Mockery wrote a trilogy with *Fifty Shades of Marker* and *Fifty Shades Fried* following *Fifty Shades of Beige*.

The list of these parody novels continues: B. Naughtie's *Fifty Shades of Black and Blue*; E. L. Balliet's *Fifty Shades of Grey: The Strange Days Parodies* and *Fifty Shades of Grey: A Graham Cracker Christmas, Even Stranger*; Twilight D. Epps's *Fifty Shades of Grayish: A Parody*; Parody Brothers' *Fifty Shades of Plaid*; Allie Beck's *Fifty Shades of Garbage*; and Riley J. Ford's *Fifty Shades of Grey: The Experiment*, Secret Anonymous's *Fifty Shades of Twilight*, just to name a few. There are also at least two cookbooks whose titles are inspired by *Fifty Shades*. One of these, F. L. Fowler's *Fifty Shades of Chicken*, makes fun of *Fifty Shades* while providing fifty recipes. The author commented to *People*:

> Like so many others, *Fifty Shades of Grey* resonated for me.… It evoked something I'd never been able to express. Then one day as I was tying up the ankles of a chicken for roasting, I realized why some of the scenes in the book were so strikingly familiar. It turns out I've been practicing BDSM for years—but with poultry [Hamm para. 2].

Similarly, Drew Ramsey and Jennifer Iserloh wrote *Fifty Shades of Kale: 50 Fresh and Satisfying Recipes That Are Bound to Please*. Some of these books have been published and are available for purchase on Amazon.com. Most are available as e-books, while some are print books. These books are creative, even though critics are most likely to argue that they lack so-called literary value. Despite this, they also demonstrate the intricate network of popular culture. Texts are adapted, revised, caricatured. Once a popular culture text is produced, it leaves the hands of the original creator and begins to live on its own.

Viral Online Media

It was in 1976 when Richard Dawkins introduced the concept of "meme" in his *The Selfish Gene* to describe "the idea of a unit of cultural transmission, or a unit of imitation" (192). Forty years later, the word is frequently used to describe the process through which cultural units are spread via the Internet (Coscia 1). Although Dawkins has recently expressed his concern that his idea had been "hijacked" by the online communities (Solon para 3), from LOLcats to planking and Leonardo DiCaprio's toasting pictures, the recent history of the Internet is filled with online memes.

Although the memes did not necessarily generate a new theme of public discussions about E. L. James's work, they nonetheless captured social sentiments about the popular story. Featuring Gene Wilder from *Willy Wonka and the Chocolate Factory*, a popular online meme series reads: "Oh, you liked *Fifty Shades of Grey*? A rich guy that wants to beat you before he fucks you? Your mother would be so proud." Clearly, this reflects a common criticism about of the book. Although it does not delve into details of abuse as some scholars and critics have, it concisely restates the gist of the story and anti-fan sentiments. Another Wilder-inspired meme reads: "So you read 50 Shades of Grey. Tell me more about how you are an expert on BDSM now." As noted in Chapter Six, *Fifty Shades* did not accurately reflect the reality of the sexual practice.

The Your-e-cards meme is rather playful. An anti-fan wrote, "I'm writing a new book. It's called 'Fifty Shades of Shut the Fuck Up.'" Another meme, this one featuring the image of a well-dressed woman speaking on the phone, reads: "Yes, it's called 'Fifty Shades of Grey.' There is a lot of 'kinky fuckery' in it…. Okay…. Laters, baby." A card featuring two women exercising stated, "I work out in hopes that one day I'll be prepared to endure Christian Grey's Red Room of Pain." Another stated, "My boyfriend is a lot like Christian Grey in that he's rich, kinky, and doesn't exist." Yet another meme stated, "I've spent all day seductively biting my bottom lip in hopes that a brooding, handsome billionaire would take notice." One particular e-card was more seriously critical of the simplistic but widely-shared idea that *Fifty Shades* was at least partially responsible for some problematic relationship behaviors. A woman, smoking a cigarette, says, "Sure, I'll show an interest in S&M after reading *Fifty Shades of Grey* just like I showed an interest in archery after reading *The Hunger Games*." The meme warns that dissenters should not be too quick to blame popular culture for the so-called deviant behaviors of some.

Even *The SpongeBob Movie: Sponge Out of Water* had a *Fifty Shades*–inspired poster that reads, "Mr. SquarePants will see you now." A picture of Squidward says, "My inner goddess is spinning like a world-class ballerina, pirouette after pirouette." SquarePants comments, "Once they [ben wa balls] are inside me, I can't really feel them—but then again I know they're there.... *Oh my....* I may have to keep these. They make me needy, needy for sex." Numerous other examples show the popularity among meme fans. A picture of a bus occupied solely by elderly people is captioned: "Fifty Shades of Grey." The "Keep Calm" series includes, "Keep calm and take me to the playroom, Mr. Grey," and "Keep calm and spank me and flog me, Mr. Grey."

Several memes point out the fact that Christian's wealth masks what could be a problematic behavior in a relationship. A "some-e-cards" meme stated, "*Fifty Shades of Grey* is only romantic because the guy is a billion-aire. If he was living in a trailer park, it would be a *Criminal Minds* episode." Similarly, a picture of Christian Grey standing by his office window is captioned, "The only reason Christian is a 'catch' ... is that he is cute and rich. Because honestly if ugly Bob down the street asked to tie you up, you would call the police, not move into his trailer." Online memes can be used as a way to raise social awareness. To call popular culture useless and worthless is easy and common. In fact, popular culture is a serious field of study.

In addition to online memes, various video parodies exist. One of the most popular pretends to be the *Fifty Shades of Grey* movie trailer. *Fifty Shades of Pink* by Shakycow uses some of the memorable lines and scenes from the movie, including the first encounter in Christian's office. However, the roles of Christian and Anastasia are flipped. In other words, it is Christian who shows up to interview Anastasia. Before long, Christian is tied up in Anastasia's play room. Furthermore, Anastasia and Christian are portrayed by Barbie and Ken dolls. Michael Tiddes directed *Fifty Shades of Black*, featuring Marlon Wayans and Kali Hawk. Its official trailer on *YouTube* has recorded over 1.8 million views. As the title suggests, Christian and Anastasia, as well as Kate and José, are black in this slapstick comedy film. Other examples, such as the ones by Brittany Furlan with almost 700,000 views, SouceFedNERD's work with over 350,000 views, and others show that playful-minded video makers spent some time to produce parody videos.

Some parody works, however, became a major hit. Tranceart Violeta's work entitled *Fifty Shades of Frozen* uses clips from Disney's recent hit movie to recreate the *Fifty Shades of Grey Trailer*. Within two years after it was posted on YouTube, the video has attracted over 5 million views. The Lego version of the trailer has become as popular, with over 5.3 million views. With approximately a million views fewer, Selena Gomez's *Fifty Shades of Blue* features Gomez and Nick Kroll. Visiting Gomez's house as a handy-man, Kroll paints the interior of Gomez's house. Gomez is sexually turned on by the sight of a poorly painted wall. The video ends with a message: "Presented by Benjamin Moore Paints."

It was not just Benjamin Moore Paints whose corporate name was associated with a *Fifty Shades of Grey* parody video. Trojan, the condom maker, features a couple who wanted to simulate the kind of sex acts described in *Fifty Shades*. In the video called *Trojan Fifty Shades of Pleasure*, the female lead says that she would like to have exciting sex, like Christian and Anastasia in *Fifty Shades of Grey*. Her male counterpart, comments that such an experiment would result only in "fifty shades of lumbar sprain." She wanted him to be "mysterious and surprising." Her partner, who has never read James's book, mistakes his role to be that of a ninja, outfitted in black from head to foot, he is mistaken by his partner to be a burglar. Instantly assuming a defense posture, she kicks him in the head. Similarly, when she asks him to be "firm and slow," he dresses as a "grandpa." An announcer for Trojan says that, instead of trying to reenact *Fifty Shades*, couples can simply use Trojan lubricants and vibrators for a positive sex experience.

Fifty Shades of Parody

With fan fiction, parody books (from novels to cookbooks), and viral online memes, the world of *Fifty Shades* has morphed into something quite different than the concept originally intended by E. L. James. However, that is what popular culture looks like as consumers gain the power to produce, claim, and reclaim cultural texts. The world of *Fifty Shades* was extended via unofficial products inspired by the trilogy. But its dynamism was beyond merchandizing efforts that were primarily driven by revenue interests. The fan activities described in this chapter are mostly for entertainment. In other words, with a few exceptions, the creators of the parodies expect no monetary gain. Although much of what fans produced may not have a high cultural value in a traditional sense, it nonetheless reflects the reality of how popular culture is produced and consumed. Most importantly, it challenges the sense of ownership of a cultural text. Just as Chapter One questioned the meaning of ownership in the era of online fandom, it is clear that active engagement, either via producing or reproducing cultural texts or by discussing the text with others online or off, is a key way for fans to consume popular culture.

Fifty Shades of Grey is not confined to the realms of the books and the movie. This chapter shows that a popular culture text can exist far away from its original intention. Furthermore, any adaptation or parody is as legitimate as popular culture. The hierarchy between the original and the copy, as the example of *Grey* suggests, cannot be made easily. In addition, one's exposure to a text may be far more significant via parodies and other forms of derivation of the original text. The same trajectory can be applied to virtually any other popular culture experiences, from sports to movies to music. If popular culture exists as an opposition to the so-called classic culture and is a form of counterculture, it also reflects the masses taking control of a text and reclaiming it as their own.

Chapter Eight

"Slap Me Like You Do"
The Movie Soundtrack and Score

Music is an essential part of a film. A soundtrack not only enhances cinematic values but also creates and instills a sense of joy, sorrow, fear, excitement, and many other feelings and sentiments in the minds and hearts of the audience. Robynn Stilwell and Phil Powrie correctly argued that "music underlines, emphasizes, inflects, *underscores* the deepest levels of film, structural and emotional" (emphasis in original) (xix). Robert T. Self also commented, "Film conveys information through five means: images, written language, spoken language, music, and sound effects. Although three of these tracks are aural, scholarship and reviews have tended to address film primarily as a visual medium" (141). Bartkowiak and Kiuchi, in their work focusing particularly on soundtracks from the 1960s and 1970s, noted that music played an integral part of various iconic films. *Fifty Shades of Grey* is no exception. Music helped create and characterize the world of Christian and Anastasia.

The soundtrack, *Fifty Shades of Grey: Original Motion Picture Soundtrack*, was released on February 10, 2015, just in time for the release of the film. Some of the songs were original to the film, whereas some others were pre-existing or remixed. Although the film made it to the top of the box-office chart during the first week after its release, the soundtrack ended second on the *Billboard* list. Drake's album, *If You're Reading This It's Too Late*, topped over the *Fifty Shades* soundtrack by selling 495,000 copies during the first week. During the same period, the *Fifty Shades* soundtrack sold 258,000 copies, 210,000 of which were non-digital album sales. By the end of March 2015, however, the album had sold more than 500,000 copies (Claufield, "Billboard 200 Chart Moves" par 4).

Although the initial sales of the *Fifty Shades* soundtrack were only a half of Drake's new album, it still was a big success for the genre. *Billboard* reports that "the album's 210,000 start is the largest sales debut for a soundtrack since Michael Jackson's *This Is It* danced in at No. 1 with 373,000 in the week ending Nov. 1, 2009" (Caulfield "Drake's Surprise," para. 15). The article continued, "*This Is It* was an all-Jackson effort, however, and behaved like a greatest hits album, so it's a bit unfair to compare it to *Fifty Shades of Grey*. So, scrolling back farther, the last *multi-artist* compilation soundtrack to debut bigger was *Get Rich or Die Tryin'*, which arrived with 317,000 at No. 2 in the week ending Nov. 13, 2005" (Caulfield "Drake's Surprise," para. 16). Aside from these two CDs, there have only been four other soundtracks that sold more than *Fifty Shades*: *Hannah Montana* (sold 281,000 and released in 2007), *Hannah Montana 2/Meet Miley Cyrus* (sold 326,000 and released in 2007), *High School Musical 2* (sold 615,000 and released in 2007), and *High School Musical 3: Senior Year* (sold 297,000 and released in 2008) (Caulfield "Drake's Surprise," para. 17). The first two were performed by Miley Cyrus whereas the other two were by cast members of *High School Musical*. The *Fifty Shades* soundtrack as a multi-artist compilation was different from these examples.

Even outside of the U.S. and the U.K., many fans commented that the music outperformed the film itself. Micah Singleton wrote:

> The *Fifty Shades of Grey Soundtrack* is the best soundtrack I've heard in years. Now, as a rule, soundtracks are generally awful amalgamations of never-before-heard artists singing never-should-have-been-sung songs, but the *Fifty Shades of Grey Soundtrack* is not that. It is a complication of magnificent songs both new and old from ... artists that form an album I would place right behind Sleater-Kiney's *No City to Love* as the best release in 2015 [para. 3].

Others were not as complimentary as Singleton. Glenn Gamboa stated that the CD "isn't all that impressive" (para. 3). Not only is she critical of Beyoncé's remix, she writes, "The haphazard collection—a Frank Sinatra track here, a Rolling Stones track there, a couple bits of Danny Elfman's score tacked onto the end—makes you wonder what other corners were cut in the movie" (para. 8). Helen Brown agrees with Gamboa, stating, "There's a pretty, scented candle sensuality to each song but the cumulative effect is so underwhelming it makes you feel like a kind of low-grade S&M submissive who gets a thrill from being put on hold for 58 minutes" (para. 4).

Perhaps more important than if reviewers and critics liked the CD or not is that analyzing its music helps us understand how it helped establish the moods and scenes that are integral to Christian's and Anastasia's worlds that E. L. James had created and the trilogy readers had already imagined.

Universal Pictures' Compilation Efforts

To ensure the success of the *Fifty Shades of Grey* album, Universal Pictures had an extensive scheme to assure a high-quality soundtrack. Tom Mackay, of Republic Records, explains, "There was a lot of back-and-forth to tailor [the music] to the scenes" (Gallo para. 6). As was the case with any other movies based on a popular novel, the film audience would include both those who were already familiar with the story and those who were not. This meant that Universal Pictures had two different groups of customers to please. The music of the film not only had to match well with the storyline to create the atmosphere appropriate for the film, it also had to match well with the images of the story that many readers had already conjured while reading the original novel. Mike Knobloch, the president of Film Music and Publishing, stated, "Knowing that the fans of the book, of which there are many, would be coming with expectations of exact songs, or at least of songs being a big part of the story, we knew we had to build something from the group up that was going to deliver a satisfying experience" (Ross para. 4).

An artist who played a significant role in ensuring the success of the soundtrack was Beyoncé. In the early phase of planning, Knobloch and his team approached her to be a part of the project. He remembers:

> I think we made a pretty good pitch.... She's being offered amazing things on a daily basis, but we gave her a compelling explanation of why the movie was going to be huge and why we felt we were making a great film that was going to do really well on a global scale. She thought it was an opportunity to do something that aligned nicely with her brand and agenda [Ugwu para. 9].

The outcome of the negotiation with Beyoncé was a remixed version of two singles, namely "Haunted" and "Crazy in Love." Universal Pictures used both for trailers and pre-release advertisements.

"Haunted" was written and produced by an American producer, Jordan Asher, more commonly known as Boots, in 2013. The remix version takes advantage of the "murky keyboards and creeping bass line" (Kot para. 8). The music was used during the sex scene in Anastasia's apartment after she e-mailed Christian, "It was nice knowing you" (James 188). Although the original and remixed versions are relatively similar, the tempo and atmosphere of the remixed music matches the visual aspects of the film. The song's lyrics also allude to kissing, biting, slapping, and engaging in foreplay.

"Crazy in Love" was more dramatically remixed. The original version was over ten years old when it was adapted for the film. It was released in 2003, featuring Beyoncé's husband, Jay Z. The song appeared as a part of Beyoncé's debut album, *Dangerously in Love*. In 2003, Kelefa Sanneh characterized the song as the best on the album and that it is "a simple, irresistible combination of triumphant horns and a wicked hip-hop beat" (para. 10). "Crazy in Love" was already a huge hit. It had won "Best R&B Song" and "Best Rap/Sung Compilation" at the Grammys in 2004 (Silverman para. 4). The song was also certified as gold by the Recording Industry Association of America in 2004. The music can be heard when Christian and Anastasia have sex in the Red Room of Pain for the first time.

Not only was it a challenge for Universal Pictures to convince a singer with many awards and accolades to her credit to be associated with the franchise, it was also difficult to ensure that the remixed version of her 2003 popular song would not disappoint fans of either the song or the film. Singleton applauds Boots's work with the remix, stating, "Sonically a complete departure from the original version, with a cacophony of creepy backing strings, the remix is sultry and sexy, and yet doesn't lose the essence of the song. It's actually better than the original" (para. 8). Helen Brown also opined that the new version of "Crazy in Love" provided "all the tension in the trailer and here still sounds mesmerizingly dirty-pretty" (para. 6). Not everyone agrees. Glenn Gamboa, for example, wrote, "The over-dramatic, breathy vocals in Beyoncé's 'Crazy in Love' work well in the commercial, but as a whole, the crawling pace of the remix feels like a slog as it nears the four-minute mark. The remix drains all the charm and giddiness of the original" (para 5).

Other singers approached by Knobloch's team composed original songs. Known for "Chandelier," a platinum-certification single released in 2014, Sia was one of them. Knobloch and Dana Sano, a music supervisor, visited Sia at her house "with a laptop and played the scene they had in mind on-site." The scene in question was when Christian and Anastasia first have sexual intercourse, or according to Christian, "rectify the situation" (Ugwu para. 10; James 110). Knobloch remembers by commenting, "She played us songs and we would say, 'That's good but could it be more of this, or less of that? ... By the end we left her spinning her wheels about what she had to do to deliver just the right song to us for the film" (Ugwu para. 11). Based on this interaction, she created an original song, "Salted Wound," which actually ended up being played during the scene in question. The song, on the one hand, is about trust. It tells Christian that he should not let her go, that he can be the man Anastasia wants him to be. But it is also about deception. It tells him to say what Anastasia wants to hear. When this music is heard as Anastasia entrusts her virginity to Christian, it hints what may come later in the story.

Another artist who contributed an original song was Ellie Goulding, a British singer known for her previous hits, including "Lights," "Anything Could Happen," "Burn," and also for singing "Your Song," to which Prince William and Kate Middleton danced at their wedding ("Ellie Goulding Sang," para. 3). Her original song for the film, "Love Me Like You Do," has become its "anthem," as characterized by Ryan Reed of *Rolling Stone*. It is perhaps the signature song on the soundtrack. Within about a month after its release on January 7, 2015, it broke the world weekly streaming record, with 15.5 million streaming hits (Copsey para. 2).

It was not just singers who had been approached and who had been made famous by the film. Stephan Moccio, a Canadian songwriter, known for co-writing Miley Cyrus's "Wrecking Ball" in 2013, met with Knobloch later in the year and was asked to write the end music for the film (Gensler para. 4). This was the beginning of his collaboration with Skylar Grey. Of course, today, those who have seen the film know that the end title song is not his "I Know You," but The Weeknd's "Earned It." For about a year after Evan Lamberg, president of North America at Universal Music Publishing, paired him with Skylar Grey in 2013, "I Know You" was slated to be the end title of the film. But Moccio recalls, "They [E. L. James and Sam Taylor-Johnson] did various screenings, and I think after a lot of thought they decided to change the ending of the movie ever so slightly.... But it meant that Sam was set on having a male vocalist. It didn't matter how incredible the song was" (Gensler para. 15). This is how Moccio started working with The Weeknd. It was in early December, about two months before the release of the film, that Taylor-Johnson approved the end credit track (Gensler para. 17).

Some of the music on the soundtrack was neither remixed nor original. For example, the movie's opening scene, in which Christian Grey is seen jogging, is accompanied by "I Put a Spell on You" (1956), written by Jay Hawkins. Although the song's original version was not a big hit at the time, many artists produced successful covers. The film uses the cover by Scottish singer Annie Lennox. Her "I Put a Spell on You" was the lead single of her 2014 album, *Nostalgia*.

Two of the songs compiled for the soundtrack are straight from the book's text, and are several decades old. The 1978 Rolling Stones' single "Beast of Burden" is heard during the scene in which Anastasia makes pancakes in Christian's apartment. Another is Frank Sinatra's vocal for "Witchcraft." The song, featuring music by Cy Coleman with lyrics by

Carolyn Leigh, was nominated for "Record of the Year," "Song of the Year," and "Best Vocal Performance," at the first Grammy Awards ceremony in 1959.

Emphasizing Female Perspective and Romance

Although the film's plot revolves around the story of a relationship in which the male character dominates the female protagonist, its soundtrack is dominated by females, both in terms of representation and perspectives. The original novel is filled with Anastasia's inner voice, or what she calls her "inner goddess." The film version, however, lacks her inner voice, letting the music speak for her. The soundtrack features eight female artists: Annie Lennox, Laura Welsh, Jessie Ware, Ellie Goulding, Beyoncé, Sia, Vaults, and Skylar Grey. It only has four male artists: The Weeknd, The Rolling Stones, Awolnation, and Frank Sinatra. Only The Weeknd and Awolnation contributed original songs to the film. Furthermore, The Weeknd has "an androgynous voice" (Farber para. 8).

What stands out about the soundtrack is not just its number of female artists but also its focus on Anastasia's perspective, which parallels the fact that the original book was written from her viewpoint. But what complicates the reading of the lyrics compiled in the soundtrack is that they frequently romanticize Christian and her relationship with him. Music rarely pictures the darker image associated with Christian's "Red Room of Pain" or the emotional pain Anastasia endures while Christian whips her with a leather belt. In other words, Anastasia's romantic conundrum is not represented by the film's music. The soundtrack tends to overly emphasize the romantic part of the relationship (helicopter and glider rides) or exotic images of BDSM (moaning and arching back), just as the movie fails to capture the depth of the psychology of the two main characters.

Songs written from Christian's perspective are also confusing, but in different ways. As Bonomi, Nichols, Carotta, Kiuchi, and Perry noted, Christian's behavior can be characterized as abusive (142). However, as the same study revealed, much of the film's audience perceived romantic features in the protagonists' relationship. Others justified Christian's actions as something they would also do if they had the means. The gap that exists in characterizing Christian's behaviors and his relationship with Anastasia, as perceived by relationship experts and their study subjects, also appear in the film's music. During the first helicopter ride, which can be characterized as Christian using his wealth to capture Anastasia's romantic attention, Ellie Goulding's music is upbeat. When Christian appears in Georgia, where Anastasia was spending time with her mother to be away from Christian, he takes her for a glider ride, again with cheerful music in the background. When Anastasia enters the Red Room of Pain, accompanying music is exotic-sounding but does not necessarily reflect the problems Bonomi, Altenburger, and Walton identified in their work.

One of the songs written from Christian's perspective is The Weeknd's "Where You Belong." The lyrics discuss Christian's psychological and physical scars. During his childhood, Christian was abused by Mrs. Robinson as her submissive. He admits that the pain from that period has never left him. Although he tells Anastasia during their walk in the woods—a scene which does not exist in the book and was added to the film—that giving up control completely can be satisfying, he also recognizes that his experience with Mrs. Robinson negatively affected his attitude toward relationships. After all, he tells Anastasia in his hotel room that his tastes are "singular." At the same time, as the movie clearly shows, Christian's chest is scarred; he does not let Anastasia touch him there.

"Where You Belong," however, suggests that Christian might be changing. Although his surprise visit to Georgia is characterized as stalking (Bonomi, Nichols, Carotta, Kiuchi, and Perry 140), the glider ride can be read as Christian's attempt to satisfy Anastasia's desire for more. ("Is this more?" he asks her.) After the ride, Anastasia asks Christian why he resists becoming romantic and being in a regular relationship. The Weeknd characterizes Christian's inner feeling as falling in love with sin. Christian knows what Anastasia wants from a relationship, and that she is aware of his psychological struggle with his past abuse, as well as his current tendency to be abusive. This may explain the fact that more than a handful of book and movie reviewers questioned who was truly in control of the relationship. It is a common observation that even though Christian was in control at the beginning, Anastasia was more in control near the end.

As The Weeknd's song develops, however, Christian's obsessive tendency begins to creep out in the lyrics. The lyrics reflect Christian gaining control while Anastasia gives up hers, Christian's desire to mark her as his own, and his need to restrain her in his own world. By the indoor swimming pool in the movie, Christian says to Anastasia, "You're mine, all mine. Do you understand?" His voice is threatening. The lyrics effectively reflect Christian's abusive and controlling tendency. The music and the singer's voice, however, do not reflect either a sense of danger or the intensity of the relationship.

The other song in the film by The Weeknd is "Earned It," which is used twice. The first time is during the car ride from Seattle to Anastasia's apartment. Prior to the drive, Anastasia and Christian have a small argument about the sleeping arrangements. The ride is interrupted by a walk in the woods, during which Christian reveals to Anastasia his past relationship with Mrs. Robinson. The second time the music is heard is the very end of the film, over the end credits. The film ends as Anastasia leaves Christian behind and tells him not to chase her on to the elevator. "No," Anastasia tells Christian with a stern voice. Never in the movie has she used such a tone. But the scene is almost identical to the end of their first encounter at Christian's office. As the elevator door closes, they say each other's name. With the final scene of the film, once again, the elevator door closes. But the tone is completely different. Anastasia has left Christian alone in his apartment. But the audience does not see either of them once the door closes. It is just the credit roll that appears on the screen. In both scenes, "Earned It" makes its audience wonder what it is that Anastasia has earned or deserves, or if it is what she truly wants.

Laura Welsh's "Undiscovered," although sung by a female singer, is more from Christian's perspective. Its lyrics do not match the level of uncertainty that Anastasia's inner goddess suggests in the *Fifty Shades* book. Instead, the words' strong message about a monogamous relationship is reflected in Christian's simple answer, "Me" when Anastasia asks what she gets out of agreeing to be his submissive (James 101). Throughout the film, Christian indeed remains committed to Anastasia. Even when she tells him that she cannot be what he wants, he says, "You're everything I want you to be" (James 509). However, Christian is also unwilling to change. At her graduation ceremony, he whispers to her, "Just try it my way, Anastasia." When she asks him if they could have a more traditional relationship, he answers, "This is the only sort of relationship I'm interested in" (James 103). He explains that going to movies and out to dinner are not "[his] thing." He is unwilling to change for her and suggests that she needs to accept him the way he is.

Although Christian's obsession with Anastasia can be heard in Welsh's lyrics, the song does not reflect the level of intensity of the protagonists' relationship. The mood that Welsh's song carries fits better as background music at a downtown apparel store than in Christian's Red Room of Pain. The same is true for "I Put a Spell on You," heard at the very beginning of the film. Originally by Screamin' Jay Hawkins, the lyrics, as the title suggests, are about obsession. There is even the element of threat in the words. Not only is the song about putting a spell on someone, it indicates—at least in this context—that Anastasia belongs to Christian, effectively depriving her of her independence and individuality. Bonomi, Altenburger, and Walton have identified Christian's tendency to control. From selling Anastasia's car without her permission to making personal hygiene and sexuality decisions while disregarding her wishes, Christian deprives Anastasia of her free will. Even when Anastasia decides to exercise her prerogative when Christian suggests she live with him but in a different bedroom, she soon complies. The contract scene, too, is restricted to Christian's wants.

Furthermore, Lennox's song tells Anastasia to stop whatever she is doing. In the context of these lyrics, she is Christian's possession. His disregard for her needs is prevalent throughout the film. He says he simply wants Anastasia to "please [him]" (James 100). Despite the unhealthy nature of the relationship, Annie Lennox's rendition is sonically unthreatening; if anything, it could be described as classy. Valerie Hoskins, E. L. James's literary agent, characterizes Christian as a man of "class" (Woolfe para 13). Jason Holland claims that the song sets a tone that evokes "longing glances in a smoky lounge someplace" (para. 4). The song even sounds elegant, matching Christian Grey's penthouse. Shannon Carlin writes that Jay Hawkins's "manic take on this track … seems more up Christian Grey's alley" (para. 17). The music downplays the risky nature of the relationship.

These examples of downplayed sexual tension and what Bonomi, Nichols, Carotta, Kiuchi, and Perry characterized as "problematic" (142) are present in other songs in the film taken from Anastasia's viewpoint. Skyla Grey's "I Know You" empathizes with Anastasia's cry to find a sense of love in Christian. It is "a beautifully performed song about longing for a man she feels she deserves" (Holland para. 11). In the film, when she tells him that she is falling in love with him, he tells her not to. But it is clear—not only visually, but aurally—that she is indeed falling for him. Skyla Grey speaks for the heartbroken young woman, who wants to break into Christian's heavily guarded world. But it, too, fails to capture the risky nature of their relationship.

"One Last Night," by Vaults, is another romantic piece. Gallo explains that this song is "the only track used on an early cut to be included in the finished film" (para. 5). Before the song is heard, Anastasia had made it clear to Christian that she wants to have a date, go to the movies, and be in a more typical relationship. When he takes her to dinner at his parents' home for the first time, Anastasia says, "I need more, I want more." Christian responds, "That's not something I know." Anastasia is left unsatisfied. This is partly why she travels, alone, to Georgia to see her mother. But Christian shows up unannounced. "One Last Night" is heard when Christian takes Anastasia for a glider ride the day after his sudden appearance. The song fits very well with the scene. Anastasia continues to want to stay with Christian. From her perspective, there are some positive signs that Christian might change for her. That is why, as Vaults sings, she wants to try one more night.

Perhaps the song most associated with the film is Ellie Goulding's "Love Me Like You Do," which, on a superficial level, sounds sweet and romantic. But from words such as "blood" and "pain" to walking a thin line between being conscious and unconscious, Goulding's lyrics actually reflect the BDMS themes in the film. What is even more troubling, though, is that Anastasia is allowing Christian to behave the way he wants to, hence the title, "Love Me Like You Do." The fact that she will let Christian establish the pace at which their relationship develops is another. Audiences must wonder what Anastasia is waiting for. Young and immature romance may be about turning a blind eye to the shortcomings of one's love interest. It may also involve complete immersion of oneself in the romance. Goulding's message is indicative of this.

The soundtrack, as a whole, speaks of relationship, sex, and sexual tension. Some sound romantic, others sound like typical love songs, a few are even classy, but all are rife with metaphors. Even Beyoncé's "Crazy in Love" is about Anastasia's affectionate dedication. Partridge characterizes the song as "trussed up with spooky synths and drumbeats that echo like boot steps on a dungeon floor" (para. 3). But even this song downplays the roughness in the relationship between the two characters. Sia's "Salted Wound" is not from either Christian's or Anastasia's perspective. Rather, it is Sia's message to Christian: Tell her how you feel. A closer look at the lyrics, however, reveals problematic messages. The song tells Christians to tell Anastasia what she wants to hear. The lyrics try to convince Christian that he is not dangerous. Farber concurs: "The eros being served up in most of the tracks rarely has much of the S&M danger that fueled the book.... More lyrics speak of romanticized sex than the rougher kind" (para. 2–3).

The popularity of the soundtrack is unqualified. It sold over half a million copies by the end of March 2015 (Claufield, "Billboard 200" para. 4). But its lyrical content romanticizes the relationship of Christian and Anastasia. It is no wonder that aural cues in general emphasize romance rather than the danger or risks that Anastasia is facing.

Danny Elfman and the Film Score

Although *Fifty Shades of Grey: Original Motion Picture Soundtrack* is considered the official soundtrack of the film, there is also another soundtrack CD for the film: *Fifty Shades of Grey: Original Motion Picture Score*. Two of the songs—"Ana and Christian" and "Did That Hurt?"— can also be heard on the soundtrack album.

Danny Elfman, an American composer with a successful career both in the film and television business, is the person behind the score of *Fifty Shades of Grey*. Known for composing the main theme title for TV shows, including *The Simpsons* and *Desperate Housewives*, and the memorable theme song for *Batman* (1989), he has won over twenty BMI Film & Television Awards, an Emmy, and a Grammy ("Danny Elfman: Awards"). *Telegraph* reported that he decided to work on *Fifty Shades of Grey* because "he was impressed by [the film's director] Sam Taylor-Johnson" (Telegraph Reporters para. 4).

About his experience of composing the score, Elfman noted that his music had to tell a story that a dialogue between Christian and Anastasia did not necessarily reflect. He stated:

> A lot of what the score is doing is that what in the book might be elation—for example, in the office, they meet, in the book she is thinking, *Oh my god, this guy is amazing*. Now the music has to mirror that in the film.... It's telling us there is something going on there beyond this simple conversation they are having ["Fifty Shades of Grey Featurette"].

He also commented that he composed his music to capture the relationship—with its tensions and hints at romance—between Christian and Anastasia. As he explained:

> My approach to the score is very simple, and playing a theme that is just about Anastasia and Christian connecting, always bringing them together, romance or not quite romance, or sexual tension. It's a very, very simple score, but I would say by far the bulk of the score is a little dark … in a romantic way, of course. Dark, meaning their inability to connect, is where there might be darkness ["Fifty Shades of Grey Featurette"].

The darkness to which Elfman refers can indeed be heard in the score. "Ana's Theme" is a very quiet and lonely piece. "Ana and Christian" is not a dark song, nor is it a romantic song. Although it is supposed to be the couple's theme, the music exemplifies the inherent tension and lack of chemistry. The same can be said about "Clean You Up." There is no romance in the song that accompanies the scene of two people sharing a bath. It is almost lifeless.

The score includes much music that seems to indicate potential. For example, "The Red Room" is led by the piano but the music does not develop too much, as if to mirror Anastasia's initial response to the room. The music's intensity builds up slowly near the end, but it stops abruptly. The same can be said about "Then Don't." Its sonic development is present, but it is not a full development. It well reflects Anastasia's uncertainty about her relationship with Christian. Some of the undeveloped potential can be read as mysteriousness. "Going for Coffee" is playful but mysterious at the same time. So is "Where Am I?" These songs are not dark, but allow the audience to wonder about their interpretation. Even "Did That Hurt?" and "Show Me" offer a sense of uncertainty.

"Counting to Six," as its title suggests, is a key piece in the film. At least in the context of *Fifty Shades of Grey*, the experience of being whipped six times is what breaks Anastasia away from Christian. The music that accompanies the scene starts slowly but develops as the whipping scene continues. Even after the scene, as Anastasia cries in her bed in Christian's apartment, she tells him, "I'm falling in love with you," he responds, "No, you can't love me." The relationship between Christian and Anastasia, characterized by Bonomi, Nichols, Carotta, Kiuchi, and Perry as "confusing" (145) can also be heard in the film score.

A Classical Inspiration

In addition to these two official soundtracks, there is also an official classical music album. The album was, in fact, one of the first official products of the *Fifty Shades* brand. Well before its movie and accompanying soundtrack came out, on August 21, 2012, EMI released *Fifty Shades of Grey: The Classical Album*. Its cover states, "Music selected by author E. L. James." James explained, "I am thrilled that the classical pieces that inspired me while I wrote the 'Fifty Shades' trilogy are being brought together in one collection for all lovers of the books to enjoy" ("'Fifty Shades of Grey' Classical Album," para. 5; O'Connell para. 4). The pieces on the CD, while not connected to the film, had been compiled to "offer some lighter fare for those working their way through [*Fifty Shades of Grey*]" (Grow para. 1). Valerie Hoskins said, "Christian is about taste, and Christian is about class" (Woolfe para 13).

Zachary Woolfe, of the *New York Times*, explains, however, that the process of producing the CD was not straightforward. At first, in July 2012, EMI created a compilation of fifty classical music pieces for downloads entitled, "Fifty Shades of Classical Music." The compilation was supposed to be "the flagship of 'the Greatest Classical Music Ever'" (para. 10). E. L. James felt that her brand was being used without her consent. Wendy Ong, the vice president for classics at EMI, remembers, "[James] was like, 'Um, what are you doing?'... And I was like, 'Oh I'm so glad you called.' And then we started talking and I said, 'Let's make an official album because I think your fans want an actual compilation and they want it stamped with your approval" (para. 11).

Fifty Shades and James became cultural icons and brands after the release of the first novel. Therefore, releasing a CD, even with classical music by Chopin, Bach, Debussy, and others, was a way to reframe these compositions from a new angle. As James explained to Woolfe, "Everyone was asking, 'When can I get the album?'" (para. 9). Kory Grow, of *Spin*, explains, "Apparently, they're on to something, too, because U.K.–based *Grey* fans purchased enough copies of 16th century composer Thomas Tallis's religious choral work, 'Spem in Alium,' referenced in the book, to push it to the top of the country's classical charts" (para. 3; Anderson). Writing for the *Guardian*, Charlotte Higgins reported that Tallis's work even outsold Luciano Pavarotti. Steve Smith stated, "I'm sure Tallis couldn't have anticipated this, but having said that there's a sort of rapture in the music, so I can understand why E. L. James would find it suitable for the purpose. It is very intense, and has [a] huge climax in it" (Higgins para. 9).

Fifty Shades has a synergistic relationship with music. From popular tunes to classical pieces, the music made the movie more popular and helped established its atmosphere. The movie, in turn, boosted the sales of many songs, even a sixteenth-century classical composition. Just as E. L. James's story frequently mentioned wine, it often detailed Christian's and Anastasia's taste in music. In addition, James's website offered a playlist for each book of the trilogy. Anne Kiplinger also compiled a list of music referenced in each book. The list included Britney Spears's "Toxic," which Christian's ex had put in his iPod, multiple songs that are on the iPod Christian gave Anastasia, and Charlene Soraia's "Wherever You Will Go," which Christian plays on the piano in the third book. In many parts of the trilogy, E. L. James specified what music was inspiring her main characters.

Fifty Shades of Scoring

Despite some of the negative reviews about the trilogy's music, such as critic Sam Kinchin-Smith's rhetorical question, "Why is so much of the

50 Shades book's blatantly misogynist (and materialist) project played out to, and through music?" (para. 1), at least the first movie features many memorable tracks that many fans liked, some even more than the film itself. Beyoncé's contribution to the soundtrack is immense. Both "Haunted" and "Crazy in Love" were remixed for the film and helped to establish the base for Christian and Anastasia's relationship. "Crazy in Love," in particular, is fitting to the scenes in the Red Room of Pain with the mixed feelings about curiosity and danger. Goulding's "Love Me Like You Do" and Vaults' "One Last Night" both sound cheerful, creating a sense of romance in the film.

Stephan Moccio, Skylar Grey, and The Weeknd also offered much to the film while benefiting from their increased exposure. Unlike Beyoncé, Sia, and Goulding, who had already been in the mainstream music scene for some time, they were less known or had not had a big hit in a while. The *Fifty Shades* film is not only made sonically more successful thanks to them but also made them more relevant in the industry.

With two exceptions, all the songs on the soundtrack were remixed or written for the film. Despite the nature of the relationship depicted, these original songs do not actually capture its danger. Christian's behavior has been characterized as stalkerish and abusive, and Anastasia's reactions as typical of an abuse victim (Bonomi, Altenburger, and Walton). The film's soundtrack, however, generally romanticizes the relationship.

A film's aural experience does not come only from its soundtrack, but from its score. Danny Elfman's music well reflects the ambivalence of Christian and Anastasia's relationship. Although there are a few upbeat songs, most are quiet. Many have a development of the sonic story, but the development is somewhat reserved. In other words, many of the motifs do not seem to have a conclusion. "The Red Room" and "Then Don't" are prime examples of this.

Fifty Shades of Grey, the film, effectively shows the power of music. On the one hand, it has the power to help the audience visualize the world of Christian and Anastasia that previously existed only in their collective imagination. On the other hand, it can also manipulate that world by romanticizing or downplaying certain parts of the storyline. The film's music may help explain to skeptics why many viewers were attracted to Christian and expressed their desire to find someone like him. The aural image provided by the soundtrack oftentimes masked the risks and dangers that some scholars have identified and instead romanticized the Cinderella-like storyline.

CHAPTER NINE

Connected in the World of *Fifty Shades*

Film Adaptation, Merchandizing, Spinoffs and Beyond

The original world of *Fifty Shades* was created by E. L. James. Her *Master of the Universe* is the origin of the story of Christian Grey and Anastasia Steel. But it was far more than just her books that exposed them to the world. For some, their first exposure to the characters came by way of the 2015 film. For others, it might have been *Grey*, the 2015 novel, told from Christian's perspective.

Even for those who refused to read the trilogy or watch the film, the title was often unavoidable. Everywhere one looked, there was *Fifty Shades*-related merchandise, both online and off. The same could have been said about *Twilight*, the basis for *Master of the Universe* and just another literary franchise that successfully engaged consumerism to the point that Natalie Wilson described it as "contemporary popular culture [promoting] addiction not only to products, but also to ideas, subcultures, and activities" (180). There were, as stated in a previous chapter, three official music CDs associated with the franchise (Burgess para. 6). In addition, E. L. put her name to a collection of *Fifty Shades* red and white wines. The title was also used to establish its line of lingerie, sex toys, and jewelry. A friend of James, whose painting was referenced in the original book, put her work on her online store to market as something that Christian Grey actually had in his office.

Examining these different ways in which the *Fifty Shades* brand was adapted, expanded, and sometimes pirated shows that fans enjoyed the franchise more than just through the original book, or even the film. Furthermore, these merchandizing efforts—both official and unofficial—

reveal how *Fifty Shades* made BDSM a reality for many consumers by offering a line of products, from paddles and handcuffs to blindfolds, while underscoring the line beyond which certain kinds of sexual activities are not considered mainstream. Regardless of how fans consumed *Fifty Shades*, classy packaging, commodification of sex and sexuality, and romanticizing a fictional relationship drove their desire to consume. However, consumption was a means, not an end, for fans. Such behavior is little different from wearing a college ring or a jacket pin to achieve a sense of belonging.

Film Adaptation

It is not surprising that the *Fifty Shades* trilogy became a commercialization frenzy. It is common for the copyright holder of a successful entertainment title to license a series of official products to generate more profit. After all, the trilogy itself is a way for the publisher, Vintage Books, to make a profit based on what was initially James's fan fiction *Master of the Universe*. In other words, *Fifty Shades* started as a spinoff, not a money-making venture.

The film adaptation of James's first book in the trilogy was released in early 2015. The film was produced by Michael De Luca, Dana Brunetti, and E. L. James, and its screenplay was written by Kelly Marcel. Made by Focus Features and distributed by Universal Pictures, the movie was released just in time for the Valentine's Day weekend. The film premiered at the Berlin International Film Festival on February 11, 2015 (Patches). Two days later, the film was released in theaters worldwide. An informational website on movies, BoxOfficeMojo.com, reports that the production budget was $40 million.

The film was an immediate success. During the opening weekend alone, the film took in over $85 million, domestically. By the end of the year, it had grossed over $166 million domestically, and over $404 million internationally ("Fifty Shades of Grey," Box Office Mojo). Brad Brevet reported that "the overall domestic box office for the calendar year [had] crossed $11 billion" (para. 1). This figure was largely pushed by *Star Wars: The Force Awakens*, which was released only two weeks before the end of the year. The film grossed over $600 million during those two weeks. Nonetheless, *Fifty Shades of Grey*'s contribution cannot be ignored.

Although the novel and the film, as expected, have differences, the general storyline remained the same. Fans' criticism about the gap between the novel and the film tended to be similar to what one would expect when such an adaptation is made. A movie, with a running time of two hours, cannot possibly capture everything that was included in a book of five hundred or more pages. There were some plot points that are all but absent from the film. For example, in the book, Anastasia's eating habits are a major part of the story: she is often resistant to Christian's demands that she eat. When Christian learns that Anastasia is a virgin, his reaction in the film is a more caring one than in the book. Similarly, José and Kate, both of whom are major characters in the book, are minor characters in the film.

Some other differences were even more noticeable. The book is written from Anastasia's perspective; the film is from the perspective of an outsider. Even though the film does not show the two characters going to their respective hotel rooms in Georgia, in the book, Anastasia meets Christian in his hotel room. This is the night before the glider ride. Christian asks her, "When did you start your period?" (James 429). Anastasia responds that it had started the day before, prompting Christian to say, "Hold on to the sink." According to Anastasia, "[Christian] reaches between my legs and pulls on the blue string—*what?!*—and gently takes my tampon out and tosses it into the nearby toilet. *Holy fuck*. Sweet mother of all" (James 430).

On the one hand, the film director's decision to cut this scene is understandable. Zipp explains that the film "did need to tone it down a bit so they could be rated R, so it makes sense" (para. 4). Taylor-Johnson, the director, commented to *Variety* that "there was not even a discussion whether or not to include the scene" (Setoodeh). On the other hand, Zipp points out that the scene is "an intriguing look at the control Christian has over Ana. The guy pulls out her tampon without warning!" (para. 3). Although it is easy to understand why the scene did not make the cut, Zipp's point is a valid one. The story is largely about control. At least in *Fifty Shades of Grey*, the story develops as Christian tries to control every aspect of Anastasia's life. Christian's excessively controlling and domineering tendencies are less emphasized in the film.

Another important difference between the novel and the film concerns Anastasia's work. In the book, she interviews for and gets an internship with Seattle Independent Publishing, or SIP. The film, however, says nothing about Anastasia's career, leaving its audience wonder how she can afford her own apartment in Seattle. Although Anastasia's career may not be a focal part of the storyline, the film does not provide an explanation for her professional independence. Of course, *Fifty Shades Darker*, James's second novel, begins with Anastasia confronted by Christian's former partner at her workplace. Anastasia and Christian have an argument about the fact that he had bought out SIP without her knowing about it. Therefore, it is assumed that the film version of *Fifty Shades Darker* will discuss Anastasia's job in one way or another. The film version of *Fifty Shades of Grey*, however, appears to be just another popular culture story that strips a woman of her profession, depicting, instead, romance as the focal point of her life.

It is easy to think that the film adaptation is a part of the original *Fifty Shades* world. But, in reality, it is only one of many productization efforts. The movie is an approximation of the novel. The differences between the two are not just a matter of condensing hundreds of pages into a two-hour running time. It is indicative of what is acceptable as a written text versus as a film (e.g., tampon removal), whose voice matters (e.g., Anastasia's perspective or an outsider's perspective), and what parts of Anastasia's life matters the most as a form of entertainment (e.g., lack of a professional life and an emphasis on romance).

Official Merchandise

The popularity of the *Fifty Shades* trilogy and film generated a significant number of products. Some are official, with an approval from E. L. James; others were made by fans, for fans. Just as James challenged the conventional idea about intellectual property and copyright issues as she wrote *Master of the Universe* as fan fiction of *Twilight*, and *Fifty Shades of Grey* as a business product, fans of James's work also pushed copyright boundaries by creating a line of *Fifty Shades*-inspired products. Regardless of the status of merchandise—official or unofficial—*Fifty Shades* products are ubiquitous.

The highest-profile official merchandise includes the aforementioned *Fifty Shades* CDs. As Chapter Eight of this book examines in depth, the soundtrack was a major success. AllMusic stated that it was a "high-thread count seduction with nary a hint of menace, suitable for any romantic evening you choose" (Erlewine para. 1). Although not a fan of the older songs included on the album, Jim Farber wrote that much of the music speaks "of romanticized sex" (para. 3). At the end of 2015, the soundtrack had sold about 862,000 copies, ranking it as the ninth-best-selling album of the year in the U.S. (Caulfield). The second CD was Danny Elfman's original score. As Elfman explains, he was intrigued by the project because "it seemed to be an unclassifiable film when it came to genre" ("50 Shades of Grey: Danny," para. 4).

Albeit less successful than the soundtrack, *Fifty Shades of Grey: The Classical Album* was released well before the film and was designed to be listened to while reading the novels. The CD features works by Bach (Jesu, Joy of Man's Desiring"), Verdi ("Prelude"), Chopin ("Prelude in E minor"), Pachelbel ("Canon in D"), and other composers. Reviewing the album, Jack Goodstein wrote, "For fans of her novels, [the album] will be more than enough. For those yet to crack the spine, the album may well add some romance to spice up its sadomasochism. For those who have no intention of reading any of the grey shades, the album will make for an hour or so of fine music" (para. 7).

Aside from the books and music CDs, Fifty Shades wine is the only item listed on E. L. James's official website. For *Fifty Shades of Grey*, James lists ten different alcoholic drinks, including Bollinger Grande Année Rosé 1999 for the graduation scene, and gin and tonic (Hendricks with cucumber) for the scene in Georgia. There are similar lists for *Fifty Shades Darker* and *Fifty Shades Freed*. In addition, the series has two official wines: 2012 Fifty Shades of Grey Red Satin and 2013 Fifty Shades of Grey White Silk. Both are available for $17.99 per bottle, or $215.88 for a case of twelve, at fiftyshadeswine.com. The red wine is described as "a delicious red blend of syrah and petite shirah that delivers plenty of fruit and [a] spicy rich finish," earning ninety points by JamesSuckling.com, a website dedicated to wine ratings and reviews. It also won a silver award at the 2015 Winemaker Challenge International Competition ("2012 Fifty Shades"). The white wine, on the other hand, has "floral aromatics of lychee, honey, and pear [that] are tempered by flavors of crisp grapefruit, mineral and lush pear with a faint hint of butterscotch" and won the 2015 Riverside International Wine Competition Gold Award ("2013 Fifty Shades"). E. L. James writes:

> Wine plays an important role in *Fifty Shades of Grey*, reflecting the sensuality that pervades every encounter between Anastasia and Christian. I've always had a penchant for good wine, so helping to create the blends Red Satin and White Silk felt like a natural extension of the *Fifty Shades* trilogy. I hope all of you curl up with a glass to savor the romance and passion ["Fifty Shades of Grey"].

For fans, the lists on James's website, as well as two special wines inspired by the story, may be appealing. But as Beggs writes, nothing about these wines is particularly unique to what *Fifty Shades* represents. More specifically, he says, "The wines are successful only in their ability to make you wonder what exactly makes them *Fifty Shades of Grey* wines" (para. 7). He continues: "Without a label, or branding of any sort that alludes to the subject matter of the movie, it's not much fun drinking them" (para. 7). The wine lists and classical music CD appear to be nothing but a way for James to expand her *Fifty Shades* product portfolio. Wilson once wrote that "*Twilight* and its surrounding commodification builds on the messages that dominate real-world advertisements, which flatten out the difference between love, desire, sex and consumerism" (180).

Marketing alcoholic beverages in connection with a movie release is not a new concept. For example, the 2015 James Bond film *Spectre* had a tie-in campaign with Heineken. Although *Fifty Shades* has no such campaigns with an alcoholic brand, throughout the trilogy, wine and other alcoholic beverages frequently appear, characterizing the relationship between Anastasia and Christian, and help identify Christian as a wealthy entrepreneur. However, James's use of wine and emphasis on her wine selections create an interesting parallel to how some scholars argued that Christian's use of wine was problematic. It was especially the case because of the recent awareness about alcohol being used to manipulate victims of sexual abuse. If Christian and Anastasia's relationship is problematic and exploitative as Bonomi, Altenburger, and Walton have alleged, marketing the film with alcohol can further fuel the criticism against the trilogy. Writing for the *Guardian*, David Robert Grimes recently characterized alcohol as "by far the most dangerous 'date rape drug.'"

Due to the many non-official *Fifty Shades* products flooding the market, it is difficult to distinguish between the authentic from the nonauthentic. One fan site, however, helps to clear up this issue. An authorized product is the *Fifty Shades of Grey* party game, available for $24.99 from various sellers, including Amazon.com. Marketed for female users eighteen years old and older, the game's object is to "reveal [their] inner goddess," and "comes complete with a set of thought-provoking and intriguing vanilla-style questions that will put you and your friends under the microscope and reveal the hidden truths about the friends you love the best." Some on the questions include:

- Which of your girlfriends would be most likely to have an affair with her boss?
- Which girlfriend is most likely to Tweet about a steamy encounter?
- Which friend would never dream of making out at the movies?
- Which friend would be most likely to insist on splitting the restaurant bill on a date?

The game also has an expansion pack of cards called the "Red Room Edition."

The reviews, however, suggest that the game is far from what one might expect. Rebecca Stevens wrote, "This is supposed to make the game racier, but it's still nowhere near as racy as the movie!" On a positive note, one reviewer says that the game delivers "plenty of laughs!" ("*Fifty Shades of Grey* Expansion Pack Card Game"). Just like the *Fifty Shades* wine, consumers appear to be disappointed with the gap between what the game offers as compared with the trilogy.

Janet Cadsawan, an American jewelry designer, offers a fine jewelry collection said to be a collaborative effort with E. L. James. She explains that her jewelry "allows the wearer to carry the essence of the story in a chic, secretive accessory" ("*Fifty Shades of Grey* Fine Jewelry," para. 1). As of late January 2016, the collection includes four necklaces and a pair of earrings. The necklace collection includes a chain with a key—available in two sizes—that conjures the image of Christian introducing Anastasia to his "play room" for the first time. There are also a *Charlie Tango* charm and a mask charm available. The earrings are designed along the lines of handcuffs. Peers Hardy Group—a corporation that sells merchandise inspired by famous brands and characters—including Hello Kitty—also offers a bracelet and key chains, as well as mugs, scented candles, stationery, and other products associated with *Fifty Shades* ("*Fifty Shades of Grey*," Peers Hardy Group).

Similarly, OPI, an American nail-product producer who distributes to more than a hundred countries, offers a line of *Fifty Shades of Grey* nail varnish ("About OPI"). Suzi Weiss-Fischmann, a co-founder of the company, explained that

> the collection captures the mood, feelings and emotions of this film with assorted hues of grey, ranging from glittering and gleaming silvers to cool grey crèmes to dark charcoal. The collection also features a rich crème red to represent passion. The collection bottles the film's passion, luxury and power in six beautiful nail lacquers ideal for expressing sensuality through beauty ["OPI is Releasing," para. 2].

Michelle Mismas, the founder of AllLaqueuredUp.com, admitted, "Even if I'm not jazzed up about the movie, I'm all in on the OPI *Fifty Shades of Grey* collection" (para. 3).

Jennifer Trouton's artistic work is also a part of the official *Fifty Shades of Grey* merchandise. Trouton, a personal friend of E. L. James, is a London-based visual artist who has had exhibitions both domestically and internationally ("Jennifer Trouton"). Trouton actually appears in *Fifty Shades of Grey*. When Anastasia first visits Christian's office for an interview, she notices "a mosaic of small paintings hanging, thirty-six of them arranged in a square." Anastasia characterizes it as "exquisite—a series of mundane, forgotten objects painted in such precise detail they look like photographs." Christian says, "A local artist. Trouton" (James 8). The print is sold for $295 in the U.S., and marketed thusly: "This is an awesome chance to own a piece of work from a very talented artist that holds a special place in the heart of the author and, of course, Christian" ("Limited Edition," para. 14). The work, entitled "Looking at the Overlooked," has thirty-six images, as Anastasia characterizes. The images include shoes, a telephone, a cup, a lantern, a pair of glasses on a book, and many other "mundane" objects. The mosaic conjures a nostalgic image that seems to hint at how childhood memories and experiences continue to affect one's life well into adulthood.

It is not a surprise that the official *Fifty Shades* merchandise includes lingerie and sex toys. KappAhl, "Scandinavia's leading fashion [retailer] with roughly four hundred stores in Sweden, Norway, Finland and Poland" with an expanding online presence, collaborated with E. L. James to start a lingerie collection ("We Are Here," para. 1). On the corporate website, James enthuses: "It has been incredibly exciting and interesting to be involved in the process, from the production of the concept through the design to the final collection. I have been deeply involved at all stages, and my thought and suggestions are clearly visible in the collection's garments" ("Fifty Shades of KappAhl," para. 2).

James explains that "it was important for all women to be able to feel comfortable and beautiful while wearing the garments." The website also states that "not surprisingly, the garments come in shades of grey with complementary colours such as red and black" ("Fifty Shades of KappAhl," para. 4). Although the online catalogue is no longer available as of late January 2016, fashiongonerouge.com has a few images of KappAhl's *Fifty Shades* collection. Aside from the model wearing a mask over her face, the lingerie itself does not look much different from what one might expect from a regular lingerie store, even from Victoria's Secret. Visitors of the website commented, "Not really anything special about this…. I've seen similar underwear a lot before." One man commented: "My woman is way too kinky for these outfits!" ("KappAhl Launches").

Similarly, Bluebella, a company selling "luxurious lingerie and sleepwear collections," carried an official *Fifty Shades* lingerie line ("Who We Are," para. 1). Its product line includes lingerie more risqué than what KappAhl's product line offered. A lot of its lingerie, especially the ones included in the Black Label Collection, evokes the image of the wearer's body being tied with a rope or a belt. Bluebella also offers a line of sex toys and accessories. It sells metal handcuffs, a spanking paddle, a feather tickler, a butt plug, a flogger, a vibrator, and even a beginners' bondage kit. All of these products are named after a quote or a scene of the trilogy. The handcuffs are called "You are mine"; blindfolds, "No peeking"; the vibrating bullet, "We aim to please"; Anastasia's "inner goddess," silver pleasure balls; the restraint kit, "hard limits," whereas wrist ties are called "soft limits" (*"Fifty Shades of Grey* Accessories"). Many of the same products are offered on Lovehoney.com, an online sex store. But additional items include lubricant, sex toy cleaner, bondage rope in red and black, and a few others. The *Charlie Tango* classic vibrator, the sweet torture vibrating nipple clamps, and a few other items are also available. These items are a part of the *"Fifty Shades of Grey* Official Pleasure Collection." James explains, "Americans were the first to succumb to the intensity of their [Christian and Anastasia's] passionate romance, and every item in this luxurious official collection has been specially chosen by me to help fans of the trilogy enjoy the *Fifty Shades* experience on a whole new level" (*"Fifty Shades of Grey* Official Pleasure," para. 3).

One of the official products, Fifty Shades of Grey Come Alive Pleasure Gel for Her, a part of the *Fifty Shades of Grey* Official Sensual Care Collection, became a topic of a lawsuit in 2015. Tina Warchol, a female customer of the product in California, sued the manufacturer of the product arguing that the gel "did not deliver the purported benefits" (Suebsaeng; Williott, para 2). Pleasure Gel is just one of the products in the collection that include Ready for Anything Aqua Lubricant, At Ease Anal Lubricant, Sex Toy Cleaner, Silky Caress Lubricant, Sensual Touch Massage Oil, and even Soothe Me After Spanking Cream. The pleasure gel's product description on the Bluebella website reads, "Heighten your pleasure with Come Alive, an intimate arousal gel from the *Fifty Shades of Grey* Official Sensual Care Collection. Experience enhanced orgasms and stimulation as every tingle, touch and vibration intensifies" ("Fifty Shades of Grey Come Alive," para. 1). The product description even pretends to quote Anastasia, who supposedly said, "I surrender, exploding around him—a draining, soul-grabbing orgasm that leaves me spent and exhausted" ("Fifty Shades of Grey Come Alive," para. 3).

By purchasing these official products, fans are actively engaging themselves in the world of *Fifty Shades*. However, it is just the feeling of the world that is conveniently packaged with grey gift wrap that they are purchasing.

Spinoff Products

Unauthorized merchandise can easily be distinguished with the lack of the *Fifty Shades of Grey* title with a trademark registration logo. These spinoff items nonetheless reveal how many *Fifty Shades* fans experienced and enjoyed the trilogy. In reality, more than the official products, unofficial products show how fans took ownership and initiative in recreating their own version of the story. Just like James originally wrote *Master of the Universe* as fan fiction, these unofficial products attest to the fact that fans are not merely passive consumers. Because of the number of unofficial products, this chapter can only examine a small fraction of them. As noted earlier, in a prosumption culture where the line between producers and consumers is blurred and where amateurs can sometimes produce goods that are equal in quality to what is produced by professionals, it is important to scrutinize even merchandise that is not recognized officially by the copyright holders.

Some of the spinoff products are completely independent from the movie or the trilogy. The only relationship to James's work, in fact, is that they carry the *Fifty Shades* name. One of the examples is "50 Shades of Earl Grey" tea available from adagio.com. A *Telegraph* article cited one of the reviewers of the tea—clearly unofficial as seen from the fact that "Fifty" is not spelled out—commented that it was "almost too sinister to be a tea" while another review described it as "commanding and decadent" (Rainey, para. 7). These reviews connect the tea to the trilogy, but it is a far-fetched effort. Other blends include "Fifty Shades of Green" and "Fifty Shades Darker."

It is not just adagio.com that connected Christian Grey's last name to Earl Grey tea. Even though it was meant as an April Fool's joke, Two Leaves and a Bud, a tea company located in Basal, Colorado, joked about its new product, also named "50 Shades of Earl Grey." The store's CEO and founder, Richard Rosenfield, explains, "Our new 50 Shades of Earl Grey is all about bringing tea lovers together with not just tea, but also other tea lovers. Or, well, any lovers at all, to be honest." He characterizes the tea to be "a little naughtier" (naomi, para. 1). He continues, "Deciding that those little bits of Viagra belonged in this new black tea blend was a big step forward for us…. Ultimately, dissolving the medication into a bit of hot water when you steep this tea has just enough oomph to increase arousal in both men and women" (para. 7). Although the news release on this fictitious new blend of tea was made as a joke, it nonetheless reflects how the film and the trilogy justified sex as a means for marketing even for a tea company.

Expectedly, there are many clothes that are inspired by *Fifty Shades*. The items that stand out more than others are a line of baby clothes. An article published in *Daily Mail* speculates that some of the baby shirts are for "expecting parents who may have the saucy books to thank for their new bundles of joy" ("Are These the Sickest," para. 2). Many of these baby clothes have writing on them: "Fifty Shades of Grey Baby"; "My Mommy pretends Christian Grey is my Daddy"; "i pretend Christian Grey is my daddy"; and "Laters, Baby." Some shirts suggest that the baby was the result of James's trilogy: "Nine months ago, my mommy read *Fifty Shades of Grey*"; "Generation Grey"; "I'm the result of my Mommy reading *Fifty Shades of Grey*"; and "By-product of *Fifty Shades of Grey*" ("'50 Shades of Grey' Products for Kids"). There is also a baby onesie that has a Grey tie printed on the front. Fans can also buy *Fifty Shades* baby-changing mats. Today, Google and Pinterest are filled with *Fifty Shades*-inspired clothes.

The list of spinoff products continues. Dog Doggin Designs offers a plush dog bone toy inspired by *Fifty Shades of Grey*, called "50 Shades of Fur." It has a picture of a chain embroidered, as well. A quick Google image reveals almost endless list of *Fifty Shades*-inspired cell phone cases, bearing such slogans as "Oh, F**k the paperwork," "Laters, Baby," "I don't make love, I fuck … hard," and "Mr. Grey will see you now." Some others poke fun at the trilogy: "Mr. Pepe will see you now," and "Keep calm and obey Mr. Grey."

There is even a special detergent called "Flirty Shades of Surf." Its commercial starts with a message on the screen that reads: "Do you know what women really want in the bedroom…?" Then a man in a pink pair of boxer briefs is seen carrying his laundry from his bedroom to his laundry room. Is this about a man who is confident enough to wear pink underwear and does not leave all the house chores to his wife or girlfriend? Is this about a man who defies stereotypes of lazy men who just watch TV and drink beer? The Surf commercial is, of course, not about caring or stereotype-defying men. The actor finds handcuffs in the washer. His laundry basket not only has his clothes but also bras. Another message then appears: "Two thirds of women across the UK admit nothing gets them more in the mood … than freshly cleaned sheets … and their men doing the laundry." After all, it is about sex. The same man is now seen with a riding crop in his hands. He then picks up handcuffs, a blind, and lingerie, only to take them out to hang outside to dry them along with bed sheets. What happens that night after he brings his laundry back inside is left to the viewers' imagination.

Another example of these spinoff products making BDSM and other "kinky" sex more visible is *Fifty Shades*-themed classes offered for those who are interested in learning about the "actual techniques to enhance [their] romance, orgasm and sexual potential" ("Fifty Shades of Pleasure," para. 1). A two-hour course, offered by Fire Horse Productions, promises to teach the "necessary foundation skills around sensuous bondage, role playing, sensation toys, how to get started safely, and more" ("Fifty Shades of Pleasure," para. 1). Similarly, another class offered by an erotic boutique called Sh! is a class for women on "a lightweight introduction to the world of BDSM" ("Sex News," para. 4). The course information states:

> Fifty Shades of Kinky Sensuality classes introduce women and couples to the erotic world of Christian Grey and Anastasia Steele, and teach basic moves and techniques to channel and empower the inner Mistress or submissive. Sh! will familiarize "students" with ways to give and receive kinky pleasures, as well as how to use props such as Love Balls, Blind Folds, Crops and Clamps in the most effective, exciting and titillating ways.
>
> For both the sexually faint-hearted and those who believe they've seen and done it all, this is a totally new class designed to open up the world of this sexual phenomenon, and give women the tools to sexually explore their own relationships. It is a lightweight introduction to the world of BDSM in a safe and playful environment where women and couples can learn together, but all activity takes place strictly away from the store ["Sex News," para. 3–4].

Martin explains that these stores had previously offered classes on BDSM. She also argues that "the novels are used to repackage what was once already sold in an attempt to capitalize on their popularity" (982).

These examples of spinoff unofficial merchandise and classes show that fans created their own version of *Fifty Shades*. Of course, these spinoff-inspired works and products are close to, if not actually, infringing on copyright- or intellectual property–related regulations. But, as fan fiction writers have demonstrated in the past and as James herself has claimed about the relationship between her work and *Twilight*, fan engagement is far more than just consuming what is offered by a publisher or a movie production company.

Fifty Shades of Spinoffs

The success of the *Fifty Shades of Grey* trilogy is clear. There is no doubt that it was one of the best-selling novels in the early 2010s and possibly for that entire decade. The trilogy had sold over 125 million copies worldwide by May 2015. The movie grossed over $500 million worldwide (Stedman). But the success can also be measured by the level of adaptation projects, official merchandise, and spinoff products. As noted above, the first film was a highly successful one, despite the number of vocal dissenters who refused to watch it. But the brand's success was not limited to those examples. The *Fifty Shades*-inspired board game may sound reasonable, especially for a wild night. But parent-and-baby screenings of *Fifty Shades* before noon is a counterintuitive way for a theater to promote itself.

The *Fifty Shades*-inspired sex toys, lingerie, and jewelry make sense. So does the soundtrack. But the collection of wine (that many critics did not particularly enjoy) is counterintuitive to the storyline of the film in which wealthy Christian Grey is portrayed as a wine connoisseur. Unofficial merchandise—from tea to cell phone cases to baby clothes—is simply entrepreneurial individuals or fans enjoying the *Fifty Shades* brand in their own way. It is easy to underestimate the value of these merchandizing efforts as trifling or to over-criticize the capitalistic drive of certain companies. It is, however, important to recognize that both fans and anti-fans experience the *Fifty Shades* brand via official and non-official—sometimes illegal knock-off—products.

Furthermore, the franchise enabled "If you like *Fifty Shades*, you will like this" type of advertisements. Rachel Deahl reported as early as 2012:

> In July, Atria acquired Jamie McGuire's originally self-published novel *Beautiful Disaster*, which is about a "good girl" named Abby who shows up at college and enters a bet with the tattooed bad boy named Travis: if she wins the bet he will take a one-month vow of abstinence, and if he is victorious she will stay in his apartment for a month. The book was sold by an agent at Valerie Hoskins Associates … and Atria filled its initial press release about the title with plenty of *Shades* references [para. 5].

Similarly, Tiffany Reisz, another erotica author, was able to have her initial printing of her work entitled *The Siren* at 60,000 copies, as well as to organize a book club meeting with DivaMoms, for whom E. L. James had a similar appearance. Authors and publishers took advantage of the popularity of *Fifty Shades* to increase their revenue.

These examples of merchandizing and spinoff products also show that a particular kind of BDSM was put into the mainstream of American and many other cultures at least for a few years. It is, however, important to note that not all kinds of sexual activities were mainstreamed. Amber

Martin explains that only "a specific brand of *Fifty Shades* BDSM" entered a part of many people's consciousness. In other words, it was the branch of BDSM that was "perceived as exciting and safe as opposed to extreme and frightening." This is why, Martin continues to posit, the sex toys "[consisted] of more lightweight items such as paddles, spankers, and blindfolds as opposed to more 'hardcore' items such as chains, gimp masks, collars, and leads" (981). As noted elsewhere in the book, *Fifty Shades'* portrayal of BDSM was far from comprehensive or representative of the actual subculture.

As a whole, *Fifty Shades* generated a wide range of associated products that made and kept the franchise highly visible. Erotica authors and publishers have taken advantage of this rare occasion for the genre's high visibility (Deahl), contributing to its success as well as to various controversies. Among other things, the trilogy was blamed for making people engage in sinful behaviors. Questions about censorship and the freedom of expression arose. Legal experts wondered if the conventional definitions of copyright and intellectual property are still valid. The list goes on and on.

Fans turned a fictional story into something more realistic. Unlike most romantic or erotic novels that do not attain the popularity anywhere close to E. L. James's work, Christian and Anastasia's world became readily consumable. Much of the story came alive for many fans, to the extent that Anastasia was depicted as writing a review for a sex toy. Merchandizing efforts—from official to unofficial and from aural to sexual—showcase the world that fans and non-fans experienced, both purposefully and non-purposefully.

On the one hand, all these works by fans and others reflect their creative work. Regardless of one's view on copyrights, there is no denying that these examples are creative works. On the other hand, these examples underscore the meaning of consumption. Wilson wrote:

> Though *Twilight* incorporates many of the consumerist messages girls and females are subject to, it also stresses the importance of friendship, community, family, dedication, trust, commitment, and love. These are things consumer culture tells us we can buy, but most of us know better. Fans may buy that *Twilight* T-shirt or bumper sticker in order to convey their love of a certain character or the saga in general, but what they really want is to continue the imaginative experience that the books represent for them, to fortify the sense of community that the fandom has wrought, to not so much "buy that *Twilight* feeling" but to live it via their immersion in the *Twilight* world [204].

Fifty Shades fans are not the only ones who wish to inhabit an imaginary world. Our attention to, and even obsession with, products—from college apparel to classic cars—is our desire to be connected in what Benedict Anderson called the imagined community that has real consequences. *Fifty Shades* merchandise, therefore, is much more than trinkets and objects of meaningless consumption.

CHAPTER TEN

Christian Grey
as an Aspirational Brand
Signs of Wealth and Materialism

Discussions on the *Fifty Shades* trilogy as well as the movie understandably tend to focus on their depictions of sex, BDSM, and Christian's stalker-like behaviors. But as Bonomi and others have shown, the audience of the film also noticed the amount of Christian's wealth displayed throughout the storyline. Of course, *Fifty Shades of Grey* is far from being the first major film to use renowned brands and merchandise to signal the wealth possessed by a character, to characterize him or her in certain ways, or to set the tone or scene for the story. In other words, movies have high-end brands to signal that a character is wealthy and low-end brands to show that the character is struggling economically. But brands also recognize that they can increase their exposure by having them displayed on the big screen. Recent James Bond movies, for example, have featured Coke Zero, Sony, and other brands. In reality, it is rare for movies today *not* to have a brand or a product represented. Furthermore, it is as rare for Hollywood moviemakers not to secure financial income by obtaining sponsorship (Hong, Wang, and Santos 104; Karniouchina, Uslay, and Erenburg 27).

As for *Fifty Shades of Grey*, some of the brands appeared in the film because its original novel by E. L. James made direct reference to them. For example, Christian gives Anastasia a MacBook Pro when he learns that her laptop is not working (James *Fifty Shades of Grey*, 178). But in some other instances, brands appeared on the big screen due to a product-placement business decision. ("Brand in *Fifty Shades*"). The scene with a glider in Georgia as depicted in the original book, for example, lacks any reference to the craft's manufacturer, even though it attained a high level of exposure in the film.

Many of the brands featured in the film are the combination of what are called aspirational brands and luxury brands. Unlike so-called luxury brands and "exclusive, high-priced often extravagant goods and services that are more likely to be purchased by upper income individuals," aspirational brands are "currently unaffordable 'dream brands' for which an individual possesses a desire to purchase upon reaching a higher professional status, income and/or social class" (Trocchia, Saine, and Luckett 331–332). Simultaneously, many of the brands that appear in the film are beyond the reach of many college students: Audi, Omega, high-end interior decor etc. The story combines a hint of realism via a MacBook or an Audi—expensive but not completely unaffordable for many—and a sign of extravagance through a helicopter or a garage full of Audis, to characterize Anastasia's experience with Christian as something that is plausible enough for the audience to relate to.

E. L. James's trilogy underscores that Christian Grey is the ideal man in multiple ways. First, Anastasia Steele's characterization of him in the book is more than enough to show how physically attractive he is. Second, it is also important to note that Christian's attractiveness is augmented by, if not dependent on, what he owns. In other words, it is not just Christian Grey that drives Anastasia or others who are similarly attracted to him. The cars Christian drives, the clothes he wears, or decorative features that adorn his apartment are integral elements. As online memes questioned, if Christian did not own any of these high-end consumer goods, would Anastasia be attracted to him? Or, would someone who has a stalking tendency be excused of his behaviors if he did not have so much money?

Brands in Media

Product placement, as defined by Pola B. Gupta and Stephen J. Gould, is a practice that "involves incorporating brands in movies in return for money or for some promotional or other considerations" is a very common practice in many forms of entertainment, including television (37). Carrie La Ferle and Steven M. Edwards, for example, published a comprehensive study on product placement in television in 2006. Kowalczyk and Royne's work focused particularly on reality shows. In other cases, this practice involves movies, as was the case with *Fifty Shades of Grey*. Regardless of the media format, the history of product placement, dating back at least to the 1920s, is extensive (Rovella, Geringer, and Sanchez;

McKechnie and Zhou). Generally, marketing research has shown that entertainment outlets, including movies, are "an appropriate vehicle to reach the consumers" (Redondo 51). This is to say that just like producing an advertisement and airing it on TV or before a movie, placing a brand logo or a particular product in a TV show or a film can have a similar effect in increasing the visibility of the brand.

Because audiences are more focused on the entertainment than the promotion of a brand, product placement might be classified as "subliminal advertising." As Siva K. Balasubramanian characterizes, product placement is "a paid product message aimed at influencing movie (or television) audiences via the planned and unobtrusive entry of a branded product into a movie (or television program)" (31). William M. O'Barr explored the lengthy history of subliminal advertising. What distinguishes subliminal advertising and product placement is the level of visibility. This is to say that just like subliminal advertising, product placement is "unobtrusive," but unlike subliminal advertising, it is visible (Cowley and Barron 89).

The outcome of product placement is assumed to be usually positive, or at least neutral, for brand recognition (Cowley and Barron 89). Writing for *Luxury Daily*, Sarah Jones explains that "branded sponsorships are common among luxury brands looking to attract consumers through a shared hobby or cause. Product placement in feature films, on the other hand, allows the brand to be viewed on a platform likely to resonate with more prospective customers" (para. 24). Reese's Pieces in *ET, the Extra-terrestrial* (1982)—one of the best-known examples of product placement in film history—clearly showed the brand logo. Similarly, seeing a DeLorean would conjure up the image of *Back to the Future* for many. Although it is unclear how much this kind of brand exposure exactly contributed to a rise in sales, d'Astous and Berrada demonstrate that product placement is usually successful in having "significant positive effects on brand recall and recognition." The authors, however, continue to argue that this practice may not necessarily have a positive effect on "brand attitude and purchase intention" (46).

Russell and Stern explain that product placement could be theorized as a "balance model" (8). They argue that the triangle with the consumer, the character, and the product or the brand exists as the base for the interactions between the product and the consumer, the consumer and the character, and the character and the product. Ultimately, product placement aims to turn media viewers into consumers. Redondo, for example, explains that "product placements are being planned in an intuitive way that increase the intrinsic positive association between moviegoers and consumers" (51). *Fifty Shades* fans have a positive association regarding Christian's wealth being indicative of his favorite brands. Simultaneously, brands, as attested by comments made by public relations officers and others, attempted to use their association to Christian to underscore that positive image.

As noted earlier, in the case of *Fifty Shades*, many of the brands and merchandise can be characterized as aspirational. They are different from more common brands that many consumers experience on a day-to-day basis, such as McDonald's, Walmart, and others. In the automotive industry, as the *Fifty Shades* film shows, Audi is an aspirational brand. Owning an Audi sends a certain message about the owner's status and taste. On the other hand, a brand like Pontiac would send a completely different message. A *SociaLogic Marketing* article explains that the AMC television series *Breaking Bad* showed Pontiac in a "less than favorable light," and the brand was "the symbol of inefficiency (admin-planb para. 4–5). What follows below is an analysis of how Christian and product-placement brands influenced each other throughout the film. On the one hand, Christian was shown as someone with a high-end appeal, due to his predilection for Audi automobiles, for example. But the brands that appeared in *Fifty Shades of Grey* were also able to take advantage of Christian's reputation for sophistication to justify their own value as exclusive brands for their potential customers.

Overall Brand Exposure for Fifty Shades of Grey

Concave Brand Tracking is a company that "records every brand's appearance and mention in entertainment as well as the context in which these occur" to "assess branding efficiency, monitor evolution over time and benchmark against competitors" ("Welcome to Concave," para. 1–2). As this quote suggests, despite the name "product placement," a film audience is exposed to what might be more accurately labeled as "brand placement." Although corporations in no way deny increased sales of a particular product due to media exposure, the aim of product placement is to take advantage of "non-traditional, alternative, non-obtrusive forms of marketing communication" for the brand rather than a particular product line (d'Astous and Berrada 45). Concave, in its effort to understand brands' strategies for their media exposure, examines how many brands appear in a movie, how long each is shown, if a logo appears, etc., rather than focusing on particular products. Because the aim of the current work is not to define these two practices, for the purpose of this chapter, these labels are used interchangeably.

According to Concave, *Fifty Shades of Grey* featured about twenty brands, accounting for a total of over sixteen minutes of the film. Based on "the number of brands, their screen time, their discernibility and their logo visibility," the brand analysis corporation determined that the film's brand visibility was higher than *The Dark Knight Rises* (2012) but slightly below *Iron Man 3* (2013). Both *Fast & Furious 6* (2013) and *Mission: Impossible: Ghost Protocol* (2011) had twice the brand visibility as *Fifty Shades of Grey*. *Skyfall* (2012), *Captain America: The Winter Soldier* (2014), and *TED* (2012) had about 50 percent more visibility ("Brands in *Fifty Shades*").

On the whole, Apple was by far the most visible brand in the film. The second-most visible brand, DG Flugzeugbau—or the brand of the glider in which Anastasia was able to experience "so much more" with Christian than what the "Red Room of Pain" offered—was over 60 percent less visible than Apple. Compared to the visibility gap between Apple and DG Flugzeugbau, the gap between DG Flugzeugbau and the rest of brands is minor. Christian's $150,000 sailplane manufacturer's visibility is only slightly higher than the third to sixth brands, namely Audi, Fazioli, Bose, and Dolce & Gabbana (Ocean para. 14; "Brands in *Fifty Shades*").

It is noteworthy that the second-most visible company brand in *Fifty Shades* is DG Flugzeugbau. The Concave website wrote, "An entire scene [was] dedicated to showing the glider off, ... the brand is associated with excitement, romance, fun and flying skill" ("Brands in *Fifty Shades*" para. 9–10). On the one hand, it is true that even the model number of the glider—DG-1001—is clearly shown on the screen. But, on the other hand, unlike Audi or Apple, for most moviegoers, DG Flugzeugbau is a foreign name. Therefore, even though the brand ranked second for its film exposure, it is somewhat questionable if much of the audience actually recognized or remembered the brand ("Brands in *Fifty Shades*").

Some brands, more than others regardless of the extent of media exposure, issued official comments about their association with *Fifty Shades of Grey* and/or Christian. Audi, for example, was not only very visible both in the film and the novels, but also was vocal about its presence in the movie, adding to the corporate value. Similarly, Covet Lounge and its partners who designed Christian's apartment and office also marketed their product lines. Reviewing how these brands and products appeared in the story and actually examining how much those items were to cost if one would purchase them reveals Christian's unique status, a status that appealed not only to Anastasia but to countless moviegoers.

Audi as a Status Symbol

Throughout the film, one automobile brand particularly stands out: Audi. A German car company whose history dates back to the early twentieth century, Audi is a global luxury automobile brand, selling over 1.7 million vehicles in 2014 alone ("Audi AG"). But it is not because of the large sales number that Christian Grey drives an Audi—it is because Audi carries an image of upper-class, exclusive wealth. Of course, E. L. James's original work depicted Christian as more than just a fan of the brand, owning an entire fleet of Audi vehicles. However, the movie's clear emphasis on the brand is not an accident. When Christian and Anastasia return to the hangar after the glider ride, an Audi is parked right next to them, even though they are in Georgia, far away from Christian's garage.

Audi, as a product placement in a major Hollywood movie, is not unfamiliar: it was also (moderately, according to Concave's study) seen in *Iron Man 3* and *Avengers: Age of Ultron* (Buss). Although movies such as *I, Robot* (2004) and *Iron Man* (2008) had far more exposure—an estimated 150 percent more—than in *Fifty Shades*, it still had more exposure than in *Skyfall* (2012) or *The Bourne Ultimatum* (2007) ("Brands in *Fifty Shades*"). *Fifty Shades*, therefore, is not unique in that it features the brand; what *is* unique about the film is that it features as many as five Audis: the 2014 R8 1 Spyder quattro S Tronic 5.2L, or "a thrillseeker's dream, [which] goes from zero to 60 mph in 3.4 seconds with the potential to reach a blistering top speed of up to 195 mph"; the 2013 S8 Quattro Tiptronic 4.0L TFSI, or a "incomparable luxury of Audi's A8 flagship sedan combined with the unparalleled performance that defines the Audi brand"; the 2012 Q7 3.0L TDI Quattro Tiptronic, or a vehicle that "is functional and comfortable for drivers and passengers alike"; the 2013 S7 Quattro S Tronic 4.0L TFSI, or a vehicle with a "4.0 liter engine [that] delivers 420 horsepower, jumping from zero to 60 mpg in only 4.5 seconds, providing performance and style"; and the 2014 A3 S Tronic TFSI 1.8L 4-cylinder that "does not compromise when it comes to design, performance, or technology" ("Audi Partners," para. 5). Audi did not have to pay any money to appear in the original *Fifty Shades of Grey* novel—it was E. L. James's personal awareness that the Audi brand would be appropriate for someone like Christian. An article, published in *SociaLogic Marketing*, concurs that

Audi's increasing revenue in general can be attributed to "the cultural relevance of [Audi's] branding" (admin-planb par. 2).

In the *Fifty Shades of Grey* story, a 2014 R8 Spyder appears several times. One of the most memorable scenes for it might be the one in which Christian and Anastasia drive to Stanley Park before a walk in the park. A 2013 S8 is also seen a few times. In addition to being lined up in the parking garage of Escala, the vehicle appears in front of Clayton's Hardware, where Anastasia works. The Audi at the gliding scene was a 2013 S7. The vehicle with the Georgia license plate may or may not belong to Christian. An Audi Q7 is what Taylor often drives, for example, from her workplace to the helicopter ride near the beginning of the movie. A 2013 A3 is what Christian gives Anastasia as a graduation gift, as well as what he has given to his previous submissives. Anastasia nicknamed the car "Submissive Special" for this reason (James *Fifty Shades Darker*, 396).

All of these cars that appear in the film, as well as others under the umbrella of Audi, benefits from the company's "branding as a sexy luxury ride with a sensual design and heart-pounding performance." It was this characteristic of Audi that "made it a natural choice in the mind of [E. L. James,] who needed a vehicle for her obscenely wealthy characters to lustfully bite their lips in" (admin-planb par. 2). So-called "cultural relevance" comes from the image that one associates with Audi, thanks to the brand's appearance in movies like *Fifty Shades*, as well as its more conventional television commercials and print advertisements (admin-planb par. 2).

As an avid brand to maintain and promote its cultural meaning, Audi was proud to be a part of the film. Giovanni Perosino, head of marketing communication of Audi, stated, "We are happy to continue our strong partnership with the film industry with this highly-anticipated project, especially after already being part of the best-selling novel" ("Audi Partners," para. 3). The director of marketing for Audi of America, Loren Angelo, also praised the collaboration by emphasizing, "It was a natural fit for Audi to be a part of 'Fifty Shades of Grey' as it's brought life in theaters.... Audi is a brand that symbolizes performance, technology and modern design. The natural inclusion of our hottest models in the series illustrates how Audi has become truly synonymous with sophisticated luxury" ("Audi Partners," para. 4). Angelo also told *Brand Channel* that Audi cars in the film "demonstrate the lifestyle of a wealthy, forward-thinking entrepreneur" (Buss para. 10).

Matthew DeBord also noted that Audi and the storyline of *Fifty Shades* was a good match. On the one hand, there are numerous luxury automotive brands. On the other hand, Audi occupies a unique space in the industry. He wrote, "Rolls-Royces and Bentleys imply lord-of-the-manor luxury, while Mercedes if often associated with aging plutocrats, and BMW is ever so slightly tainted by being the preferred vehicle of Hollywood talent agents." He continues, "Audi's sweet spot is the under-40, hard-charging, techno-finance crowd. The cars especially are widely admired for sleek designs that attract praise from the creative echelons of the upper-crust. Audis are German, but they are *sexy* German" (emphasis in original) (para. 8–9). Of course, the luxury automotive industry has Lamborghini, Ferrari, and Porsche. DeBord, however, offers, "While those cars are stunning, they also carry with them an adolescent hangover. Somehow, it doesn't seem right to be wearing a Bespoke suit, à la Mr. Grey, while tearing around in a bright yellow Lambo Hurácan" (para. 18).

Apple Makes Its Mark

Just like Audi, Apple is not new to product placement. In 2011 alone, Apple appeared close to nine hundred times on TV shows. Marketing literature explains that "from hi-tech spy comedies to hip hop teen dramas, Apple products have appeared anytime characters are portrayed as technologically savvy and up-to-date" (admin-planb para. 6). There is no question that Apple continues to carry the "cool" image compared to Dell or other computer manufacturers. Similarly, iPhones continue to attract customers worldwide. But it is not just because of the images that viewers associate Apple with that make it an ideal brand to depict. The same marketing article states: "To top it all off, they've spent no money on the exposure—they simply give their products to TV shows who request them" (admin-planb para. 6). Apple strategically makes itself attractive to entertainment producers by offering its product for free. In return, it receives a high media exposure with little financial investment on its part.

Among about twenty brands that appeared in *Fifty Shades of Grey*, Apple had the highest visibility ("Brands in *Fifty Shades*"). Christian Grey's office receptionists use Apple desktop computers. Anastasia's roommate, Kate, uses an Apple laptop. Christian uses an iPhone. On the one hand, the original novel references a MacBook Pro as a gift from Christian to Anastasia. On the other hand, it was the filmmaker's choice to feature the brand used by Christian's receptionists. Albeit minor, seeing the logo for Dell or Acer in his office would not have created the same ambiance.

Apple's screen time in the film amounted to over four minutes. Of these four minutes, the brand's logo or name was visible 43 percent of the time. In terms of discernibility, Apple products were shown close-up 10 percent of the time, while 41 percent of the time it was considered "subtle," and 49 percent "discrete" ("Brands in *Fifty Shades*"). The visibility of Apple would have been higher if Anastasia also used an iPhone. But instead she uses a flip phone by LG, ranked seventh in brand visibility. Apple, probably one of the most affordable of all the brands that Christian owns, is popular among college students like Anastasia. It is, therefore, no surprise that Christian gifts Anastasia with an Apple laptop.

Compared to other movies featuring Apple's brand, according to Concave, *Mission: Impossible: Ghost Protocol* (2011) had more than double the brand visibility in *Fifty Shades*, racking up a screen time of more than six minutes. *Flight* (2014) and *I Am Legend* (2007) had less than a half of *Fifty Shades*, and *Captain America: The Winter Soldier* (2014) less than a third ("Brands in *Fifty Shades*"). Even though Christian buys Anastasia a BlackBerry and not an iPhone, Christian uses an iPhone, and both use Apple laptops.

Interior Design

Much of the interior design for Christian's apartment was taken care of by Covet Lounge and its partners: Boca do Lobo, Delightfull, Brabbu, and Koket (Covet Lounge). Covet Lounge press director, Filipia Mendonça, stated, "'Fifty Shades of Grey' was one of the most expected and waited for [films in recent years].... The movie was an excellent way to promote our partner brands and their pieces.... It allowed [us] to show the elegance and luxury of the pieces that are absolutely delightful" (Jones, para. 15–16).

Covet Lounge's press release explains that "each piece was carefully selected to fit its designated environment style, from bold and avant-garde, to organic and feminine, aiming to mirror the film and brand's common qualities" (sic) (para. 4). Janet Morais, creative director and founder of Koket, stated:

> My passion and mission with Koket is to create highly desirable, empowering statement pieces. The essence of my pieces dreamily complements the film's aura of desire, passion and power. Although I never thought my collection would be powerful enough to grace the set of *Fifty Shades of Grey*, our inclusion has revealed the influence of exceptional design [Koket].

Mendonça added:

> Our pieces were chosen to reflect Christian Grey's extravagant lifestyle and millionaire taste. The timeless elegance and refinement of each piece suits the story's

environment perfectly—luxury and an elite world filled with raw, natural passion, with a touch of feminine perspective, all attributes found in each of Covet Lounge's brands [Jones para. 16].

Jones explains that Universal Pictures, in an attempt to promote its film, created a virtual tour of Christian's apartment. On their website, fans can see not only the interior of his apartment decorated with Covet Lounge's furniture and design features, but also "explore the assortment of Audi vehicles" (para. 17). The website offers an opportunity for fans to virtually "visit" the *Fifty Shades* world. It creates an entertainment experience for fans while promoting the brands associated with the film.

Justin Ocean estimates that wallpaper for one of the rooms alone would cost $12,000. He continues:

There's marble everywhere—moody course-grained slabs for the floors and lighter grey ... in a bathroom. That's a Blue Stone freestanding tub (from $7,150) they get busy in, by the way. Those appliances in the kitchen are a Wolf range (from $1,805) and integrated Sub-Zero fridge (from $7,030), like any self-respecting urbanite. Fresh flowers—orchids—are delivered every three days [para. 19].

The list of extravagant furniture continues. The redwood and brass side table in Christian's apartment was designed by Brabbu Design Forces; its price is available only upon request. A similar version of the redwood dining room table costs over $17,000, with each of its Milo Baughman dining chairs costing approximately $1,200 for reproductions (Ocean para. 21).

A memorable scene in the film has Christian playing the piano, with Anastasia, wrapped in a bed sheet, standing across the room. The piano on which he plays Chopin's "Prelude to E-Minor" is a $268,999 Fazioli F278 Grand Piano, handmade "in Italy over three years using red spruce ... with some parts plated in 18K gold" (Ocean para. 22). Concave Brand Tracking states, "The grand piano is associated with sex and female attraction. Indeed, in the scene when Christian plays the instrument and in which it gets most of its exposure, a naked Anastasia Steele is drawn to him. She then proceeds to interrupt his playing in order to initiate another round of sex" ("Brands in *Fifty Shades*," para 16).

Omega Watches a Questionable Choice

Christian is also a fan of Omega watches. Although TAG Heuer or Hublot may be more apt brands for him, especially because of their aggressive marketing—including Hublot's official sponsoring of soccer's largest event, FIFA World Cup, for over four events (South Africa in 2010, Brazil in 2014, Russia in 2018, and Qatar in 2022)—Christian is seen with an Omega. Omega has also placed its brand in *Casino Royale* (2006) to discriminate itself from its rival brand, Rolex. In the film, Vesper Lynd asks James Bond if he is wearing a Rolex. Bond responds, "Omega," to which Lynd simply states, "Beautiful." While Christian never makes a direct reference to his watch in the movie, Bond's 2006 film is more explicit about product placement.

Watch connoisseurs may say that the aforementioned brands (or a rarer brand, like Richard Mille) may be more appropriate for Christian (Ocean para. 5). Ocean argues that E. L. James's decision to portray Christian as an Omega user was probably because of her personal lack of knowledge on watches. Nonetheless, Christian owns several Omega watches, as seen in the opening sequence in which he opens the drawer with accessories as he puts his shirt on. The first watch shown is a Seamaster Aqua Terra, following the café scene. After Christian saves Anastasia from a biker who almost runs into her, he holds her face with his Omega adorning his left wrist. The image was used in many of the film's promotional materials. The watch costs $7,200. It also appears in *Fifty Shades Darker*:

> Christian launches into his story. He was flying with Ros, his number two in *Charlie Tango* to deal with a funding issue at WSU in Vancouver. I can barely keep up I'm so dazed. I just hold Christian's hand and stare at his manicured fingernails, his long fingers, the creases on his knuckles, his wristwatch—an Omega with three small dials [James *Fifty Shades Darker*, 460].

The other watch, an Omega Speedmaster Moonwatch Co-Axial Chronograph, is a pricier one, costing $26,000.

In *Fifty Shades Freed*, Anastasia is also depicted as an Omega user:

> He clasps that hand, too, turning it gently over to examine my wrist. The platinum Omega watch he gave me at breakfast on our first morning in London obscures the red line. The inscription still makes me swoon.
>
> > Anastasia
> > You are my More
> > My Love, My Life
> > Christian
>
> In spite of everything, all his Fiftyness, my husband can be so romantic [*Fifty Shades Freed* 56].

Despite the detailed depictions of her watch, the platinum Omega that Christian gave Anastasia in *Fifty Shades Darker* does not seem to exist. Writing for an Omega online forum, a contributor named dsio states emphatically that Omega "does NOT make any solid platinum ladies wristwatches, and while they have many decades ago produced ladies watches in platinum, those watches are far too small to carry an inspection anywhere near that size" (para. 14). Of course, as a fictional story, *Fifty Shades* has no reason to adorn its characters with watches that are available in real-life stores. But, on one level, fans look to find the exact model these characters wear to reflect their own emotional investment in the story or the brand. On another level, it shows how product placement can be a legitimate way to reach a large audience.

Dressed for Success

The *Fifty Shades of Grey* team hired Mark Bridges as the costume designer. Bridges is known for his involvement with *Silver Linings Playbook* (2012), *The Fighter* (2010), and *Captain Phillips* (2013). He also won an Academy Award for *The Artist* in 2012 (Scharf). According to Ocean, "Bridges kept the wool lightweight and Italian, the cuts classic, and the buttons were mainly limited to one" (para. 10). For the movie, Bridges designed most of the clothes himself, rather than utilizing existing lines of apparel (Cheng). Some of Anastasia's clothes are not original, though. The knit she wears when she first sees the Red Room of Pain is a Ralph Lauren 2013 fall flutter-sleeve top. The blue jacket she wears when Christian kisses her in the elevator is a Theysken's Theory biker jacket. The pink jacket she wears to meet Christian's family is from Zara. Princess Victoria of Sweden was also seen wearing the same jacket. Nordstrom's Brass Plum brand produced the brown leather moto jacket ("Fifty Shades of Grey Movie Fashion"). Aside from these exceptions, Bridges avoided using existing clothes so the movie would not be associated with a certain year. He comments,

> You'll sit in the theater and someone owns something from the Anthropologie, and they're like, oh my god that's Anthropologie, and I have that! But it's like a year old, it's from fall of 2013 and now its spring of 2015. If you can tell when we shot the film because of what clothes we are using, I don't dig that at all ["Fifty Shades of Grey Movie Fashion," para. 16].

Bridges also explains that a billionaire like Christian would not go out to a department store to buy a shirt or a suit. His closet should be filled with custom-made apparel.

In an interview, Bridges told Ocean that David Beckham, David Gandy, and other well-dressed international stars were the inspirations for Christian's attire (Ocean para. 10). His appearance, therefore, is "luxurious, body conscious, intimidating at first, and then comfortable" ("Fifty Shades of Grey Movie Fashion," para. 12). Bridges argues that there is an "arc" in Christian's character. At first, he is

> very buttoned-up and off putting, and as we get to know him, and as Anna gets to know him, the textures soften. The language and the choices of the clothes change. By the time he introduces her to the glider pilot and refers to her as his girlfriend, he seems like a regular guy—granted he's a billionaire, but it's sort of more normal, accessible, let-down-your-guard clothes. If you put the glider outfit next to the first time we meet him, he's softening. In a way, he said plainly [to Anastasia], you're changing me ["Fifty Shades of Grey Movie Fashion," para. 12].

As for Anastasia, she makes a transformation from the beginning to the ending of the first movie. Initially, she is shown as a college student who is not very keen on fashion. Before she leaves for Christian's office for an interview, Kate asks her, "You're wearing that?" questioning her fashion choice. Bridges characterized her outfit as "awkward." He comments:

> I always start from the feet up, so here's boots that everyone thinks is really cute, these Fiorentini + Baker boots. They're probably way more expensive than this actual girl could use, but it's the best possible reality it could be. She trips into his office, so I felt a heavy foot would be more awkward. The tights make it not super sexy in a short skirt, but the skirt was a silk skirt, so if it does move, it's pretty. Her blouse was made from [a] Liberty of London print which is kind of fuddy duddy, but we used the wrong side of the fabric, so it looks like something she got from the thrift store or used for a very long time. I made the toggle coat. I needed it to feel like a rain coat, but also [to] give the imagery of kids waiting for the bus in a toggle coat. But then everywhere you look, designers have done a riff on the toggle coat, so it feels kind of fresh, but to me it's old-fashioned. All that thought when into one outfit ["Fifty Shades of Grey" Movie Fashion," para. 7].

The designer's choices are smart. During the first encounter, Christian is immediately attracted to Anastasia. For this to be plausible, Anastasia has to look pretty and attractive, while remaining naïve. The clumsiness and old-fashioned images are well represented with the clothes Bridges chose for her. As the story develops, however, her appearance changes. Bridges explains that the change must be felt, without being noticed:

> What happens is, the fit of things gets more slick. She goes from heavy shoes to $700 flats. Everything becomes more body conscious; the peach dress feels floaty and feminine. The white shirt that she wears when she leaves him with the slick jeans and the slick shoes. It's a real departure from [the] clunky feet and flowered shirt in the beginning. If you put the picture of her at the first interview, and the picture of what she's wearing when she leaves him, it's basically, this girl is a woman now kind of thing ["Fifty Shades of Grey Movie Fashion," para. 11].

For example, when Anastasia sits down for a contract negotiation dinner with Christian, Bridges adorns her in a form-fitting dress which "leverages in her direction, because she looks so fantastic" (Cheng para. 8).

Christian is seen wearing shirts sewn by Anto Beverly Hills, each costing at least $300 (Ocean para. 11). During the contract negotiation scene, Christian wore Dunhill silver Knot and Rod cufflinks that are sold for $991. His belts, briefcases, bags, and wallet are all leather and made by Yves Saint Laurent, costing between $375 and $5,975 (Ocean para. 6). Christian's ties are also made by Anto Beverly Hills. Ocean explains that Bridges only used Prada shoes from a store because of time constraints. The list of expensive clothing continues with Christian's casual outfit. His underwear, Zimmerli boxer briefs, are a Swiss brand that cost $100 a pair. His Ralph Lauren jeans ($495), boots ($850), Malo cashmere sweaters ($289), and Dolce & Gabbana jacket ($4,195 and above) are all good examples of aspirational products. When he takes Anastasia out for gliding, he wears a $980 Bottega Veneta windbreaker and a $198 T-shirt by John Varvatos. When he wears sweats, he still wears a pair of James Perse costing $135, and a Wings + Horns hoodie costing $195 (Ocean para. 12–13). Most of what Christian wears at work is custom-made, as are Anastasia's clothes.

Bridges's involvement with the film did not allow apparel brands to place their logo in the movie very much. Even though there is a long list of pre-existing clothes that Anastasia and Christian wear, a great majority of clothes were custom-designed and custom-made. Furthermore, even the clothes that were available from stores lacked logos. Therefore, apparel is one of the few areas in which product placement was rather absent.

Fifty Shades of Branding

Despite many examples of product placement in *Fifty Shades of Grey*, Tonya Garcia believes that some brands could have been more apparent. For example, a company like Steinway & Sons could have had its corporate name shown whenever Christian played the piano. After all, the film is full of classical music. Similarly, aside from DG Flugzeugbau, no aircraft manufacturer logos appear on the screen. Even Christian's helicopter, *Charlie Tango*, is brand-less in the film.

In various forms of entertainment—from movies to television shows and even computer games—product placement has become the norm, and not a novel marketing tactic. Compared to augmented reality-based marketing, product placement is an old tactic. But it is far from how Mark Ritson mockingly characterizes the practice in his essay in *Marketing*

Week. He writes, "Apparently [the film] is all about BDSM. As I have no clue what that acronym means, I am going to assume it stands for Brands Doing Stupid Marketing" (para. 10). In reality, product placement is a way for a brand to remain culturally relevant. This is why Leon Angelo, of Audi, commented that Christian and Anastasia's lives "have become a cultural phenomenon that has attracted so many fans round the world—and what better brand than Audi to bring to life the story and this sentiment on the big screen" (Buss para. 10). A brand's image cannot be fully established and maintained with conventional advertisements and commercials alone.

As was the case with Audi in the *Fifty Shades* novel or Apple in a great number of TV shows, often the company does not even have to pay for its product to appear onscreen. Simply supplying a vehicle, a laptop (or whatever the product may be) for free will grant them a low-investment advertisement opportunity. At the same time, TV and movie makers are able to take advantage of the pre-established images and values of such brands to set the scene or create an identity. *Fifty Shades* readers and viewers may not visit an Audi dealer or an Omega seller on their way home from a theater or a book club meeting, but the use of these products reinforce their brand image while portraying Christian, Anastasia, and other characters in a positive light.

Christian Grey, without doubt, is wealthy. *Forbes* in 2013 estimated his net worth to be about $2.2 billion ("#8 Christian Grey"). Justin Ocean writes for *Bloomberg* that

> the luxury porn starts with Christian's sleek glass office and continues as little Ana from Savannah hops into a helicopter for their first date. From there, she encounters endless fine suits, high-end watches, museum-quality art, expensive sound equipment, fancy hotels, that fleet of Audis, and of course, high-end bondage gear [para. 3].

Christian's helicopter, known as *Charlie Tango*, cannot be exactly how it is described in the novel because of the aviation law in Seattle. However, his Eurocopter EC130 is estimated to be over $3 million (Ocean para. 14). A three-bedroom penthouse at Escala sold for $6.2 million in 2013 (Ocean para. 18). When Christian shows off his wealth in this way and uses it to draw Anastasia to him, one cannot help but question what Christian would be and how his relationship with Anastasia would be if he was not a billionaire.

Despite one's personal preferences, both Jamie Dornan and Dakota Johnson are attractive individuals. What the brands and signs of wealth do is to help the movie create an even dreamier, but unrealistic, world.

Stephanie Marcus opines that Christian is not the dream lover he seems to be, at least on a surface level.

> It's only Christian's extreme wealth ... that barely mask what's really just completely creepy behavior. In any other movie, a man or woman who tracks down another person at their job, local bar, home and oh, their *mother's home* in Georgia, a plane ride away, would probably end up in back of a police car [para. 3].

She goes on to say that Christian can get what he wants because of his wealth. The first-edition of *Tess of the D'Urbervilles*, a laptop, a new Audi, and other material gifts are "manipulating and controlling [Anastasia] into being with him on his terms" (para. 7). Hardy's first-edition books cost about $14,000. A night at the Heathman Hotel costs at least $329 a night. Similarly, Sancerre, Pouilly-Fumé, Hendricks, and Bombay Sapphire are not usually on the list of daily drinks for a recent college graduate who owns a flip phone. Christian's Bacarrat crystal wine glasses also cost over $100 each (Ocean para. 15–16). Would Anastasia be drawn to Christian if he was the same person with the same sexual preferences and controlling tendencies, only without wealth?

On one level, the producers' decision to integrate products and brands is a common practice and is nothing new. Its original novel included many of such products as significant parts of the story, as well. On another level, because the story is about what could be seen as a problematic relationship, it is also important to note how brands and products might have lured Anastasia, and presumably Christian's previous partners, into a particular kind of relationship. This is not to say that the *Fifty Shades* trilogy and similar works are dangerous, worthless, immoral, or unethical. But these stories provide an opportunity to challenge how one's perception about an individual or a relationship could be altered by an image associated with wealth or brands.

CHAPTER ELEVEN

The International Reception
Japan

Although *Fifty Shades of Grey* is considered an American movie, because of the location of its setting as well as the nationality of its production companies—Michael De Luca Productions and Trigger Street Productions—and its distributors, its original trilogy and their reach are international. E. L. James is a London-born British author. Stephenie Meyer, the author of *Twilight*, on which *Fifty Shades* was based, is American. Its film version was directed by Sam Taylor-Johnson, a British filmmaker. The screenplay, however, was written by Kelly Marcel, a British writer. Christian Grey is portrayed by Jamie Dornan, a Northern Irish actor.

Fifty Shades' reach is far more international than its West-dominated production team. The trilogy has been translated into over fifty languages and had sold over 125 million copies internationally (Johnson para. 5; Stedman para. 4). According to *Forbes*, James was "the highest-earning author of 2013, with an estimated income of $95 million" (Alter para. 14). During the first weekend after the international release of *Fifty Shades of Grey* right before Valentine's Day of 2015, the movie ranked number one in fifty-four territories. The weekend box-office take was $20.8 million in the U.K., $14.1 million in Germany, and $12.3 in France. Similarly, Russia recorded $11 million, Brazil $8.3 million, and Mexico $8.1 million as well (Tartaglione para. 1). Writing for *Deadline*, Nancy Tartaglione summarized:

> The film remains the biggest bow of all time in thirteen markets: Croatia, Czech Republic, Hungary, Latvia, Lithuania, Paraguay, Poland, Slovakia, Slovenia, South Africa, Ukraine, Uruguay, and Venezuela. Also for an R-rated film—or an equivalent abroad—*Fifty Shades* tours the biggest opening abroad even for an adult film, beating the previous record holder *The Matrix Revolutions* at $117M [para. 1].

These positive outcomes abroad are important for *Fifty Shades*. During the first few days, the movie made just above $80 million in the U.S., while the international figure was well above $230 million (Tartaglione para. 2).

These numbers from global markets do not mean that international readers and moviegoers always enjoyed *Fifty Shades*. They simply mean that there was hype about it, as was the case in the U.S. Furthermore, the U.S. witnessed varying degrees of enjoyment about the trilogy and the film, as well as diverse reactions, including religion-based rejections to capitalism-driven merchandizing. Consumers outside the U.S. also reacted to the trilogy in varying ways.

Why Examine Fifty Shades of Grey *in Japan?*

The way in which the Japanese market reacted to *Fifty Shades* is by no means representative of what happened in other Asian markets. Japanese fans also expressed a unique kind of criticism: namely the quality of censorship to make the film released as an R-15 film. In order to maximize the movie's exposure, Japan's movie industry created a list of censorship-related changes that had to be made so that it could be viewed by audience members of fifteen years old and above. The list was shared with the U.S. film producer. The quality of censorship—censorship bars, pixilation, and blurring—was disastrous. Japanese fans were not quiet about their dissatisfaction.

Japan also has a long history in playing an important role in the production and distribution of world's popular culture, from the so-called *otaku, ganguro,* computer games including *Pokémon,* and other youth cultures and subcultures. It is, however, also important to note that Japan represents a clash of the past and the present. Writing for the Japan Foundation, Michelle Pham stated that Japan was "a land where traditional and modern culture somehow coexist in unity" (para. 1). This is to say that, on the one hand, Japan remains highly traditional and conservative. It is not just observable through visible cultural icons, such as sumo and the Kinkakuji Temple in Kyoto, but also through intangible cultural values and beliefs. For example, the World Economic Forum's study showed that Japan ranked 104th out of 142 countries assessed on their gender equality ("Japan Remains"). The country's employment system also tends to be conservative with its adherence to lifetime employment, behavior—rather than performance-based evaluations (*Traditional Employment*). Websites for foreign visitors to Japan, such as thinkjapanblog, frequently emphasize the importance of tradition in Japanese society.

Japan can also be extremely progressive and liberal. It is particularly so when it comes to sexuality. Japan's tabloid newspapers often have a page with an erotic novel series, adult movie reviews, and/or a review of a local red-light district establishment. It is common to find a middle-aged businessman reading such a page in a commuter train without any hint of embarrassment or guilt. Others around him also do not seem to think twice about it. Next to an ATM at a convenience store exists a shelf for numerous R-rated magazines. From anime-based to online pornography, the erotic industry flourishes in Japan. It was only in 2014 that Japan banned the possession of child pornography (Hellman).

Although pornography and sexual materials tend to be more visible in public in Japan than in many Western societies, sex in this context is often consumed as a commodity by men only. It is usually men who frequent the so-called back room of a DVD-rental store. Japanese 7–11 convenience stores stock adult magazines for men, but none for female readers. Sex and women do not mix, at least in public, in Japan.

In addition, despite its omnipresence, sex is a major concern among many Japanese couples. According to a survey conducted by a condom manufacturer, Durex, in 2006, about 60 percent of Japanese couples surveyed stated that they had not had sex in a week, and only 15 percent claimed to be sexually satisfied (Goto). Similarly, according to Sagami Gomu, a Japanese condom maker, over 55 percent of marriages in Japan are sexless. But it is only less than a quarter of such couples who state they want to have more sex (Sagami Gomu). The percentage of sexless couples in Japan is much higher than, for example, the U.S. where the percentage is estimated to be about 15 percent (Parker-Pope para. 2). Sex, therefore, is a significant part of entertainment in Japan.

These characteristics of Japan's society create a unique environment where *Fifty Shades* was consumed. Unlike in France, where the movie was categorized as PG-12 by Le Centre National du Cinéma et de L'image Animée "because of the casualness with which the movie presents sadomasochism" (Denham para. 4), Japan's Film Classification and Rating Committee had the film classified as R-15 with a substantial amount of sex-related depictions blurred for censorship; the R-18+ version was released with less censorship, but at a very limited number of theaters. Despite such a restriction, numerous fans commented on the film and the trilogy online and created a rich environment for a study of this kind.

Additionally, the Japanese market has been in transition for the last decade. During this period, non–Japanese movies initially accounted for over 65 percent of its market share, or about $1.4 billion. In 2012, however, the number fell to 34.3 percent, or $689 million (Schilling para. 1). According to Ileigh Schoeff and Miho Hoshino, Japanese movies have "accounted for more box office revenue than imported films" (para. 1). Although there are fewer than half the number of movie theaters than there were in the late 1950s, the number has increased in the past twenty years. In addition, despite the industry's decline in 2011, the Japan's movie industry has grown since then ("60 Nen Amari"). This is to say that Japan's movie industry is doing relatively well, although the success of the industry has been driven mostly by domestic, rather than foreign, movies. This is a shift from the early twenty-first century.

In this context of Japan's film industry, *Fifty Shades of Grey* became a much-discussed movie well before its release in Japan in mid–February 2015. The movie's trailers, available in Japanese as well, were featured on websites a few months before the movie's release. Backed up by this fervor, it was released at over three hundred theaters across Japan on the same day as the U.S. opening, and recorded over sixty thousand viewers and about $800,000 in revenue in the first two days, ranked as the fifth-most popular movie release of that weekend. Although these numbers are smaller than those in the U.S., it was nonetheless a successful debut.

Overall Fan Reaction

As noted above, numerous media outlets had talked about *Fifty Shades of Grey* well before its release. In reality, ever since the publication of the original trilogy, many websites have discussed its popularity, both in Japan and abroad. Some of the articles discussed the film's music, especially Beyoncé's involvement, due to her popularity in Japan. Others were about the novel and movie's sexual content, as characterized by its often-used descriptor, "mommy porn." It was only natural that, driven by the hype, the movie attracted attention after its release, and numerous reviews were written by Japanese audience members and critics.

Through examining reviews available on Japanese blogs and websites, several distinct themes appear. The first is about the main characters. Expectedly, many fans voiced their satisfaction or dissatisfaction about Dakota Johnson as Anastasia Steele and Jamie Dornan as Christian Grey. Some simply liked, or did not like, these actors. Others shared their views on their acting. The second is about the gaps between the novel and the film. As is frequently the case with any film based on a novel, viewers tend to feel that the movie does not do justice to the original source. Such a review is almost a cliché. Although it may be unfair to expect a book of a few hundred pages to be condensed into a two- to two-and-a-half-hour film, many viewers of *Fifty Shades* who had read the novel agreed that the film version was not as good. The third kind of audience reviews were an almost unanimous criticism about the R-15 version of the film, with its censored images. The final type of reviews connected the message of the film to social issues. Although most reviewers agreed that the film could have done a better job portraying the psychology of the two lead characters and the intricacy of their relationship, it was acknowledged that the movie could serve as a means to discuss socially important issues, namely about what it means to exercise control in a romantic relationship and how we normalize certain sexual behaviors, including BDSM.

Generally, fans liked the film, although many agreed that it was hardly the best film of the year. It had many flaws. But reviewers tend to appreciate the movie. Many, for instance, felt that the music was successful. As noted elsewhere in this book, even those who did not like the film in the U.S. or England similarly commented that the film's soundtrack deserved proper recognition, outperforming the film itself. Japanese film critic Kuwae noted that the soundtrack was very enjoyable; she also admired the camera work, stating that the skyline of Seattle at night was very beautiful. Concurring with Kuwae, a blogger using the pseudonym Lady M characterized the film as "beautiful like a music video" (para 2). Maya also wrote that "the film did not give an impression of a filthy porn" ("Fifty Shades of Grey No," para. 3).

Johnson as Steele, and Dornan as Grey

On a superficial level, many reviews agreed that Jamie Dornan was handsome enough to justify going to see the movie or that Dakota Johnson was a more convincing actor than her co-star. Kanae wrote, "Anastasia is so beautiful. She is so cute. Her back is sexy. There is nothing to complain about her…. She is like a human version of a perfume commercial" (para. 3 and 7). "Kagehinata no Review" wrote that Johnson was able to enact Anastasia's kindness and weakness. She was also able to show happiness and a sign of sadness after hearing her mother and her fourth husband laugh because Anastasia wanted a similar relationship, rather than the one Christian was offering. In general, although this was Johnson's starring debut, she was very successful in showing the subtleties of Anastasia's psychology.

Of course, individual tastes in actors differ. Leen, one reviewer's pseudonym, wrote, "I enjoyed this movie mostly because I like Jamie Dornan" ("Fifty Shades of Grey No Review," para 1). Kanae wrote that in the first part of the movie, he looked "so hot" (para. 6). It is common for reviewers to focus on Christian's muscular back as he takes off or puts on a shirt throughout the film. As will be discussed later, in some scenes, Christian's body was blacked out almost in its entirety, much to fans' dismay.

Although many Japanese fans seem to like the looks of Dornan, many argued that his acting was not the strength of the movie. Lady M wrote that Johnson brought Ana's innocent, typical college student to life. As for Dornan, even though the actor was handsome and has a "nice body," there was no depth in his acting. She added that he "did not make her want to know more about Christian or to understand how Christian ended up the way he was" (Lady M para. 1). Another review discussed that "this kind of story is a very boring one when it fails to show why the handsome man is doing what he is doing or what exists as a part of his dark history" ("Kagehinata no Review," para 14). Although both reviewers admit that it probably was not completely the actor's fault and it might have been influenced by the original novel and the screenplay, they concluded that Dornan's acting did not do justice to Christian's complex past and personality. Lady M also noted that she did not "feel the HOT chemistry between the actors" (emphasis in original, para. 3). Writing under the pseudonym LandBLUE, one reviewer stated: "Anastasia only is facing difficult decisions because Christian is rich and handsome.... If it was the opposite, there was no way she would even consider him" ("Fifty Shades of Grey No," para. 23).

Comparing the Movie to the Novel

Comparing the movie to the first book of the trilogy and being unsatisfied with what the movie offered is not unique to Japanese fans. Neither is this unique to *Fifty Shades of Grey*. Lady M succinctly noted: "Books don't necessarily translate into movies" (para. 3). The movie's ending, for example, was very much different from that of the book. Japanese reviewers commented on the gap. For example, Kuwae noted that even though the first part of the movie was relatively loyal to the original book, the ending made those who had not read the book feel that the story was about "a strange man with money [who] had BDSM sex with a virgin" (para. 11). Zoo also wrote, "I cannot like the way the movie ended" (para.

4). Kuwae continues that the movie, unlike the book, lacked the depiction of Christian's and Anastasia's psychology. Without it, the movie was essentially "softcore pornography with no depth" (para. 12).

Another issue addressed by viewers is the film's cringe-worthy dialogue: lines adapted from the novel sound awkward when said aloud. A review on "Minna no Kuchikomi" stated, "The movie just made me laugh" (Enjoy_Cinema para. 12). Another reviewer was amused as well: "Everything that the male protagonist said and did was comedic and made me laugh. It was as comical to see the heroine who was totally mesmerized by such a man. At the end of the film, I was simply convinced that they were a perfect couple because of their comedic life" (para. 16). From the catchphrases "Laters, baby" to "I'm fifty shades of fucked-up," Christian's awkward choice of words were evident even translated into Japanese.

Numerous non–Japanese websites enumerated the differences between the film and the novel. Jessica Rawden listed fourteen disparities between the two, from Christian's purchasing of a coverall to the movie's underplaying of Christian's obsession about Anastasia's eating habits. Writing for the *Huffington Post*, Jessica Goodman wrote about ten differences; Eliza Thompson wrote about fourteen. Some of them are related to sex and sexual depictions. Others are not. But in general, fans were understanding of the need for the movie to be slightly different from the novel— rather than a boat house, for example, Anastasia and Christian visit an indoor swimming pool—and the necessity of certain cuts due to time constraints.

For Lady M, the movie, despite its R-18+ categorization in Japan, did not have as many sex scenes as she had expected, and the ones which are included are too "soft" (para. 2). She continues: "If this movie was just a common love story, beautiful love scenes like a music video would suffice. But because *Fifty Shades of Grey* is about sex, the movie did not do justice to the theme especially when the movie only showed three or four items in Christian's secret Red Room being used" (para. 2). Lady M graded the film a low 50 out of 100.

Poor Censorship Quality

One of the most common comments—or rather complaints—about the film took aim at the R-15 version of the movie. As noted earlier in this chapter, it was released both in R-15 and R-18 formats. Although both versions were censored due to the movie's sexual content, the R-15 version was, understandably, more censored than its racier counterpart. Many argue that even though the film's content was probably not suitable for high school students, fans speculate that the Japanese distributing company wanted to increase the exposure, hence making censorship efforts so the movie could be released as an R-15 work.

The presence of the R-15 and R-18 versions did not mean that fans were given choices between the two on the release day; the only option for Japanese moviegoers was the R-15 version. It was not until February 25, 2015, that six movie theaters in Tokyo showed the R-18 version due to "the requests by many women over 20 years old" (Ito para. 5).

The list of short review comments compiled by Enjoy_Cinema immediately after the release of *Fifty Shades of Grey* is filled with audience frustrations about censorship. One disgruntled reviewer wrote, "The story of the innocent protagonist who is drawn to a dangerous world is appealing. She is very cute. The actress is doing a great job but all her work is overshadowed by censorship pixilation" (para. 3). Another wrote that the movie lacked excitement and there was nothing left for audience to enjoy (para. 5). Yet another unsatisfied customer stated, "There were so many blurred scenes [that] it did not work as a movie" (para. 4). These comments, generally speaking, are not questioning the need for censorship, but the amount of it. The issue addressed time and again was how censorship interfered with the quality of the film. Numerous Tweets shared this view. Nico wrote, "I watched 'Fifty Shades of Grey' in the R-18 version. The R-18 version is way better." Hana tweeted, "I watched *Fifty Shades of Grey* in the R-18 version, without black censorship bars. It was beautiful."

"Kagehinata no Review" also noticed that sometimes the film used black censorship bars while, at other times, it had more translucent blurs. The reviewer wrote, "They must have tried to make the movie an R-15 film so they could invite more audience [members]. But there must have been a better way to censor this film" (para. 4). That reviewer also admitted to having laughed out loud during the screening because of the black circles that suddenly appear on the screen, in three separate instances covering up more than a half the image. One such scene offered a glimpse of Anastasia's pubic hair as the camera focused on the lower half of her body. Another instance, when Anastasia has sex for the first time, about 60 percent of the screen is blacked out. The last is Christian's entire body being blacked out.

Even the reviews that praise the movie are highly critical of such techniques. One frustrated individual commented, "All was good until the two characters started being sexually intimate. But after that, everything collapsed [because of the blurred image]" (Enjoy_Cinema para. 20). Another concurred: "There are many scenes that made no sense because of the blurs but the scenes that are not blurred are actually very good" (Enjoy_Cinema para. 28). One metaphorically gifted writer summed up the viewing experience this way: "It was nothing but a gag comedy that the main character inserts [his penis into] the giant censorship black hole" (Enjoy_Cinema para. 18).

While some movies have depictions of sex as non-essential parts of the main story, for *Fifty Shades of Grey*, sex is indeed significant. "Eiga no Kansou" comments:

> [This] is a love story between a handsome guy who likes S&M and a cute college girl. It is originally an adult fiction. So sex scenes are vital. You cannot remove them. But they want many people to see the movie. I don't personally think high school students should be able to see it, but I think they wanted them too. It is nothing but a comedy that rather than using translucent pixilation, they blacked out parts of the movie....
>
> In the first part of the movie, because the room on the screen was dark, you could live with awkwardness of half of the screen blacked out.... But as the depiction of sexual acts got more and more hardcore, the play room had more light. So when the main character whipped [Anastasia] in a well-lit play room, the blacked out parts are more than just annoying. They are almost comedic. There is a scene in which [Christian] disappears into a large black area in the middle of the screen and his arm begins to grow out of it....
> Here comes the black hole as [Christian] unzips his pants.
> Here comes the black hole between two legs on the bed.
> Here comes the black hole dancing between two characters.
> It is a torture not to laugh when you are shown so many black holes [Manabu para. 13–19].

These critical views can be summarized by one short comment left by an anonymous reviewer: "What is the Japanese distributing company doing by showing a movie in which a whole character is blurred?" (Enjoy_Cinema para. 46). Another reviewer also commented that, in one scene during which Anastasia's entire body was blurred, he could not even contextualize the scene to the rest of the film (Enjoy_Cinema para. 52).

Ito, however, explains that Japan's Film Classification and Rating Committee was not actually responsible for the poor censorship work. The U.S. distributor contacted the committee and asked what needed to be done to release it as an R-15 film. In response, the committee simply created a list of adjustments for the request to be fulfilled. Ito speculates that the U.S. filmmakers were afraid that either the movie would be changed by a third-party entity or the content of the movie—a highly anticipated one well before its release—to be leaked. Based on the feedback from the Film Classification and Rating Committee, the American production company censored the film for the Japanese market. Ito concludes that the only positive outcome of the "censorship controversy" was that it revealed that Japan's censorship technique would not have interfered with the quality or the integrity of the film. The fact that fans were critical of *how* censorship happened and not *that* it happened makes a good contrast to the censorship debate in the U.S., as discussed in Chapter Four.

Japanese Popular Culture

Popular culture never exists in a vacuum. When it is consumed, it is consumed in its context. Both positive and negative views on a text, therefore, are contingent upon their surroundings. Just as there were many mixed reviews in the U.S. and the U.K.—the largest market and the home country of the trilogy, respectively—Japanese reviews were mixed. Reasons for these positive and negative views underscore experiences in each society. Of course, some reviews are rather general. It is common for viewers to say that a film made them think. One reviewer, for example, simply said, "The ending of the film was shocking and made me deeply think about the relationship between the two characters" (Enjoy_Cinema para. 35). Another reviewer agreed with a comment captured by a study conducted by Bonomi et al., by questioning who was truly in control of the relationship. In the study, several subjects implicated Anastasia in what the authors called a problematic relationship. In other words, Anastasia was controlling Christian, more than the other way around. As "Minna no Kuchikomi" writes:

> In fact, in any relationship, the closer [a] relationship you have with your partner, the more diverse it gets [concerning] what you like and what you seek. Nobody can say where "normal" ends and where "abnormal" starts. Even in this case [between Anastasia and Christian], it makes you wonder who is actually in charge [Enjoy_Cinema para. 42].

Yasuko, apparently sharing a widely held view, also asked in her review, "Who really was in control?" ("Fifty Shades of Grey No," para. 11). Others felt that the protagonists were truly in love. Christian, of course, had said, "I don't do the girlfriend thing" (James 47). But one reviewer argues that Christian's confusion when he learned Anastasia was a virgin was moving and touching, as well as a sign of his caring for her. ("Fifty Shades of Grey No," para. 2).

Although Christian's behavior is problematic, some Japanese viewers were attracted to his dominating personality. Critics argue that this was because Japan lacks aggressive men. Amy Chaves writes:

> My Japanese girlfriends complain that there are no interesting guys out there. Could they be right? It seems that these days the average Japanese guy is, well, you know, kinda boring. Kinda quiet. Nothing wrong with being quiet of course, especially if you have nothing to say.
>
> The Japanese media has coined these men "herbivores" or "grass-eaters." ... They are non-competitive, concentrate on personal grooming (yay!), are frugal, and lack an interest in sex. Now, I am totally for the quiet contemplative, sensitive type. Frugal? Okay. But no sex? Sex is free [para. 1–2].

Furthermore, both single and married Japanese men reportedly lack interest in sex. Media outlets attribute this to the men's so-called "pandafi-cation." Yuzukibuka explains that panda bears are in heat for only three to seven days during a period of three to six months. Japanese men are not much different (para. 8). Additionally, Japanese workers' long working hours, small houses and apartments where privacy is difficult to secure, and the fear of pregnancy in a country where raising a child is not always affordable all contribute to a lack of sex. In this context, Futamatsu argues that Christian's strong drive and controlling nature appears very attractive to many Japanese women. Christian, in other words, represents the car-nivorous man Japanese women find unattainable.

Futamatsu continues to explain that many women's hearts are lit when a handsome man like Christian whispers something sweet in their ear. She enumerates six reasons why Christian may appeal to many Japa-nese women. The first is the typical Cinderella-type storyline. Anastasia, who is described as a regular college student, finds a very handsome, very rich man. Second, although the story is unrealistic, the abundance of sex is enough to enjoy the story. Third, the sex is not mundane. They have sex in a boat house, in the Red Room of Pain, on the couch, and so on. Fourth, many female readers identify with Anastasia and experience her sense of guilt and pleasure. Fifth, the story shows its readers a new world. For many Japanese married women, dildos, clamps, duct-tape, and other such items are taboo, giving them a sense of excitement. Finally, Futamatsu states that the story is just plain sexy.

Put in contrast with the perspective analyzed in the work by Bonomi et al., Futamatsu's analysis can be seen problematic: women's sexual agency is ignored. Instead, women are portrayed as passive participants in men's sexual behaviors. At the same time, there is a strong interest among women to be more sexually active. In addition, Futamatsu's essay reflects Japan's relative lack of awareness about relationship violence.

These three themes—lack of recognition about women's sexual agency, the presence of women's interest in sex, and low awareness about relationship violence—allow us to connect *Fifty Shades* to larger social issues in Japan.

As noted above, Japan is a traditional society in which women are expected to be sexually reserved. For example, Seishin Girls High School in Yokohama Prefecture on its website states that women have been stereotyped as sexually passive. Shuichi Fujita also makes the point that women in Japan are culturally taught to be passive about their sexuality. Although stereotyping female sexuality as negative is not unique to the Japanese society, women in Japan who have been brought up with such cultural messages tend to empathize with Anastasia, who is naïve about her own sexuality and who takes a passive role, especially in the first movie's early scenes.

Of course, just because women in Japan are taught to be subdued about their sexuality does not mean they are asexual. After all, a traditional society like that of Japan is not immune to change. Universal Studios' Japanese promotional website for the film comments that Japanese women are drawn to the love in the world of *Fifty Shades* ("Fifty Shades of Grey" Universal). Although studies have shown that professional responsibilities, housework, and other external factors contribute to a sexless state, many women express their innate desire for an active personal life. An office worker in Tokyo in her early thirties responded to an interview published in *Nikkan Spa!* by saying, "I know it is fiction. But I cannot help but think I wish it was true…. Now that I'm in my thirties, I want more fulfilling sex than I did in my twenties." Other respondents in their thirties agreed with her and generally underscored their rarely expressed sexual desire. *Fifty Shades* provides Japanese women with an opportunity to explore and express their sexual desires, serving as an example of popular culture assisting and mirroring the process of social change. But as Futamatsu's analysis revealed, few people in Japan critically examined the relationship between Christian and Anastasia. It was rare for Japanese reviewers to pose a question if their relationship is healthy. Instead, a great majority of reviews romanticized their relationship. As noted earlier in this book, it is partly because the film's music characterizes the connection between the two characters in a positive light. But as for Japanese perceptions, it is also because there is less awareness about relationship violence in the country.

Typically, discussions on relationship violence focus on domestic violence, or violence within a family. It may involve parents abusing their children, adult children abusing their elderly parents, or a spouse abusing his or her partner. Either way, there is far less awareness about non-marital relationship violence, including date rape. This is particularly troublesome. Shiori Ino, a college student at the time, was murdered after she and her family made repeated reports to the police about harassments from her stalker and his peers. This high-profile incident, which took place in 1999, revealed the law enforcement's lackadaisical attitude about stalking and a general tendency to blame the victim. Although Ino's death made the term "stalking" known in Japan, gender-based violence continues to be discussed in the context of domestic violence.

The Gender Equity Bureau of Japan's Cabinet Office, for example, regularly releases reports about gender discrimination and violence. Out of the sixteen reports posted on its website, fifteen deal with Japanese cases—the other examines an incident in East Asia. Out of these fifteen, only four deal with non-domestic gender violence. This relatively low awareness about relationship violence may explain Japanese viewers' positive response to Christian. A blogger using the pseudonym of leira3mitz37 characterized Christian as "stalkerish," but never called his behaviors—showing up at Anastasia's work, tracking her location, flying to Georgia uninvited, just to name a few—stalking (para. 4). Another reviewer, Melou, wrote, "Christian is a control freak and has a stalking tendency, but he is sincere and deeply loves Anastasia" (para. 1). Melou is not alone in minimizing Christian's stalking behaviors; it is even characterized as a sign of his love and affection.

Fifty Shades *and Popular Culture*

The way in which Japanese fans reacted to *Fifty Shades of Grey* was not necessarily unique. Similar reactions—both positive and negative—were shared in other parts of Asia, as well as in the West. But exploring Japanese reviews reveals similarities and differences in different societies. Comments about the two lead actors and their believability, for example, are common both inside and outside Japan. But the film suffered from censorship, something to which the film was not subjected in the U.S. It interfered with the quality of the film, and, ultimately, the enjoyment of the Japanese viewers. A simple comparison of this kind shows that even an international popular culture icon like *Fifty Shades* can suffer from local regulations and restrictions. In addition, and probably more significantly, the trilogy and its film adaptations serve to examine Japan's view on female sexuality as taboo. In this unique context, *Fifty Shades* gave many women an opportunity to publicly express their sexual desires.

Popular culture, as a form of entertainment, does not necessarily bear the responsibility to educate the public about important issues, including date rape. But it does help us better understand the context in which it is consumed when we explore how it is received in a particular society.

Bibliography

Ackman, Dan. "How Big Is Porn?" Forbes Media, 25 May 2001. Web. 25 Aug. 2016.

Adams-Curtis, Leah E., and Gordon B. Forbes. "College Women's Experiences of Sexual Coercion: A Review of Cultural, Perpetrator, Victim, and Situational Variables." *Trauma, Violence, & Abuse* 5.2 (2004): 91–122. Web. *Sage*. 8 Dec. 2015.

Adams, Mark. "'Fifty Shades of Grey' Jumps from Book Clubs to a Nearby Brothel." *Las Vegas Weekly*, 12 Feb. 2015. Web. 3 Aug. 2016.

admin_planb. "Symbols, Sales, and Sado-Masochism: 50 Shades of Grey & Audi's Increased Revenue." SociaLogic Marketing, 15 Aug. 2012. Web. 7 Mar. 2016.

"Affirm the Freedom to Read During the Banned Books Week, Sept. 21–27, 2014." *Plus Media Solutions*, 24 Sep. 2014. *LexisNexis*. Web. 8 July 2015.

Alpers, Paul. "Lycidas and Modern Criticism." *English Literary History* 49.2 (1982): 468–496. Print.

Alter, Alexandra. "'Fifty Shades' Fan Fiction Assumes a Life of Its Own." *New York Times*, 19 June 2015. Web. 2 Aug. 2016.

"American Women Use Book Club Membership in Dating Field." The University of Kansas, 24 Aug. 2015. Web. 3 Aug. 2016.

Anderson, Benedict. *Imagined Communities: Reflections on the Origin and Spread of Nationalism*. New York: Verso, 2006. Print.

Anderson, Kyle. "'Fifty Shades of Grey' Mention Spikes Sales for 16th-Century Classical Composer." *Entertainment Weekly*, 16 July 2012. Web. 16 July 2016.

Andrews, David. "Toward a More Valid Definitions of 'Pornography.'" *The Journal of Popular Culture* 45.3 (2012): 457–477. Print.

Angelowicz, Ami. "5 Crimes Inspired by *Fifty Shades of Grey*." Crime Feed, 13 Feb. 2015. Web. 10 Aug. 2015.

"Are These the Sickest Baby Clothes Ever? Parents Celebrate the *Fifty Shades of Grey Children*." *Daily Mail*, 5 Nov. 2012. Web. 7 Apr. 2015.

Arndt, William B., John C. Foehl, and F. Elaine Good. "Specific Sexual Fantasy Themes: A Multidimensional Study." *Journal of Personality and Social Psychology* 48.2 (1985): 472–480. Web. *ProQuest*. 21 Dec. 2015.

Associated Press. "Miller Explains 'Brokeback' Call: He Canceled Move Due to Concern Over Breakup of Families." *Desert News*, 6 Apr. 2006. Web. 27 July 2016.

Atlas, James. "Really? You're Not in a Book Club?" *New York Times*, 22 Mar. 2014. Web. 3 Aug. 2016.

Attwood, Feona, and Caroline Walters. "*Fifty Shades* and the Law: Regulating Sex and Sex Media in the U.K." *Sexualities* 16.8 (2013): 974–979. *Sage*. Web. 28 Mar. 2015.

"Audi AG: New Record Year with Over 1.74 Million Deliveries in 2014." Audi of America, 9 Jan. 2015. Web. 7 Apr. 2016.

"Audi Partners with Universal Pictures for Film Adaptation of 'Fifty Shades of Grey.'" Audi of America, 14 Nov. 2014. Web. 7 Apr. 2016.

AyeltsHayley. "My Mom Reads 50 Shades of Grey?!" YouTube, 2 Sep. 2012. Web. 7 Apr. 2015.

Baelo-Allué, Sonia. "From *Twilight* to *Fifty Shades of Grey*: Fan Fiction, Commercial Culture and Grassroots Creativity." In *The Twilight Saga: Exploring the Global Phenomenon*, ed. Claudia Bucciferro. Lanham, MD: Scarecrow Press, 2013. Print.

Baker, Meg. "Consent is a Grey Area?: A Comparison of Understandings of Consent in *Fifty Shades of Grey* and on the BDSM Blogosophere." *Sexualities* 16.8 (2013): 896–914. Web. *Sage*. 28 Mar. 2015.

Balasubramanian, Siva K. "Beyond Advertising and Publicity: Hybrid Messages and Public Policy Issues." *Journal of Advertising* 23.4 (1994): 29–46. Print.

Balson, Ronald H. "Bestseller Success Stories that Started Out as Self-published Books." *Huffington Post*, 8 Oct. 2013. Web. 9 Apr. 2015.

Barna. "The Books Americans Are Reading." *Barna Group*, 13 June 2013. Web. 9 Dec. 2015.

Bartkowiak, Mathew, and Yuya Kiuchi. *The Music of Counterculture Cinema: A Critical Study of 1960s and 1970s Soundtracks*. Jefferson, NC: McFarland, 2015. Print.

Beggs, Alex. "*Fifty Shades of Grey* Wine, Reviewed." *Vanity Fair*, 12 Jan. 2015. Web. 18 Jan. 2016.

Behm-Morawitz, Elizabeth, Melissa A. Click, and Jennifer Stevens Aubrey. "Relating to Twilight: Fans' Responses to Love and Romance in the Vampire Franchise." In *Bitten by Twilight: Youth Culture, Media, and the Vampire Franchise*, ed. Melissa A. Click, Jennifer Stevens Aubrey, and Elizabeth Behm-Morawitz. New York: Peter Lang Publishing, 2010. Print.

Belmont, Cynthia. "Claiming Queer Space in/as Nature: An Ecofeminist Reading of Secretary." *Interdisciplinary Studies in Literature and Environment* 19.2 (2012): 317–335. Print.

Bender, Kelli, and Alex Heigl . "How Does *Fifty Shades of Grey* Compare to Other Film's Sex-to-Runtime?" *People*, 15 Feb. 2015. Web. 15 July 2016.

Bentley, Paul. "'Mummy Porn' *Fifty Shades of Grey* Outstrips Harry Potter to Become the Fastest Selling Paperback of All Time." *The Daily Mail*. Associated Newspapers, 17 June 2012. Web. 29 Mar. 2015.

Bixby, Scott. "The 13 Most Ridiculous, Insipid, No-Good, Terrible Passages from 'Fifty Shades of Grey.'" *Mic*, 7 Feb. 2015. Web. 10 May 2015.

Blumenthal, Ralph. "Porno Chic: 'Hardcore' Grows Fashionable and Very Profitable." *New York Times*, 21 Jan. 1973. Web. 7 Apr. 2015.

Bodnick, Marc. "Will Public Libraries Become Extinct?" *Forbes*, 2 Oct. 2012. Web. 6 Aug. 2015.

Bonomi, Amy, Emily M. Nichols, Christin L. Carotta, Yuya Kiuchi, and Samantha Perry. "Young Women's Perceptions of the Relationship in *Fifty Shades of Grey*." *Journal of Women's Health* 25.2 (2015): 139–148. Web. 3 Dec. 2015.

Bonomi, Amy, Lauren E. Altenburger, and Nicole L. Walton. "'Double Crap!' Abuse and Harmed Identity in *Fifty Shades of Grey*." *Journal of Women's Health* 22.9 (2013): 733–744. Print.

Boone, John. "All the 'Fifty Shades of Grey' Sex Scenes by the Numbers." *ETOnline*. CBS Studios, 12 Feb. 2015. Web. 15 July 2016.

Bosman, Julie. "Discreetly Digital, Erotic Novel Sets American Women Abuzz." *New York Times*, 9 Mar. 2012. Web. 29 Apr. 2015.

_____. "For 'Fifty Shades of Grey,'" More than 100 Million Sold." *New York Times*, 26 Feb. 2014. Web. 29 Mar. 2015.

_____. "Libraries Debate Stocking 'Shades.'" *New York Times*. 22 May 2012. *LexisNexis*. Web. 8 July 2015.

Bowker. "Who's Really Reading *50 Shades*?" *Bowker*. n.d. *ProQuest*. Web. 25 Mar. 2015.

Boyle, Karen. *Everyday Pornography*. New York: Routledge, 2010. Print.

"Brands in *Fifty Shades of Grey*." Concave Brand Tracking, 23 Feb. 2015. Web. 7 Mar. 2016.

Brennan, Joseph, and David Large. "'Let's Get a Bit of Context': *Fifty Shades* and the Phenomenon of 'Pulling to Publish' in *Twilight* Fan Fiction." *Media International Australia* 152.1 (Aug. 2014): 27–39. Web. *Sage*. 15 July 2016.

Brevet, Brad. "2015 Box Office Totals a Record of $11 Billion." *Box Office Mojo*. IMDb, 30 Dec. 2015. Web. 12 Jan. 2016.

Briscoe, Tony, and John Keilman. "Ex-high

School Water Polo Player: I Was Sexually Assaulted During Game." *Chicago Tribune*, 25 July 2016. Web. 25 July 2016.

Brown, Helen. "50 Shades of Grey Soundtrack, Review: 'Better for washing sheets than being tied up in them.'" *Telegraph*, 10 Feb. 2015. Web. 2 Apr. 2015.

Burger, Pamela. "Women's Groups and the Rise of the Book Club." *JSTOR Daily*, 12 Aug. 2015. Web. 3 Aug. 2016.

Burgess, O'Jay. "Billboard Charts Top 5 Classical Music Albums." *Classicalite*, 23 Oct. 2012. Web. 17 Jan. 2016.

Busby, Karen. "*Every Breath You Take*: Erotic Asphyxiation, Vengeful Wives, and Other Enduring Myths in Spousal Sexual Assault Prosecutions." *Social Science Research Network*. n.p., 15 June 2012. Web. 22 Aug. 2016.

Buss, Dale. "Audi Extends 'Fifty Shades of Grey' Tie-in to Movie Product Placement." *BrandChannel*, 17 Nov. 2014. Web. 7 Mar. 2016.

Busse, Kristina, and Karen Hellekson, eds. *Fan Fiction and Fan Communities in the Age of the Internet: New Essays.* Jefferson, NC: McFarland, 2006. Print.

Buxton, Ryan. "BDSM Experts Critique 'Fifty Shades of Grey': What It Gets Right and Wrong about BDSM." *Huffington Post*, 11 Feb. 2105. Web. 1 Dec. 2015.

Carlin, Shannon. "Every Song on the 'Fifty Shades of Grey' Soundtrack, Ranked by Sexiness." *Radio.com*. WordPress, 10 Feb. 2015. Web. 10 Apr. 2015.

Caulfield, Keith. "Adele's '25' Rules as Nielsen Music's Top Album of 2015 in U.S." *Billboard*, 5 Jan. 2016. Web. 17 Jan. 2016.

_____. "Billboard 200 Chart Moves: 'Fifty Shades' Album Whips Past Half-Million in Sales." *Billboard*, 27 Mar. 2015. Web. 7 Apr. 2015.

_____. "Drake's Surprise Album Debuts at No. 1 on Billboard 200." *Billboard*, 18 Feb. 2015. Web. 7 Apr. 2015.

Cavicchi, Daniel. "Fandom Before 'Fan': Shaping the History of Enthusiastic Audiences." *Reception: Texts, Readers, and Audiences, History* 6 (2004): 52–72. Print.

Chaves, Amy. "Herbivorous Men, Where's the Beef?" *The Japan Times*, 17 Dec. 2011. Web. 15 July 2016.

Cheng, Andrea. "Everything You Need to Know about Anastasia Steele's Outfits in Fifty Shades of Grey." *InStyle*, 9 Feb. 2015. Web. 19 Sep. 2016.

Christian, Scott. "10 Reasons Why You Should Quit Watching Porn." *GQ.* Condé Nast, n.d. Web. 27 July 2015.

Clark, Roy Peter. "What Writers Can Unlearn from 'Fifty Shades of Grey.'" *The Poynter Institute*, 24 Nov. 2014. Web. 10 May 2015.

Clarke, Suzan. "Florida County Library Lifts Ban on '50 Shades of Grey.'" *ABC News*, 30 May 2012. Web. 6 Aug. 2015.

Cochrane, Kira. "Stephenie Meyer on Twilight, Feminism and True Love." *The Guardian*, 11 Mar. 2013. Web. 25 Apr. 2015.

Cohen, Stanley. *Folk Devils and Moral Panics.* New York: Routledge, 1972, 2002. Print.

Connolly, Pamela, H. "Psychological Functioning of Bondage/Domination/Sado-Masochism (BDSM) Practitioners." *Journal of Psychology & Human Sexuality* 18.1 (2006): 79–120. Web. *Taylor & Francis Online.* 1 Dec. 2015.

Considine, Austin. "A Satirist Goes for None-Too-Subtle Shading." *New York Times*, 2 May 2012. Web. 5 Aug. 2016.

Coppa, Francesca. "A Brief History of Media Fandom." In *Fan Fiction and Fan Communities in the Age of the Internet: New Essays,* ed. Karen Hellekson and Kristina Busse. Jefferson, NC: McFarland, 2006. Print.

Copsey, Rob. "Ellie Goulding's Love Me Like You Do Breaks Worldwide Streaming Record." *Official UK Charts Company*, 19 Feb. 2015. Web. 9 Apr. 2015.

Coscia, Michele. "Competition and Success in the Meme Pool: A Case Study on Quickmeme.com." Michelecoscia.com. n.p., n.d. Web. 15 Aug. 2016.

Covet Lounge. "Feel the Passion in the *Fifty Shades*" Design Set." *Covet Lounge*, n.d. Web. 14 Apr. 2016.

Cowley, Elizabeth, and Chris Barron. "When Products Placement Goes Wrong: The Effects of Program Liking and Placement Prominence." *Journal of Advertising* 37.1 (2009): 89–98. *JSTOR.* Web. 7 Mar. 2016.

Critelli, Joseph W., and Jenny M. Bivona. "Women's Erotic Rape Fantasies: An Evaluation of Theory and Research." *The Journal of Sexual Research* 45.1 (2008): 57–70. Web. *Taylor & Francis Online.* 9 Dec. 2015.

Crothers, Lane. *Globalization & American Popular Culture.* Lanham, MD: Rowman & Littlefield, 2013. Print.

Crouch, Rachel. "Fanfiction and Fanart: The World Beyond *Fifty Shades of Grey.*" *The Mary Sue,* 1 Dec. 2015. Web. 2 Aug. 2016.

Cunningham, Todd. "'Fifty Shades of Grey' Sex Toy Sales Bulging and Universal Is Not Turned On." *The Wrap News,* 5 Feb. 2015. Web. 2 Apr. 2015.

Damon, Will. "Dominance, Sexism, and Inadequacy." *Journal of Psychology & Human Sexuality* 14.4 (2003): 25–45. Web. *Taylor & Francis Online.* 1 Dec. 2015.

"Danny Elfman: Awards." *IMDb,* n.d. Web. 13 Apr. 2015.

d'Astous, Alain, and Chemsi Berrada . "Communication Strategies to Enhance the Effectiveness of Product Placement in Movies: The Case of Comparative Apparel." *International Journal of Arts Management* 14.1 (2011): 45–55. *JSTOR.* Web. 7 Mar. 2016.

Dawkins, Richard. *The Selfish Gene.* New York: Oxford University Press, 1976. Print.

Deahl, Rachel. "E.L. James: PW's Publishing Person of the Year." *Publishers Weekly,* 30 Nov. 2012. Web. 25 Apr. 2015.

_____. "The 'Fifty Shades' Tail: How Long, and Far, Will It Stretch?" *Publishers Weekly.* 259.33 (2012). *ProQuest.* Web. 8 July 2015.

DeBord, Matthew. "It Makes Perfect Sense that Kinky Billionaire Christian Grey Drives an Audi." *Business Insider,* 16 Feb. 2015. Web. 7 Apr. 2016.

de Certeau, Michel. *The Practice of Everyday Life.* Berkley, CA: University of California Press, 1984. Print.

De Lacey, "'It's Not Even Sexy!: E.L. James' Fifty Shades of Grey Dismissed as 'Terribly Badly Written' by Novelist Barbara Taylor Bradford." *Daily Mail.* Daily Mail, 17 June 2013. Web. 27 July 2015.

Deller, Ruth A., Sarah Harman, and Bethan Jones. "Introduction to the Special Issue: Reading the *Fifty Shades* 'Phenomenon.'" *Sexualities* 16.8 (2013): 859–863.

Demarest, Erica. "Not Enough Evidence Against UIC Student in 'Shades of Grey' Case: Judge." *DNAInfo Radio,* 19 Mar. 2015. Web. 10 Aug. 2015.

Denham, Jess. "Fifty Shades of Grey Movie Only Gets a '12' Rating in French Cinemas." *Independent,* 12 Feb. 2015. Web. 30 June 2016.

Denison, Jim. "3 Reasons You Must Not See 'Fifty Shades of Grey.'" *The Christian Post,* 14 Feb. 2015. Web. 27 July 2015.

Derecho, Abigail. "Archontic Literature: A Definition, A History, and Several Theories of Fan Fiction." In *Fan Fiction and Fan Communities in the Age of the Internet: New Essays,* ed. Karen Hellekson and Kristina Busse. Jefferson, NC: McFarland, 2006. Print.

Dines, Gail. "Putting the Text in Context: What is Pornography Really About?" *Off Our Backs* 37.1: 56–57. *JSTOR.* Web. 10 Aug. 2015.

"Dr. Cox on Regeneration." *The Millennial Harbinger. LexisNexis.* Web. 13 Oct. 2015.

Doll, Jenn. "Is 'Fifty Shades of Grey' Bad for Teenage Girls?" *The Atlantic Monthly,* 12 July 2012. Web. 31 Mar. 2015.

dsio. "Omega in *Fifty Shades of Grey.*" *Omega Forums.* n.p., 20 July 2012. Web. 3 June 2016.

Duckett, Jodi. "Revisit 'Fifty Shades' in Sexy, Funny, 'Spank!!'" *Tribune Business News.* 15 Mar 2013. *ProQuest.* Web. 30 Mar. 2015.

Edington, Melissa. "A Plea for Christians to Decide Now Not to Watch 50 Shades of Grey." *Your Mom Has a Blog.* n.p., 19 June 2014. Web. 27 July 2015.

"8 Ways 50 Shades of Grey Amps up the Romance." *Cafemom.* CIM Marketing, n.d. Web. 3 June 2015.

"Ellie Goulding Sang at Royal Wedding." *MTV.* Viacom International, 30 Apr. 2011. Web. 9 Apr. 2015.

Erlewine, Stephen Thomas. "AllMusic Review." *AllMusic,* Web. 17 Jan. 2016.

Eveleth, Rose. "Americans Are More into BDSM Than the Rest of the World." *Smithsonian.com,* 10 Feb. 2014. Web. 1 Dec. 2015.

Faharty, Allanah. "Immerse Yourself in This Sexy Fifty Shades of Grey Fan Fiction!" *Movie Plot*, 13 Feb. 2015. Web. 2 Aug. 2016.

Falcon, Karen. "OPI Fifty Shades of Grey, the Limited-Edition Collection Swatched." *Beautygeeks*, 12 Dec. 2014. Web. 3 Mar. 2016.

"Fans not Joyous over Hunnam, Johnson for '50 Shades.'" *Telegram & Gazette.* 4 Sep. 2013. *ProQuest.* Web. 2 Apr. 2015.

Farber, Jim. "Album Review: 'Fifty Shades of Grey' Features Beyoncé, Sia, Ellie Goulding and Jesse Ware Singing of S&M and Bondage." *NYDailyNews*, 3 Feb. 2015. Web. 10 Apr. 2015.

Feldscher, Kyle. "Feds Say Michigan State Had a 'Sexually Hostile Environment' for Students and Staff." *MLive*, 1 Sep. 2015. Web. 16 Aug. 2016.

"Fifty Shades—Dakota Johnson Featurette." *YouTube*, n.d. Web. 29 June 2015.

"Fifty Shades of Censorship?" *Newsletter on Intellectual Freedom* 61.4 (2012): 145, 147–148. Print.

"50 Shades of Domestic Abuse." *50 Shades of Domestic Abuse.* n.p., n.d. Web. 24 July 2016.

"*Fifty Shades of Grey.*" *Belfast Telegraph Online*. 31 Mar. 2015. *LexisNexis.* Web. 10 Aug. 2015.

"Fifty Shades of Grey." *Box Office Mojo.* IMDb, n.d. Web. 12 Jan. 2016.

"Fifty Shades of Grey." *Fifty Shades of Grey Wine*, n.d. Web. 17 Jan. 2016.

"*Fifty Shades of Grey.*" *Peers Hardy Group*, n.d. Web. 19 Jan. 2016.

"Fifty Shades of Grey." *Universal Studio*, n.d. Web. 15 July 2016.

"*Fifty Shades of Grey* Accessories." *Bluebella*, n.d. Web. 21 Jan. 2016.

"Fifty Shades of Grey by E.L. James." *PrincetonBookReview.com*, n.d. Web. 3 Aug. 2016.

"Fifty Shades of Grey: CCTV Captures Couple Having Sex in Erotic Museum at Film-Inspired Event." *Mirror*, 7 Mar. 2015. Web. 10 Aug. 2015.

"'Fifty Shades of Grey' Classical Album Coming in August." *Billboard*, 7 Aug. 2012. Web. 17 Jan. 2016.

"Fifty Shades of Grey Come Alive Pleasure Gel for Her, 30ml." *Bluebella*, n.d. Web. 5 Mar. 2016.

"50 Shades of Grey: Danny Elfman on Composing the Score." *Telegraph*, 13 Feb. 2015. Web. 26. July 2016.

"'Fifty Shades of Grey' Draws Male Fans: Tale of Sand M and Bondage Appeals to More Than Just Women." *NYDailyNews*, 27 Apr. 2012. Web. 25 Mar 2015.

"*Fifty Shades of Grey* Expansion Pack Card Game." *Amazon*, n.d. Web. 17 Jan. 2016.

"*Fifty Shades of Grey* Fine Jewelry. *Cadsawan Jewelry*, n.d. Web. 19 Jan. 2016.

"Fifty Shades of Grey (James)." *LitLovers*, n.d. Web. 3 Aug. 2016.

"Fifty Shades of Grey Movie Faison: What Anastasia Wore." *On Screen Style*, n.d. Web. 19 Sep. 2016.

"Fifty Shades of Grey No Review." *Eiga.com*, n.d. Web. 8 June 2016.

"*Fifty Shades of Grey* Official Pleasure Collection Launching in U.S." *50 Shades Movie Fansite.* WordPress, 6 Mar. 2013. Web. 19 Jan. 2016.

"*Fifty Shades of Grey* Party Board Game." *Amazon*, n.d. Web. 17 Jan. 2016.

"*50 Shades of Grey* Party Board Game is More Fun with Sarah Heyward." *Huffington Post*, Web. 19 Jan. 2016.

"'50 Shades of Grey' Products for Kids." *BuzzFeed*, 4 Nov. 2012. Web. 3 Mar. 2016.

"Fifty Shades of KappAhl." *KappAhl*, n.d. Web. 21 Jan. 2016.

"Fifty Shades of Pleasure Revealed." *Fine Horse Productions.* n.p., n.d. Web. 9 Apr. 2016.

Firger, Jessica. "With 'Fifty Shades of Grey,' BDSM Goes Mainstream." *CBS News*, 13 Feb. 2015. Web. 25 Mar. 2015.

Fishelov, David. *Metaphors of Genre: The Role of Analogies in Genre Theory*. University Park, PA: Pennsylvania State University Press, 1993. Print.

Flood, Alison. "American Library Association Releases its 10 Most Challenged Books of 2013." *The Guardian*, 14 Apr. 2014. *LexisNexis.* Web. 8 July 2015.

Ford, Luke. *A History of X: 100 Years of Sex in Film.* Westminster, MD: Prometheus Books, 1999. Print.

Fowler, Tara. "Jamie Dornan Hopes *Fifty Shades of Grey* Will Spice Up Your Sex

Life." *People*, 12 Feb. 2015. Web. 25 July 2016.

Friedel, Reva. "'Why I Will Not Read or Watch 'Fifty Shades of Grey.'" *The AP Party*, 12 Feb. 2015. Web. 27 July 2015.

Friedman, Jaclyn. "Adults Hate 'Yes Means Yes' Laws: The College Students I Meet Love Them." *Washington Post*, 14 Oct. 2015. Web. 3 Dec. 2015.

Fuchs, Barbara. *Romance*. New York: Routledge, 2004. Print.

Fujita, Shuichi. "Seiyakuwari no Juyousei to Joseizou ni Kansuru Kenkyu [Study on Passive Sexual Roles and Image of Womanhood]." *Josai Daigaku*, n.d. Web. 15 July 2016.

Futamatsu, Mayumi. "Mommy Porno de Shitakunaru Tsuma Zoukachu [An Increasing Number of Wives Are Hornier Because of Mommy Porn]!" *NewsDig*, n.d. Web. 15 July 2016.

Fyre, Northrop. *Anatomy of Criticism: Four Essays*. Princeton, NJ: Princeton University Press, 1957. Print.

Gajewski, Ryan. "'Fifty Shades of Grey': College Student Arrested for Sexual Assault Inspired by Film." *Hollywood Reporter*, 25 Feb. 2015. *LexisNexis*. Web. 10 Aug. 2015.

Gallo, Marissa, and Bryna Zumer. "Harford Library Stands Behind Decision Not to Carry 'Fifty Shades' Trilogy." *McClatchy*, 31 May 2012. *ProQuest*. Web. 8 July 2015.

Gallo, Phil. "How the '50 Shades of Grey' Soundtrack Is Being Deployed to Sell the Steamy Movie." *Billboard*, 2 Feb. 2015. Web. 7 Apr. 2015.

Gamboa, Glenn. "'Fifty Shades of Grey' Soundtrack Review: Unimpressive." *Newsday*, 9 Feb. 2015. Web. 2 Apr. 2015.

Ganteau, Jean-Michel. "Fantastic, but Truthful: The Ethics of Romance." *The Cambridge Quarterly* 32.3 (2003): 225–238. Print.

Garcia, Tonya. "There Were a Lot of Missed Marketing Opportunities in *Fifty Shades of Grey*." *AdWeek*, 13 Feb. 2015. Web. 7 Mar. 2016.

Gensler, Andy. "How 'Fifty Shades of Grey' Is Helping Stephan Moccio's Songwriting Star Rise." *Billboard*, 14 Feb. 2015. Web. 7 Apr. 2015.

Geraldine. "50 Reasons Why I Won't Be Reading 50 Shades of Grey." *Everywhereist*. n.p., 5 June 2012. Web. 27 July 2015.

"Global Publishing Industry 2012–2017: Trend, Profit, and Forecast Analysis." *PR Newswire*, 8 Oct. 2012. *ProQuest*. Web. 10 Apr. 2015.

Goldstein, Meredith. "Boston College Bookstore Pulls '50 Shades.'" *Boston Globe*, 12 Mar. 2015. Web. 5 Aug. 2015.

Goode, Erich, and Nachman Ben-Yehuda. "Moral Panics: Culture, Politics, and Social Construction." *Annual Review of Sociology* 20.1 (1994): 149–171. Print.

Goodman, Jessica. "All the Differences Between the 'Fifty Shades of Grey' Book & Movie." *Huffington Post*, 11 Feb. 2015. Web. 15 July 2016.

Goodrich, Diana S. "Introduction: Genre Studies." *Disposition* 15.39 (1990): iii–xi. Print.

Goodstein, Jack. "Music Review: Various Artists—Fifty Shades of Grey: The Classical Album." *Seattle pi*, 15 Sep. 2012. Web. 17 Jan. 2016.

Goto, Yuriko. "Shoushika no Mottomo Shinkoku na Mondai [The Most Serious Issue Related to the Decline in the Number of Children]." *Blogos*. LINE Corporation, 14 Nov. 2014. Web. 8 July 2016.

Green, Emma. "Consent Isn't Enough: The Troubling Sex of *Fifty Shades*." *The Atlantic*, 10 Feb. 2015. Web. 10 Aug. 2015.

Gresh, Dannah. "I'm Not Reading *Fifty Shades of Grey*." *Pure Freedom*, n.d. Web. 27 July 2015.

Grey, Jordan. "7 Things Men Can Learn from Fifty Shades of Grey." *Jordan Grey*, n.p., 7 Oct. 2014. Web. 21 Sep. 2106.

Grigg, Casilda. "The Fifty Shades Effect: Why Sex Talking 'Clubs' Are the New Book Clubs." *Telegraph*, 23 Feb. 2016. Web. 3 Aug. 2016.

Grimes, David Robert. "Alcohol is by Far the Most Dangerous 'Date Rape Drug.'" *The Guardian*, 22 Sep 2014. Web. 17 Jan. 2016.

Grinberg, Emanuella. "Explaining 'Fifty Shades' Wild Success." *CNN*. Cable News Network, 17 Jul. 2012. Web. 7 Apr. 2015.

Grow, Kory. "Get Ready for 'Fifty Shades of Grey: The Classical Album.'" *Spin*. Spin, 7 Aug. 2012. Web. 15 Apr. 2015.

Gueren, Casey. "25 Facts about BDSM that You Won't Learn in 'Fifty Shades of Grey.'" *BuzzFeed*, 12 Feb. 2015. Web. 1 Dec, 2015.

Gunelius, Susan. "The Shift from CONsumers to PROsumers." *Forbes*, 3 Jul. 2010. Web. 10 May 2015.

Gupta, Pola B., and Stephen J. Gould. "'Consumers' Perceptions of the Ethics and Acceptability of Product Placements in Movies: Product Category and Individual Differences." *Journal of Current Issues and Research in Advertising* 14 (Spring 1997): 37–50. Print.

Hamm, Liza. "*Fifty Shades of Grey* Inspires a Naughty Chicken Cookbook." *People*, 19 Sep. 2012. Web. 5 Aug. 2016.

Hana (anelaliko). "I watched *Fifty Shades of Grey* in the R-18 version, without black censorship bars. It was beautiful." 26 Feb. 2015. 10:06 p.m. Tweet.

Harman, Sarah, and Bethan Jones. "Fifty Shades of Grey: Snark Fandom and the Figure of the Anti-fan." *Sexualities* 16.8 (2013): 951–968. Web. *Sage*. 15 July 2016.

Hawley, Patricia H., and William A. Hensley IV. "Social Dominance and Forceful Submission Fantasies: Feminine Pathology or Power?" *The Journal of Sex Research* 46.4 (2009): 568–565. Web. *Taylor & Francis Online*. 9 Dec. 2015.

Hazen, Helen. *Endless Rapture: Rape, Romance, and the Female Imagination*. New York: Scribner, 1983. Print.

Hébert, Ali, and Angela Weaver. "An Examination of Personality Characteristics Associated with BDSM Orientations." *The Canadian Journal of Human Sexuality* 23.2 (2014): 106–115. Print.

Hellekson, Karen. "A Fannish Field of Venue: Online Fan Gift Culture." *Cinema Journal* 48.4 (Summer 2009): 113–118. *ProjectMuse* Web. 15 July 2015.

Hellman, Melissa. "Japan Finally Bans Child Pornography." *Time*, 18 June 2014. Web. 30 June 2016.

Hetgner, Steven A. "Using Social Norms to Regulate Fan Fiction and Remix Culture." *University of Pennsylvania Law Review* 157.6 (2009): 1869–1935. Print.

Hicks, Tony. "'Fifty Shades of Grey' Reenactor Charged with Sexual Assault." *San Jose Mercury News*, 24 Feb. 2015. *LexisNexis*. Web. 10 Aug. 2015.

Higgins, Charlotte. "Fifty Shades of Grey Sends Sales of Thomas Tallis's Spem in Alium Soaring." *The Guardian*,16 July 2012. Web. 16 July 2016.

Highfill, Samantha. "*Fifty Shades of Grey*: Let's Talk about That Ending." *Entertainment Weekly*, 14 Feb. 2015. Web. 9 June 2015.

Hill, Heather, and Marni Harrington. "Beyond Obscenity: An Analysis of Sexual Discourse in LIS Educational Texts." *Journal of Documentation* 70.1 (2014): 62–73. Print.

Hilzik, Michael. "'Deep Throat' Numbers Just Don't Add Up." *Los Angeles Times*, 24 Feb. 2005. Web. 7 Apr. 2015.

Holland, Jason. "'Fifty Shades' Soundtrack Just as Dark as Film." *Stylusonline*. WordPress, 20 Feb. 2015. Web. 10 Apr. 2015.

Holley, Peter. "College Student Accused of Rape Claims He Was Re-enacting 'Fifty Shades of Grey.'" *Washington Post*, 23 Feb. 2015. Web. 10 Aug. 2015.

Hollows, Joanne. *Feminism, Femininity and Popular Culture*. Manchester: Manchester University Press, 2000. Print.

Hong, Soonkwan, Yong Jian Wang, and Gilberto De Los Santos. "The Effective Product Placement: Finding Appropriate Methods and Contexts for Higher James Brand Salience." *Journal of Promotion Management* 14.1–2 (2009): 103–120. *Taylor & Francis Online*. Web. 7 Mar. 2016.

Hume, Kathryn. "A Perdurable Pattern." *College English* 36.2 (1974): 129–146. *JSTOR*. Web. 4 May 2015.

Humphrey, Steven. "Fifty Terrible Lines from *Fifty Shades of Grey*." *The Stranger*. Index Newspaper, 14 Feb. 2015. Web. 10 May 2015.

Hunter-Kilmer, Meg. "Why I Hate Mr. Darcy." *Held by His Pierced Hands*. WordPress, 18 Aug. 2012. Web. 27 July 2015.

_____. "Why I Won't Read Fifty Shades of Grey." *Held by His Pierced Hands*. WordPress, 18 Aug. 2012. Web. 27 July 2015.

Hyde, Lewis. *The Gift: Creativity and the Artist in the New World*. New York: Vintage, 1983, 2007. Print.

"Interview with Fifty Shades of Trilogy Author E.L. James." Henry Cavill, 24 Jan. 2013. Web. 1 Dec. 2015.

Irwin, Heather. "'Fifty Shades of Grey' Means a Lot of Green." *Tribune Business News*, 21 Oct. 2012. *ProQuest*. Web. 30 Mar. 2015.

"Is It a Mortal Sin to See 'Fifty Shades' of Grey?" *Crux Catholic Media*, 6 Apr. 2015. Web. 24 July 2016.

Italie, Leanne. "'Fifty Shades of Grey' Marketing Goes Mainstream." *The Journal News*, 23 Aug. 2012. *ProQuest*. Web. 31. Mar. 2015.

Ito, Tokuhiro. "Bokashi Shori ga Zatsu [Poor Quality Blur]." *Sankei News*, 22 Feb. 2015. Web. 6 July 2016.

Jalabi, Raya. "New Charges for Teenager in 'Fifty Shades of Grey' Sexual Assault Case." *The Guardian*, 4 June 2015. *Lexis-Nexis*. Web. 10 Aug. 2015.

James, E.L. *Fifty Shades Darker*. New York: Vintage, 2012. Print.

_____. *Fifty Shades Freed*. New York: Vintage, 2012. Print.

_____. *Fifty Shades of Grey*. New York: Vintage, 2012. Print.

Jameson, Fredric. "Magical Narratives: Romance as Genre." *New Literary History* 7.1 (1975): 135–163. Print.

"Japan Remains Near Bottom of Gender Gap Ranking." *The Japan Times*, 29 Oct. 2014. Web. 30 June 2016.

Jason, Sharon. "Not All Gays Heading to Altar." *The Desert Sun*, 7 July 2013. *ProQuest*. Web. 1 Dec. 2015.

Jenkins, Henry. *Textual Poachers: Television Fans and Participatory Culture*. New York: Routledge, 1992, 2013. Print.

Johnson, Steve. "Tribune Archive: Interview with E.L. James, 'Fifty Shades of Grey' Author." *Chicago Tribune*, 27 Feb. 2015. *ProQuest*. Web. 30 Mar. 2015.

_____. "Who Is E.L. James?: 'Fifty Shades' Author and Her Fans Bond over Improbable Success Story." *Chicago Tribune*, 3 May 2012. Web. 28 Apr. 2015.

Johnson, Zach. "*Fifty Shades of Grey* Release Date Pushed Back to February 13—Just in Time for Valentine's Day." *EOnline*, 13 Nov. 2013. Web. 29 Mar. 2015.

Jones, Barbara M. "Controversy in *Fifty Shades of Grey*." *American Libraries Magazine* 43.5/6 (2012): 21. Print.

Jones, Bethan. "Fifty Shades of Exploitation: Fan Labor and *Fifty Shades of Grey*." *Transformative Works and Cultures* 15 (2014). Web. 11 May 2015.

Jones, Ralph. "*Fifty Shades of Grey*, Tacky Merchandise." *The Guardian*, 8 Feb, 2015. Web. 12 Jan. 2016.

Jones, Sarah. "Fifty Shades of Luxury Product Placement." *Luxury Daily*, 18 Feb. 2015. Web. 7 Apr. 2016.

"Just How Realistic Is the S and M in 50 Shades of Grey?" *Stylist*, n.d. Web. 3 Dec. 2015.

"KappAhl Launches '*Fifty Shades of Grey*' Inspired Lingerie Line." *Fashion Gone Rogue*, 24 Nov. 2013. Web. 21 Jan. 2016.

Karniouchina, Ekaterina V., Can Uslay, and Grigori Erenburg. "Do Marketing Media Have Life Cycles? The Case of Product Placement in Movies." *Journal of Marketing* 75 (2011): 27–48. Web. 7 Mar. 2016.

Kelley, Annie J. "'Fifty Shades' of Controversy." *Battle Creek Enquirer*, 13 May 2012. *ProQuest*. Web. 8 July 2015.

Kennerly, Britt. "50 Shades to Return to Brevard County Library Shelves." *Florida Today*, 26 May 2012. *ProQuest*. Web. 8 July 2015.

_____. "Racy Tale Back on Brevard's Bookshelves Tomorrow." *Florida Today*, 29 May 2012. *ProQuest*. Web. 8 July 2015.

_____. "Residents Speak Up About 'Fifty Shades of Grey' at Library Board Meeting." *Florida Today*, 17 May 2012. *ProQuest*. Web. 8 July 2015.

_____. "Residents Want Brevard Libraries to Once Again Carry Steamy Best-seller." *Florida Today*, 14 May 2012. *ProQuest*. Web. 8 July 2015.

Kinchin-Smith, Sam. "Many Shades of Beige: Abuses of Music and the Fifty Shades Phenomenon." *Drowned in Sound*, 31 Oct. 2012. Web. 15 Apr. 2015.

Kingkade, Tyler. "Texas Tech Frat Loses Charter Following 'No Means Yes, Yes Means Anal' Display." *Huffington Post*, 8 Oct. 2014. Web. 3 Dec. 2015.

Kiplinger, Anne. "Fifty Shades of Grey: The Music." *Chicago Now*, 28 May 2012. Web. 15 Apr. 2015.

Kittner, Gena. "Fifty Shades of Reaction to 'Mommy Porn." *Tribune Business News*, 26 May. 2012. *ProQuest*. Web. 30 Mar. 2015.

Kot, Greg. "'Beyoncé' Album Review: More

Than the Delivery Is a Surprise." *Chicago Tribune*, 14 Dec. 2013. Web. 9 Apr. 2015.

Kowalczyk, Christine M. and Marla B. Royne. "Are Products More Real on Reality Shows? An Exploratory Study of Product Placement in Reality Television Programming." *Journal of Current Issues & Research in Advertising* 33.2 (2012): 248–266. *Taylor & Francis Online*. Web. 7 Mar. 2016.

Kutchingsky. "Pornography and Rape: Theory and Practice? Evidence from Crime Data in Four Countries Where Pornography is Easily Available." *International Journal of Law and Psychiatry* 14 (1991): 47–64. Print.

Kuwae, Nanko. "Eiga [Film]." Spotnote, 13 Feb. 2015. Web. 8 June 2016.

Lady M. "Fifty Shades of Grey wo Mita Shoujiki na Kansou [Honest Thoughts after Watching Fifty Shades of Grey]." *Ameblo*, 1 Mar. 2015. Web. 8 June 2016.

La Ferle, Carrie, and Steven M . Edwards. "Product Placement: How Brands Appear on Television." *Journal of Advertising*. 35.4 (2006): 65–86. *JSTOR*. Web. 7 Mar, 2016.

Lascala, Marisa. "How does 'Fifty Shades of Grey' the Movie End? Here's Your Definitive Spoiler Alert." *Bustle*, 12 Feb. 2015. Web. 9 June 2015.

Lawler, Emily. "1 in 4 Female Michigan State University Undergrads Sexually Assaulted, According to Survey." *MLive*, 21 Sep. 2015. Web. 16 Aug. 2016.

Leavenworth, Maria Lindgren. "Variations, Subversions, and Endless Love: Fan Fiction and the *Twilight Saga*." In *Bringing Light to Twilight: Perspectives on the Pop Culture Phenomenon*, ed. Giselle Liza Anatol. New York: Palgrave Macmillan, 2011. Print.

Lee, Linda J. "Guilty Pleasures: Reading Romance Novels as Reworked Fairy Tales." *Marvels & Tales: Journal of Fairy-Tale Studies* 22.1 (2008): 52–66. Print.

Lehnardt, Michelle. "Motherhood Matters: Letting Your Teenager Read, Watch 'Fifty Shades of Grey' Is a Terrible Idea." *Desert News*, 10 Feb. 2015. Web. 30 Mar. 2015.

Lewis, Andy. "'Fifty Shades of Grey' Parody Skewers the Erotic Hit. *The Hollywood Reporter*, 9 Aug. 2012. Web. 5 Aug. 2016.

"Limited Edition Prints from Artist Featured in *Fifty Shades of Grey*." *50 Shades Movie Fansite*, WordPress, 27 Nov. 2012. Web. 19 Jan. 2016.

Lindgren, James. "Defining Pornography." *University of Pennsylvania Law Review* 141.3 (Apr. 1993): 1153–1275. *JSTOR*. Web. 10 Aug. 2015.

Little, Jane. "*Master of the Universe* versus *Fifty Shades* by E.L James Comparison." *Dear Author Media Network*, 13 Mar. 2012. Web. 11 May 2015.

Lizerbram, David. "Copyright Fair Use: Fifty Shades of Grey." *David Lizerbram & Associates: Attorneys at Law*, 17 Feb. 2015. Web. 11 May 2015.

Luscher, Kurt, and Barbara Grabmann . "Gay and Lesbian Couples and Parents: Ambivalences in the Institutionalization of Private Life." *Zeitschrift fur Soziologie der Erziehung und Socialisation* 22.1 (2002): 47–63. Web. *ProQuest*. 1 Dec. 2015.

Luscombe, Belinda. "The Grey Area." *Time*, 6 Feb. 2015. *EBSCO*. Web. 31 Mar. 2015.

Lush, Tamara. "Some Libraries Ban 'Fifty Shades of Grey.'" *Charleston Daily Mail*, 10 May 2012. Web. *LexisNexis*. 8 July 2015.

Makinen, Merja. "Embodying the Negate: Contemporary Images of the Female Erotic." In *Image and Power: Women in Fiction in the Twentieth Century*, ed. Sarah Sceats and Gail Cunningham. New York: Longman, 1996. 41–50. Print.

"Man Stands Trial after Deadly '50 Shades of Grey' Sex Game with Girlfriend." *Opposingviews.com*, 28 Jan. 2013. Web. 10 Aug. 2015.

Marcs, Stephanie. "'Fifty Shades of Grey' Isn't a Movie about BDSM, and That's a Problem." *Huffington Post*, 16 Feb. 2014. Web. 3 Dec. 2015.

Martin, Amber. "*Fifty Shades of Sex Shop*: Sexual Fantasy for Sale." *Sexualities* 16.8 (2013): 980–984. Print.

Mason, Callum, and Alex Shaw. "Student Outrage as Yale Fraternity Suspected for 'No Means Yes' Chants Establishes Chapter at Edinburgh." *Independent*, 17 Feb, 2014. Web. 3 Dec. 2015.

McAlister, Jodi. "Breaking the Hard Limits: Romance, Pornography, and Genre in the *Fifty Shades* Trilogy." *Interdisciplinary.net*, n.d. Web. 21 Sep. 2016.

McCormick, Rich. "Find the Next Fifty Shades of Grey in Wattpad's Erotic Fan Fiction App." *The Verge*, 26 Feb. 2015. Web. 2 Aug. 2016.

McKechnie, Sally A., and Jia Zhou. "Product Placement in Movies: A Comparison of Chinese and American Consumers' Attitudes." *International Journal of Advertising* 22.3 (2015): 349–374. *T and F Online*. Web. 7 Mar. 2016.

McSpadden, Kevin. "*Fifty Shades of Grey* Inspired Student's Sexual Assault, Prosecutors Say." *Time*, 24 Feb. 2015. Web. 10 Aug. 2015.

Meisel, Keith. "More Than 1,000 County Residents on Library Waiting List for 'Fifty Shades.'" *McClatchy*, 30 May 2012. *ProQuest*. Web. 8 July 2015.

Melou. "Jouge Kan wo Yomi Oete [After Reading Books 1 and 2]." *Amazon*, 8 Feb, 2015. Web. 18 July 2016.

"Men Are Reading 'Fifty Shades of Grey,' Too." *CBS News*, 26 Apr. 2012. Web. 25 Mar. 2015.

Merricks, Trenton. "On the Incompatibility of Enduring and Perduring Entities." *Mind* 194.415 (1995): 523–531. Print.

Messer, Lesley. "Jamie Dornan Defends the Romantic Aspect of '50 Shades of Grey.'" *ABC News*, 2 Jan. 2015. Web. 3 June 2015.

Mietus, John. "If Mr. Grey Asks to See You Now, Run Away. Fast." *The Shakerite*, WordPress, 23 Mar. 2015. Web. 10 Dec. 2015.

Miller, Gregory. "Fan Fiction Writers Speak Out Against 'Fifty Shades of Grey.'" *New York Post*, 7 Feb. 2015. Web. 11 May 2015.

Miller, Julie. "Even Oprah Has Read *Fifty Shades of Grey*." *Vanity Fair*, 15 Oct. 2012. Web. 3 Aug. 2016.

Mismas, Michelle. "OPI Fifty Shades of Grey Swatches & Review." *All Lacquered Up*, 17 Dec. 2014. Web. 3 Mar. 2016.

Moffitt, Mary Anne. "Articulating Meaning: Reconceptions of the Meaning Process, Fantasy/Reality, and Identity in Leisure Activities." *Communication Theory* 3.3 (1993): 231–251. Web. 25 July 2016.

Morrissey, Katherine. "Fifty Shades of Remix: The Intersecting Pleasures of Commercial and Fan Romances." *Journal of Popular Romance Studies* 4.1 (2014): 1–17. Web. 23 June 2015.

Moser, Charles, and Peggy J . Kleinplatz. "Introduction: The State of Our Knowledge on SM." *Journal of Homosexuality* 50.2–3 (2006): 1–15. Web. *Taylor & Francis Online*. 1 Dec. 2015.

Mulligan, Christina. "The Most Scandalous Part of 'Fifty Shades of Grey' Isn't the Sex and Bondage." *Washington Post*, 11 Feb. 2015. Web. 11 May 2015.

"My Mom is Reading 50 Shades of Grey?" *Yahoo! Answers*, Web. 7 Apr. 2015.

"My Problem with 'Fifty Shades of Grey.'" *Brain Fuzzies*, Tumblr, 18 Mar. 2012. Web. 30 May. 2015.

Myers, Abigail E. "Edward Cullen and Bella Swan: Byronic and Feminist Heroes … or Not." In *Twilight and Philosophy: Vampires, Vegetarians, and the Pursuit of Immortality*, ed. Rebecca Housel and J. Jeremy Wisnewski. Hoboken, NJ: John Wiley & Sons, Inc., 2090. Print.

naomi. "Bring Tea Drinking to a Boil with 50 Shades of Earl Grey." *Two Leaves and a Bud*, n.p., Apr. 2015. Web. 3 Mar. 2016.

Newmahr, Staci. "Rethinking Kink: Sadomasochism as Serious Leisure." *Qualitative Sociology* 33.3 (2010): 313–331. Web. *Springer*. 3 Dec. 2015.

"#8 Christian Grey." *Forbes Fictional Fifteen*, Forbes Media, 2003. Web. 3 June 2016.

O'Barr, William. "'Subliminal' Advertising." *Advertising & Society Review* 13.4 (2013). *ProjectMUSE*. Web. 7 Mar. 2016.

Ocean, Justin. "Every Expensive Thing in *Fifty Shades of Grey*, Explained." *Bloomberg Business*, 11 Feb. 2015. Web. 10 Dec. 2015.

O'Connell, Michael. "'Fifty Shades of Grey' Readies a Kinky, Classical Soundtrack." *Hollywood Report*, 7 Aug. 2012. Web. 15 Apr. 2015.

Office of Intellectual Freedom. "OIF Statement on 'Fifty Shades of Grey' Controversy." *American Library Association*, 10 May 2012. Web. 6 Aug. 2015.

Ohlheiser, Abby. "Need a Reason Not to See 'Fifty Shades of Grey'? Here Are a Few." *Washington Post*, 13 Feb. 2015. Web. 27 July 2015.

"OPI Is Releasing a 'Fifty Shades of Grey' Collection—Includes Shades of Grey." *Styleblazer*, 18 Nov. 2014. Web. 3 Mar. 2016.

Ortmann, David M., and Richard A. Sprott. *Sexual Outsiders: Understanding BDSM Sexualities and Communities.* New York: Rowman & Littlefield, 2013. Print.

Outlaw, Kofi. "'Fifty Shades of Grey' Review." *Screen Rant*, 16 Feb. 2015. Web. 7 Apr. 2015.

Paglia, Camille. *Vamps and Tramps: New Essays.* New York: Vintage, 1994. Print.

Parker-Pope, Tara. "When Sex Leaves the Marriage." *New York Times*, 3 June 2009. Web. 8 July 2016.

Parkin, Rachel Hendershot. "Breaking Faith: Disrupted Expectations and Ownership in Stephenie Meyer's Twilight Saga." *Jeunesse: Young People, Texts, Cultures* 2.2 (Winter 2010): 61–85. Web. *Project Muse.* 9 Apr. 2015.

Partridge, Kenneth. "Album Review: The 'Fifty Shades of Grey' Soundtrack Hits Hard Enough to Leave a Lasting Mark." *Billboard*, 10 Feb. 2015. Web. 7 Apr. 2015.

Patches, Matt. "Striving for Legitimacy, 'Fifty Shades of Grey' Books Berlin Film Festival Premiere." *HitFlix*, 22 Dec. 2014. Web. 12 Jan. 2016.

Pew Research Center. *E-Reading Rises as Device Ownership Jumps: Three in Ten Adults Read an E-book Last Year; Half Own a Tablet or E-Reader.* 16 Jan. 2014. Web. 9 Apr. 2015.

_____. *Online Video 2013.* 10 Oct. 2013. Web. 10 Aug. 2015.

Powrie, Phil, and Robynn Stilwell, eds. *Changing Tunes: The Use of Pre-existing Music in Film.* Burlington, VT: Ashgate Publishing, 2006. Print.

Prinzivalli, Fallon. "'Fifty Shades of Grey': Stephenie Meyer Speaks Out." *MTV News.* Viacom, 29 May 2012. Web. 10 May 2015.

Pugachevsky, Julia. "Here's Why You Should See 'Secretary' Before 'Fifty Shades of Grey.'" *BuzzFeed*, 24 Jul. 2014. Web. 11 Mar. 2016.

Pugh, Sheenagh. *The Democratic Genre: Fan Fiction in a Literary Context.* Bridgend, Wales: Seren, 2005. Print.

Quale, Amy E. *Pursuit of Empowerment:* *The Evolution of the Romance Novel and Its Readership in* Fifty Shades of Grey. MA thesis. Minnesota State University, 2014. *ProQuest.* Web. 24 June 2015.

Radway, Janice. *Reading the Romance: Women, Patriarchy, and Popular Literature.* Chapel Hill, NC: University of North Carolina Press, 2007. Print.

Raine, Lee, and Andrew Perrin . "Slightly Fewer Americans Are Reading Print Books, New Survey Finds." *Pew Research Center*, 19 Oct. 2015. Web. 3 Aug. 2016.

Rainey, Sarah. "Fifty Shades of Grey" The Most Ridiculous Merchandise." *Telegraph*, 12 Feb. 2015. Web. 3 Mar. 2016.

Rawden, Jessica. "14 Big Differences Between the Fifty Shades of Grey Book and Movie." *CinamaBlend*, n.d. Web. 15 July 2016.

Rea, Michael C. "What is Pornography?" *Noûs* 35.1 (Mar. 2001): 118–145. Web. *JSTOR.* 10 Aug. 2015.

Reagin, Nancy, and Ann Rubenstein. "'I'm Buffy, and You're History': Putting Fan Studies into History." *Transformative Works and Cultures* 6 (2011).

Redondo, Ignacio. "Product-Placement Planning." *Journal of International Consumer Marketing* 18.4 (2006): 33–60. *Taylor & Francis Online.* Web. 7 Mar. 2016.

Reed, Ryan. "Hear Ellie Goulding's sensual '50 Shades of Grey' Anthem." *RollingStone*, 7 Jan. 2015. Web. 9 Apr. 2015.

Regis, Pamela. *A Natural History of the Romance Novel.* Philadelphia, PA: University of Pennsylvania Press, 2003. Print.

Richards, Neil. "The *Fifty Shades of Grey* Paradox." *Slate*, 13 Feb. 2015. Web. 9 Apr. 2015.

Richtel, Matt. "For Pornographers, Internet's Virtues Turn to Vices." *New York Times*, 2 June 2007. Web. 25 Aug. 2016.

Richters, Juliet, Richard O. DeVisser, et al. "Demographic and Psychosocial Features of Participants in Bondage and Discipline, "Sadomasochism" or Dominance and Submission (BDSM): Data from a National Survey." *The Journal of Sexual Medicine* 5.7 (2008): 1660–1668. Web. *Wiley Online Library.* 1 Dec. 2015.

Ritson, Mark. "The Fifty Shades of Stupid Marketing." *Marketing Week*, 18 Feb. 2015. Web. 7 Mar. 2016.

Ritzer, George, and Nathan Jurgenson. "Production, Consumption, Prosumption: The Nature of Capitalism in the Age of the Digital 'Prosumer.'" *Journal of Consumer Culture* 10 (2010): 13–37. Print.

Rivadeneira, Caryn. "Why I Still Haven't Read *Fifty Shades of Grey.*" *ThinkChristian*, 21 Mar. 2013. Web. 27 July 2015.

Rojas, John-Paul. "Gardener Cleared of Assault after *Fifty Shades of Grey* Sex Session." *Telegraph*, 22 Jan. 2013. Web. 10 Aug. 2015.

Romance Writers of America. "About the Romance Genre." *RWA*, n.d. Web. 2 June 2015.

_____. "The Romance Genre: Romance Industry Statistics." *RWA*, n.d. Web. 2 June 2015.

Ross, Amy. A. "Universal Picture's Film Music President Talks 'Fifty Shades of Grey' Soundtrack." *Northwestern University School of Communication*, 5 Mar. 2015. Web. 9 Apr. 2015.

Ross, Janell. "The Myth of the 'Anchor Baby' Deportation Defense." *Washington Post*, 25 Aug. 2015. Web. 24. July 2016.

Rovella, Michelle, Susan D. Geringer, and Rudy Sanchez. "Viewer Participation of Product Placement in Comedic Movies." *American Journal of Management* 15.1 (2015). Web. 7 Mar. 2016.

Russell, Cristel Antonia, and Barbara B. Stern. "Consumers, Characters, and Products: A Balance Model of Sitcom Product Placement Effects." *Journal of Advertising.* 35.1 (2006): 7–21. *JSTOR.* Web. 7 Mar. 2016.

Salmon, Catherine. "The Pop Culture of Sex: An Evolutionary Window on the Worlds of Pornography and Romance." *Review of General Psychology* 16.2 (2012): 152–160. Web. *American Psychological Association.* 10 Aug. 2015.

Sanneh, Kelefa. "Music: The Solo Beyoncé: She's No Ashanti." *New York Times*, 6 Jul. 2013. Web. 9 Apr. 2015.

Saul, Heather. "University Student Charged with Rape Claimed He Was Re-enacting Fifty Shades of Grey Film." *Independent*, 24 Feb. 2015. Web. 10 Aug. 2015.

Scharf, Lindzi. "Meet 'Fifty Shades of Grey' Costume Designer Mark Bridges." *Entertainment Weekly*, 4 Dec. 2013. Web. 7 Mar. 2016.

Schilling, Mark. "Why Hollywood Movies Are Plummeting at Japan Box Office." *Variety*, 23 Oct. 2013. Web. 30 June 2016.

Schimmel, Kimberly S., C. Lee Harrington, and Denise D. Bielby. "Keep Your Fans to Yourself: The Disjuncture Between Sport Studies' and Pop Culture Studies' Perspectives on Fandom." *Sports in Society* 10.4 (2007): 580–600. Print.

Schmadeke, Steve. "In 'Fifty Shades of Grey' Rape Case, Female Student Set to Testify." *Chicago Tribune*, 19 Mar. 2015. Web. 10 Aug. 2015.

_____. "Judge Throws out Case against UIC Student Charged with '50 Shades of Grey' Assault." *Chicago Tribune*, 20 Mar. 2015. Web. 10 Aug. 2015.

_____. "Prosecutors: UIC Student Charged with Assault Said He Was Re-enacting 'Fifty Shades of Grey.'" *Chicago Tribune*, 24 Feb. 2015. Web. 14 Oct. 2015.

Schoeff, Ileigh, and Miho Hoshino. "A Study of Japan's Film Industry." *U.S. Commercial Service*, Mar. 2016. Web. 30 June 2016.

Schwabach, Aaron. *Fan Fiction and Copyright: Outsider Works and Intellectual Property Protection.* Burlington, VT: Ashgate Publishing, 2011. Print.

Sciortino, Karley. "Breathless: Has *Fifty Shades of Grey* Made S&M Too Mainstream?" *Vogue*, 12 Feb. 2015. Web. 31 Mar. 2015.

Scott, Catherine. *Thinking Kink: The Collision of BDSM, Feminism and Popular Culture.* Jefferson, NC: McFarland, 2015. Print.

"Seikinou to Seiyakuwari [Sexual Functions and Sexual Roles]." Seishin Girls High School, 1 July 2003. Web. 16 July 2016.

Self, Robert T. "The Sounds of *MASH.*" In *Close Viewings: An Anthology of New Film Criticism,* ed. Peter Lehman. Tallahassee, The Florida State University Press, 1990. 141–157. Print.

Setoodeh, Ramin, "'50 Shades of Grey' Won't Include Infamous Tampon Scene." *Boston Herald Radio*, 21 Jan. 2015. Web. 14 Jan. 2016.

Sewell, Melissa. "'Brokeback Mountain' Stirring Up Controversy." *Washburn Re-*

view Online, 10 Jan. 2007. Web. 27 July 2016.

"Sex Just Not Novel Enough Grey Marriage." *Sydney MX*. 12 Nov. 2012. *LexisNexis*. Web. 10 Aug. 2015.

"Sex News: Sh! Women's Store Offers 50 Shades Lessons." *Cliterati*, 30 July 2013. Web. 9 Apr. 2016.

Shachar, Hila. "A Post-Feminist Romance: Love, Gender and Intertextuality in Stephenie Meyer's Saga." In *Theorizing Twilight: Critical Essays on What's at State in a Post-Vampire World*, ed. Maggie Parke and Natalie Wilson. Jefferson, NC: McFarland, 2011. Print.

Shetty, Raksha. "Huge Decline in Book Reading." *CBS News*, 8 July 2004. Web. 3 Aug. 2016.

Silverman, Stephen. "Much Grammy's 'Love' for Beyoncé, OutKast." *People*, 8 Feb, 2004. Web. 9 Apr. 2015.

Singleton, Micah. "The Fifty Shades of Grey Soundtrack Is One of the Best Albums of 2015." *The Verge*, 11 Feb. 2015. Web. 2 Apr. 2015.

Skurnick, Lizzie. "'50 Shades of Grey,' A Self-published E-book, Is the Future of Publishing." *The Daily Beast*, 17 Mar. 2012. Web. 9 Apr. 2015.

Smith, Anna Marie. "'What Is Pornography?': An Analysis of the Policy Statement of the Campaign Against Pornography and Censorship." *Feminist Review* 43 (Spring 1993): 71–87. Web. *JSTOR*. 10 Aug. 2015.

Smith, Anna. "Fifty Shades of Grey: What BDSM Enthusiasts Think." *The Guardian*, 15 Feb. 2015. Web. 1 Dec. 2015.

_____. "The 10 Best BDSM Movies." *The Guardian*, 10 Feb. 2015. Web. 1 Dec. 2015.

Smith, Haley Morgan. "The Problem with 50 Shades of Grey." *Haley Morgan Smith.com*, 17 Feb. 2015. Web. 24 July 2016.

Snitow, Ann. "Mass Market Romance: Pornography for Women Is Different." In *Powers of Desire: The Politics of Sexuality*, ed. Ann Snitow, Sharon Thompson, and Christine Stansell. New York: Monthly Review Press, 1983. 245–263. *Gale Literature Resource Center*. Web. 24 June 2015.

Sollee, Kristen. "How 'Fifty Shades of Grey' Changed Your Sex Life: Not to Mention Your Reading Habits." *Women's Health*, 29 July 2014. Web. 25 July 2016.

Solon, Olivia. "Richard Dawkins on the Internet's Hijacking of the Word 'Meme.'" *Wired*, 20 June 2013. Web. 15 Aug. 2016.

Somarriba, Mary Rose. "50 Shades of Yawn." *Verily*, 27 July 2012. Web. 27 July 2015.

Sonderholm, Jorn. "Having Fun with the Periodic Table: A Counterexample to Rea's Definition of Pornography." *Philosophia* 36 (2008): 233–236. Web. *Springer*. 10 Aug. 2015.

Stagg, Natasha. "The Reality of People: An Interview with Dian Hanson." *The Paris Review*, 18 Mar. 2015. Web. 9 Apr. 2015.

Stedman, Alex. "'Fifty Shades' Spinoff 'Grey' Copy Reportedly Stolen from Publisher." *Variety*, 10 June 2015. Web. 5 Mar. 2016.

Stewart, Thomas. "Which 5 Book Genres Make the Most Money?" The Richest, 31 Jan. 2014. Web. 2 June 2015.

Stiles, Beverly L., and Robert E. Clark. "BDSM: A Subcultural Analysis of Sacrifices and Delights." *Deviant Behavior* 32.2 (2011): 158–189. Print.

Stover, Bob. "'Fifty Shades of Grey' Removal by Brevard Libraries Not Best Option." *Florida Today*, 7 May 2012. *ProQuest*. Web. 8 July 2015.

"Student Accused of Re-enacting '50 Shades of Grey' Cleared by Judge." *News Point*, 21 Mar. 2015. *LexisNexis*. Web. 10 Aug. 2015.

Suebsaeng, Asawin. "'Fifty Shades of Grey' Author Sued Over Mediocre Sex Lubricant." *The Daily Beast*, 9 Feb. 2015. *ProQuest*. Web. 8 July. 2015.

Suh, Jennifer. "'Fifty Shades' Pulled from BC Bookstore." *The Heights*, 12 Mar. 2014. Web. 5 Aug. 2015.

Sunstein, Cass. "Pornography and the First Amendment." *Duke Law Journal* (1986): 589–627. Print.

Tapscott, Don. "Four Principles for the Open World." TED. Jun. 2012. Lecture.

_____. *Grown up Digital: How the Net Generation is Changing Your World*. New York: McGraw-Hill, 2009. Print.

_____, and Anthony D . Williams. *Wikinomics: How Mass Collaboration Change Everything*. New York: Penguin Group, 2008. Print.

Tartaglione, Nancy. "'Fifty Shades' Higher in Global Bow at $266.6M: Record R-Rated Opening Overseas—Tuesday Update." *Deadline*, 17 Feb. 2015. Web. 8 June 2016.

"Teaching *Fifty Shades of Grey*." *The Popular Romance Project*, Web. 9 Apr. 2015.

Teotonio, Isabel. "Erotic Trilogy Puts Libraries in Bind: Some U.S. Sites Bow to Demand to Stock Popular Fifty Shades Bondage Books While Others Ban Them." *Toronto Star*, 25 May 2012. *Lexis Nexis*. Web. 8 July 2015.

Thomas, Brownen. "What Is Fanfiction and Why Are People Saying Such Nice Things about It?" *StoryWorlds: A Journal of Narrative Studies* 3 (2011): 1–24. Print.

Thompson, Anne. "6 Reasons Why 'Fifty Shades of Grey' Is a Classic Romance (Review & Roundup)." *Thompson on Hollywood*. Indiewire.com, 10 Feb. 2015. Web. 3 June 2015.

Thompson, Eliza. "14 Ways the 'Fifty Shades of Grey' Movie Differs from the Book." *Cosmopolitan*. Hearst Communications, 11 Feb. 2015. Web. 15 July 2016.

Thornton, Neil. "The Politics of Pornography: A Critique of Liberalism and Radical Feminism." *Journal of Sociology* 22.1 (Mar. 1986): 25–45. Web. *Sage*. 10 Aug. 2015.

Tofler, Alvin. *The Third Wave*. New York: William Morrow and Company, 1980. Print.

"Top Ten Reasons 'Secretary' Beats '50 Shades of Grey'." *SundanceTV*. SundanceTV, 28 Jul. 2014. Web. 11 Mar. 2016.

Tosenberger, Catherine. "Mature Poets Steal: Children's Literature and the Unpublishability of Fanfiction." *Children's Literature Association Quarterly* 39.1 (2014): 4–27. Print.

"Traditional Employment Practices in Japan." *DISCO*. DISCO Inc, 2012. Web. 30 June 2016.

Traywick, Catherine. "What Letting MSU's Basketball Players Off the Hook for Sexual Assault Tells Us About Campus Rape." *Generation Progress*. Generation Progress, 4 Oct. 2015. Web. 16 Aug. 2016.

Trina. "Fifty Shades of Grey Sex: 20 Naughty Tricks to Grey Up Your Sex Life." *YouQueen*. YouQueen, 14 Sep. 2014. Web. 25 July 2016.

Trocchia, Phillip J., Ruby Q Saine, and Michael G. Luckett. "I've Wanted a BMW Since I Was a Kid: An Exploratory Analysis of the Aspirational Brand." *Journal of Applied Business Research* 31.1 (2015): 331–344. Print.

Tsaros, Angelika. "Consensual Non-consent: Comparing EL James's *Fifty Shades of Grey* and Pauline Réage's *Story of O*." *Sexualities* 16.8 (2013): 864–979. Web. *Sage*. 28 Mar. 2015.

"Twilight." *Box Office Mojo*. IMDb.com, n.d. Web. 25 Apr. 2015.

"2013 Fifty Shades of Grey White Silk." Fifty Shades of Grey Wine, n.d. Web. 17 Jan. 2016.

"2012 Fifty Shades of Grey Red Satin." Fifty Shades of Grey Wine, n.d. Web. 17 Jan. 2016.

"Tying Up Classmate with Belts in His Dorm Before Whipping and Raping Her in Attempt to Recreate Scene from Fifty Shades of Grey." *Hiru Times*. 27 Feb. 2015. *LexisNexis*. Web. 10 Aug. 2015.

Ugwu, Reggie. "Why the 'Fifty Shades of Grey' Soundtrack Is Better Than It Has Any Right to Be." *Buzzfeed*, 26 Feb. 2015. Web. 9 Apr. 2015.

United States. Department of Justice. *Criminal Victimization, 2013*. Sep. 2014. Web. 25 July 2016.

"USCCB Reclassified Gay Western 'Brokeback Mountain' After Complaints." *Catholic News Agency*. CNA, 16 Dec. 2005. Web. 27 July 2016.

Varga, Talya. "50 Shades of Grey—Is This Really What Women Want?" *UCA Journalism*. UCA Journalism, 13 May 2012. Web. 25 Mar. 2015.

Vetter, Chris. "'Grey' Hot: Libraries Can't Keep Race Bestseller on the Shelves." *The Leader-Telegram*. 12 May 2012. *Lexis-Nexis*. Web. 8 July 2015.

Vino, Lauren. "How to Talk to Your Mom about Her Creepy 'Fifty Shades' Obsession." *MTV News*. Viacom, 22 Aug. 2014. Web. 7 Apr. 2015.

Walsh, Matt. "To the Women of America: 4 Reasons to Hate 50 Shades of Grey." *The Matt Welsh Blog*. TheMattWelshBlog, 25 July 2014. Web. 27 July 2015.

"Washington: College Student Accused of Sexual Assault Uses 'Fifty Shades of

Grey' As a Defense." *Plus Media Solutions*. 6 Mar. 2015. *LexisNexis*. Web. 10 Aug. 2015.

"We Are Here." *KappAhl*. n.p., n.d. Web. 21 Jan. 2016.

Weber, Bruce. "Joel J. Tyler, Judge Who Pronounced 'Deep Throat' Obscene, Dies at 90." *New York Times*. New York Times, 12 Jan. 2012. Web. 7 Apr. 2015.

Weinberg, Martin S., Colin J. Williams, and Charles Moser. "The Social Constituents of Sadomasochism." *Social Problems* 31.4 (1984): 379–389. Web. *JSTOR*. 1 Dec. 2015.

Weisman, Aly. "Here Are the Actors Who Passed on the 'Fifty Shades of Grey' Lead Roles. *Business Insider*. Business Insider, 17 Feb, 2015. Web. 24 July 2016.

Weiss, Margot D. "Mainstreaming Kink: The Politics of BDSM Representation in U.S. Popular Media." *Journal of Homosexuality* 50.2–3 (2006): 103–132. Print.

_____. *Techniques of Pleasure: BDSM and the Circus of Sexuality*. Durham, NC: Duke University Press, 2011. Print.

"Welcome to Concave Brand Tracking." *Concave Brand Tracking*. Concave Brand Tracking, n.d. Web. 7 Mar. 2016.

Wells, Jane. "Fifty Shames of Earl Grey: The Fifty Shades Parody." *CNBC*. CNBC, 23 Aug. 2012. Web. 5 Aug. 2016.

Westen, John-Henry, and Dawn Hawkins. "'Fifty Shades of Grey' Will Lead to Spike in Abuse of Women." *CNS News*. CNSNews.com, 16 Feb. 2015. Web. 2 Apr. 2015.

Whitehead, Deborah. "When Religious 'Mommy Bloggers' Met "Mommy Porn': Evangelical Christian and Mormon Women's Responses to *Fifty Shades*." *Sexualities* 16.8 (2013): 915–938. *Sage*. Web. 28 Mar. 2015.

"Who We Are." *Bluebella*. Bluebella, n.d. Web. 21 Jan. 2016.

"Why Does My Mom Read 50 Shades of Grey?" *Yahoo! Answers*. Yahoo, n.d. Web. 7 Apr. 2015.

"Why Is It, When Women Say No, They Really Mean Yes?" *Quora*. n.p., n.d. Web, 16 Aug. 2016.

Wiley, Clare. "We Spoke to the Women Protesting Against the '50 Shades of Grey' Film." *Vice*. Vice, 10 Feb. 2015. Web. 24 July 2016.

Williott, Carl. "Women Sues 'Fifty Shades of Grey' Lube for False Advertising." *MTV.com*. MTV.com, 10 Feb. 2015. Web. 5 Mar. 2016.

Wilson, Natalie. *Seduced by Twilight: The Allure and Contradictory Messages of the Popular Saga*. Jefferson, NC: McFarland, 2011. Print.

Wismeijer, Andreas A.J., and Marcel A.L.M. van Assen. "Psychological Characteristics of BDSM Practitioners." *International Society for Sexual Medicine* 10 (2013): 1943–1952. Web. *Wiley Online Library*. 3 Dec. 2015.

Woolfe, Zachary. "For Those in the Mood, Some Music." *New York Times*. New York Times. 18 Sep. 2012. Web. 15 Apr. 2015.

Yujia, Ma. "Businessman Jailed in 'Fifty Shades of Grey' Crime." *China.org.cn*. China.org.cn, 1 Apr. 2015. Web. 10 Aug. 2015.

Yuzukibuka, Tsubasa. "Kikon Josei no Roku Wari ga Sexless [60% of Married Women Are Sexless]." *KoiGaku*. KoiGaku, 17 Aug. 2015. Web. 15 July 2016.

Zickuhr, Kathryn, and Lee Raine . "A Snapshot of Reading in America in 2013." *Pew Research Center*. Pew Research Center, 16 Jan. 2014. Web. 3 Aug. 2016.

Zipp, Michele. "'Fifty Shades of Grey' Movie Leaves Out Important Sex Scene." *The Stir*. CMI Marketing, 21 Jan. 2015. Web. 14 Jan. 2016.

Zoo. "Eiga Fifty Shades of Grey Kansou [Film Review Fifty Shades of Grey]." *Hatena*. Hatena, 6 Aug. 2015. Web. 19 July 2016.

Index

201